THE
ATOMIC
ESTABLISHMENT

H. PETER METZGER

SIMON AND SCHUSTER • NEW YORK

First printing

SBN 671-21351-2
Library of Congress Catalog Card Number: 72-83090
Designed by Eve Metz
Manufactured in the United States of America

ACKNOWLEDGMENTS

I WOULD LIKE to thank Dr. Gary H. Higgins of the Lawrence Livermore Laboratories, Livermore, California; Dr. Harry J. Otway, of the Los Alamos Scientific Laboratory, Los Alamos, New Mexico; and Mr. William L. Oakley of the Atomic Energy Commission's headquarters in Washington, for their valuable suggestions and help in obtaining much of the information which was necessary to write this book. Although I have never required access to secret data, the difficulties inherent in obtaining ordinary information from the AEC would make it seem that much of what I needed was classified. These men, without ideological bias, facilitated the free flow of information to me, information to which any citizen is entitled, but which until recently required a friend's help to obtain.

I am also indebted to Robert D. Siek of the Colorado Department of Public Health for providing access to pertinent records of both his department and those of the health departments of the other uranium-mining states.

I am particularly grateful for the help of Anthony Ripley of *The New York Times,* whose several unpublished interviews I have included, and whose observations made during our many conversations have helped shape this book.

DEDICATION

This book is dedicated to the citizen activist. He is so far the only force shown to be capable of taming the unrestricted extension of self-serving technology. Like the little boy in Hans Christian Andersen's fairy tale "The Emperor's Clothes," he resists the hypnotic effect of past grandeur and sees things as they are and not as they claim to be or promise to become.

CONTENTS

III · THE TURNING POINT: ATOMIC FALLOUT   79

IV · RADIATION ON THE JOB: THE URANIUM MINERS   115

VII · THE REAL PROBLEMS WITH ATOMIC ENERGY TODAY   239

THE
ATOMIC
ESTABLISHMENT

I
HOW THE MEANS BECAME THE ENDS

Fanaticism consists in redoubling your efforts when you have forgotten your aim.

—George Santayana[1]

1 · THERE WAS A TURNING POINT

IT'S THE WAY of the institutions of government: They begin dedicated to a greater purpose, and they end up serving themselves. Sometimes the change is imperceptible or lost in history. No one can remember, for example, when the Army, the Navy or the Air Force subordinated its own interests in favor of the general good of the combined military services. In other cases, the loss of original purpose and the subsequent slip into self-interest was more recent and catalyzed by a single issue. That was the way it was with the United States Atomic Energy Commission (AEC) and its watchdog in Congress, the Joint Committee on Atomic Energy.

But viewed from the inside, no such degeneration took place at all. Congressman Chester Earl Holifield (D., Calif.), the most pivotal individual controlling the destiny of atomic energy in the United States, is one of only two men who have served continuously on the Joint Committee since it was first formed in 1946. The chairman of that committee for many years,* he has grown to expect people to listen to his words—industrialists, scientists, military leaders and Presidents—and they do, not because he is a compelling speaker but because of his power.

* No longer. The current chairman is Senator John O. Pastore.

When recently interviewed in Washington's Rayburn House Office Building, he went over to a bookcase and pointed to the rows of bound volumes of testimony taken during the twenty-four years of work of the Joint Committee. They were not in the usual green paper wrappers common to congressional reports, but were bound in leather. "I look at this proudly, for t is 's my life's work," he said, motioning to the volumes, pulling out a ew and thumbing through them to show the thoroughness of debates over the years.[2]

Indeed, there was reason to be proud of many of the volumes, for they contained some of the great scientific and military debates over atomic power that have taken place during those many years. Nobel Prize winners in science, generals, admirals and national leaders debating the great issues of war and peace that are tied to the mighty nuclear warheads—all have appeared before his committee.

But "Chet" Holifield, as he prefers being called, noted bitterly that the nation's atomic establishment now is under fire from irresponsible men whose credentials he thought were as poor as their upstart ideas. He labeled them "kooks" and men with "axes to grind," and grandly dismissed them. "They have all been discredited," he said. "We have tried to bring into existence a great new good for mankind—a new form of energy. I believe we've done a superb job."

But somewhere among the bound volumes the chairman so proudly displayed, a very significant bookmark was missing. That bookmark should indicate the turning point among the millions of words, charts and diagrams when the flame went out in the debates before the Joint Committee, when the assumptions were no longer questioned, when witnesses began to soothe the committee instead of stimulate it, when the fierce committee watchdogs became only household pets, when the uses of atomic power became ends unto themselves, exaggerated out of all proportion to the risks they involved.

The turning point came in connection with radioactive fallout from our nation's testing of atomic weapons in the atmosphere. In 1957, at hearings before the Joint Committee,[3] the AEC represented the nuclear tests as safe, strongly committing itself to certain points of view regarding its assessment of those dangers, and the

Joint Committee believed what the AEC had to say. It was soon apparent that the AEC had made several serious errors, the most obvious in connection with strontium 90, carbon 14 and iodine 131, and by the time the 1962 Joint Committee hearings came around[4] there was no ready answer to the public outcry and the international embarrassment caused by such glaring incompetence (see Chapter III).

At that time the AEC could have acknowledged its errors and welcomed constructive criticism from the outside. The Joint Committee could have assigned blame and demanded a housecleaning at the AEC. But to have done so would have been for each to admit to its own incompetence. Instead, those in charge chose to harden their attitudes and justify statements made almost ten years earlier. From that time on, their attitude has been much the same every time they have been caught in an error: the AEC and Joint Committeemen harden their attitudes, justify their former position and refuse to acknowledge that their critics are, after all, correct, despite the fact that every constructive change at the AEC since fallout days has been initiated by outside criticism.

The purpose of this book is to show how the Joint Committee and the AEC changed from healthy adversaries into pals: how the committee was transformed from a critic into an apologist, from an attacker of the AEC into its defender, while the AEC itself was reduced to a fanatically defensive protectionist clique of tenured bureaucrats who have been drawing job security and prestige from the miraculous achievement of the Manhattan Project over twenty-five years ago, and whose best efforts since then have been divided between wildly inappropriate technological adventures and the justification of their past mistakes.

2 · RUBBER CHECKS AND BALANCES

THE TURNING POINT was vital in the history of this nation, for in atomic matters it marked the breakdown of the traditional checks and balances which have been a key to the survival and growth of American government. If that breakdown had occurred in some minor line of government endeavor, perhaps the loss of traditional constitutional rules might have been a small matter to be corrected by some future board of inquiry or an ambitious senator. But it was not. It involved an awesome new form of energy and all of its peaceful and wartime uses. It included the mighty nuclear bombs as well as the development of nuclear-powered electric generating stations, a technology which sooner or later will be the main source of energy for America.

Atomic energy began as a government effort, a child of war, and was sought as a superweapon for use by the United States Army during World War II. It brought that war to a dramatic end with the atomic bombing of the Japanese cities of Hiroshima and Nagasaki in 1945.

The immediate job after the war was to decide who would control the bomb: civilians or soldiers. Perhaps because of this nation's long prewar history of civilian dominance, the military temporarily lost control. But although today most AEC men still react with indignant fury over any suggestion that the military be put in charge of its own programs, the fact is that there is no civilian control over atomic weapons beyond the President's button. Even on a scientific level the distinction between the AEC and the military is hard to find. All three men who have served as top scientific directors of the Department of Defense in recent years were also directors of one of the AEC's main weapons laboratories, the Lawrence Livermore Laboratory in Livermore, California. The men are Herbert F. York, Harold Brown and John S. Foster, Jr. The AEC's Director of Military Applications today, as in the past, is a general. And just before his retirement in 1971, AEC Chairman Glenn T. Seaborg, in a remarkably frank concession, stated that "most of the weapons . . . have become the charge of the Department of Defense . . ." But, by way of justifying his agency's continued "control," Seaborg added that the AEC "still exerts an influence and we have the elements of civilian control with the involvement of the AEC."[5]

Connecticut Senator Brien McMahon's bill,[6] the Atomic Energy Act of 1946, passed Congress, and set up a five-man Atomic Energy Commission—all civilians—to serve as the President's arm in the secret technical world of the atom. The same act set up a Joint Committee on Atomic Energy, made up of nine senators and nine representatives, and gave the committee unusually great powers.

Some of the reasons for granting those special powers then, and over the next decade, had to do with America's postwar obsession with anti-Communism. Triggered by events in China, Korea, Czechoslovakia and Berlin, America's nervousness increased immeasurably when Russian scientists came up with their own atomic bomb. We developed a national hysteria complete with atomic spies, the reign of terror of Senator Joseph M. McCarthy, the hurling of "Soft on Communism" charges against the Democratic Party, and the scramble to outdo the Soviet Union in every field. Though the worst of it all trailed off during the 1950s, the obsession itself remained largely intact until the latter stages of American involvement in the Vietnam War. And so, with the Communist threat in the background, the powers given to the Joint Committee did not seem so unusual then as they do today.

The Atomic Energy Act gave the committee the right to use "services, information, facilities and personnel" of the executive branch of government. Accordingly, the Joint Committee can, among other things, order files or investigations by such closely held executive departments as the Central Intelligence Agency and the Federal Bureau of Investigation. Although this arrangement obviously violates the separation-of-powers idea of the federal Constitution, it is perhaps because the Joint Committee gained its special advantages against the background of the Cold War that the legal basis for this unique arrangement has never been tested in the courts.

The AEC was charged with keeping the Joint Committee "fully and currently informed" of its activities; the committee took this as a strict rule, demanding that it be included in the decision-making process of the executive branch of government. The committee rapidly extended its mandate and even moved into the fiscal phase of government, taking over control of all spending in atomic matters, and at times even pressing unasked-for funds on an unwilling AEC or a reluctant President.[7, 8] While appropriations are properly the function of congressional committees, budget and spending matters are the function of the executive.

Except for the obvious violation of the separation of powers into which this arrangement finally degenerated, the "fully and currently informed" concept seems, on the surface at least, to have been a good idea. But the Joint Committee was at a great disadvantage because, unlike nontechnical fields, the free flow of knowledge between the AEC and the Joint Committee (and the Joint Committee and the rest of Congress, for that matter) was severely hampered by the scientific complexity of the new science itself. Information could be easily withheld (and was) from the Joint Committee by the AEC, just as effectively as if it all had been classified as secret, and Congress was refused a clearance.

For if there is one thing that all federal bureaucrats know well (the system weeds out those who don't learn this lesson), it's the care and feeding of their watchdogs in Congress. Writing reports that gloss over errors and exaggerate achievements in order to support requests for money is the normal occupation of the federal functionary. But the technical complexities of the new world of the atom made congressional scrutiny of AEC reports virtually impossible.

Accordingly, the AEC was able to divert the attention of the Joint Committee from some of its most embarrassing mistakes by scientific smokescreens (see Chapter III).

Whether the AEC was correct or not in its technical judgments was a matter that Congress trusted to the Joint Committee. The Joint Committee in turn left all that up to the experts of the AEC. And so when independent scientists began discovering AEC mistakes, they found themselves in the paradoxical position of having their scientific credentials challenged by the Joint Committee on the basis that AEC experts must be more qualified because they had been closer to the situation for a longer time. Unfortunately, this is still true today.

Under the 1946 Atomic Energy Act, responsibility for the promotion of nuclear energy rested with the AEC. The concept was that the AEC, as a technical organization, would initiate ideas and then present them to the public. The Joint Committee, as the representative of the public's interest, would then hold open hearings where AEC ideas could be discussed, modified, rejected or accepted. Instead, in what was probably its greatest overreaching for power, the Joint Committee itself originated many of the ideas from the start and directed the AEC to develop the appropriate technology and sell it to the public, occasionally with disastrous results (see Chapter VI). With the role of promoter often reversed, the public had nowhere to go in order to reject an idea but to its author, an unlikely place for a fair hearing.

Senator Henry M. Jackson (D., Wash.), who has served on the Joint Committee both as a member of the House and as a senator, wrote that "in the case of certain vital policy decisions, the urging from the Joint Committee has played so powerful a role that it can be said the Committee made the decisions, with the advice and consent of the executive branch."[9]

The Joint Committee has muscled aside almost every executive agency with which it has worked, including even the President himself. In 1962, Holifield, leading the Joint Committee Democrats in their boldest move, went so far as to force the President to appoint their own chief administrative assistant as one of the five Atomic Energy Commissioners. There were two openings on the commission, and the Democrats announced they would accept no nominations unless their staff director, James T. Ramey, was one of those nominated. The White House at first balked at this flagrant violation of the doctrine of separation of powers and refused; the matter hung in the air for a month before President Kennedy finally capitulated.[10] Since Ramey's appointment, insiders concede that he has exerted a single-handed veto inside the AEC over every matter that Representative Holifield of the Joint Committee on Atomic Energy did not favor. Thus, two men, Holifield and Ramey, dictate atomic energy policy in the United States.

Before long, the Joint Committee insisted on designing and promoting its own programs, unresponsive to Presidential or AEC initiatives. It did not watch the AEC, it simply took over management. Commission Chairman Lewis L. Strauss resisted during his stormy tenure at the AEC. But it was a losing fight, generally abandoned by his successors, Dr. John A. McCone and Dr. Glenn T. Seaborg. A personal hostility between Strauss and Senator Clinton Anderson of New Mexico led to the kind of revenge that a member of Congress can extract: further limiting the powers of the commission itself in order to strike at his enemy, Strauss. But after Strauss's resignation in 1958, the tense climate suddenly and dramatically changed. Senator Anderson was already close friends with the new chairman, John McCone, but by this time the Joint Committee had solid hold and the two adversary groups became partners.

Another important reason for the no-questions-asked attitude as the Joint Committee increased its power was the awesome air of magic mystery about the atom itself. The first chairman of the AEC, David E. Lilienthal, wrote:

The atom had us bewitched. It was so gigantic, so terrible, so beyond the power of imagination to embrace that it seemed to be the ultimate fact. It would either destroy us or bring around the millenium. It was the final secret of Nature, greater by far than man himself. . . . Our obsession with the atom led us to assign to it a separate and unique status in the world. So greatly did it seem to transcend the ordinary affairs of men that we shut it out of those affairs altogether; or rather tried to create a separate world, the world of the atom.[11]

Consider the words of Senator Brien McMahon in 1945:

... when the bomb bay doors of the B-29 opened over Hiroshima when the first atomic bomb exploded almost 90 days ago, in my opinion there occurred, as I said the other day, the most momentous development in the 2,000 years of the world's history since the birth of Jesus Christ.

Eve tempted Adam, and Adam succumbed and partook of the fruit of the tree of knowledge, and as a result Adam and Eve were banished from Paradise.

Man today has tasted the fruit of the secret of energy; he has finally discovered the secret of matter, and I say that unless this momentous development is handled wisely and judiciously, unless it leads to peace and righteousness among men and among nations, all mankind will be banished from the face of the earth.[12]

These were the pressures on the eighteen men of the Joint Committee. When they reached for excess power their request was unquestioned, because it was a noble cause, a just mission to hurry along a fumbling bureaucracy. Also, the matter was one of highest national security, requiring the rest of Congress to accept the decisions of the Joint Committee on faith, not facts.

More cynical Americans prefer to see the Joint Committee members as reaching out to feather their own political nests or seeking power for its own sake. To some degree this might be true, for it is the perennial temptation of politicians, but these were not evil men with evil designs who were guided only by a lust for power. The members who took an active role in the affairs of the Joint Committee were not even the vain stags who strut the halls of the Senate; they were only the drab and routine pragmatic politicians like Representative Holifield. The only thing that sets them apart is that they have listened long enough to scientific jargon to think they understand it and to be able to ask stylish and occasionally penetrating questions. So when the hearings before the committee became friendly, with the questions and answers sounding often like rehearsed affairs, which they were in some cases (see Chapter V), a measure of public control had broken down. The other form of control in this nation, control by competition and controversy, never existed.

Though voices in Congress are beginning to irritate the Joint Committee, men like Senator Mike Gravel are not strong enough yet to counteract the carefully built political machine that maintains the Joint Committee. The power of its members, through seniority in the Congress and through pork-barrel politics, is hard to beat— even for the President.

But it is easy, especially today, for Americans to forget the importance of the division of powers between the executive and legislative branches, between the President and the Congress. It is part of the checks-and-balances system of American government, the *single device* we have to keep a person or an agency from becoming an unchallenged dictator. It is one thing for a congressional committee to oversee Presidential programs—to criticize, to make sure things are being done right, to point out errors and inconsistencies—but it is quite another thing for the same committee to devise its own programs and directions and still try to pose as the watchdog. Instead of criticizing others, the Joint Committee shortly found itself in the position of criticizing its own works and judgments, a corruptible position even among the noblest of men.

And that is what has happened in the government of the atom in this country. The Joint Committee and the AEC were transformed from healthy adversaries into pals, the committee changed from being a critic into being an apologist, from an attacker into a defender. The watchdog grew rubber teeth.

3 · MONEY TALKS

"THE PRODUCTION of the atomic bomb was a great big scientific success story," wrote David E. Lilienthal. "The doors of the treasury swung open and money poured out. For the physicist who had waited for years to test his theories on equipment too expensive for anyone to buy, it was a dream come true."[11]

In the field of scientific research it is best to think of money as fertilizer, to spread it everywhere very thickly and hope that something worthwhile comes up. Besides, a rich nation can afford to be careless with research money: it buys more than simply increasing the possibility of a scientific breakthrough, it also buys support for the donor agency in Congress, and that support is needed to insure the continuation of government funding.

AEC spending has been directed annually to all fifty states in recent years (also the District of Columbia, Japan, Puerto Rico, Johnstown Island and other spots around the globe). This is not the classic federal spending for post offices, federal buildings, or public works; instead it is spending for things the states want even more: "clean" industries connected with science, electronics, engineering, metallurgy and a host of other exotic subjects. Further, the people brought into areas on AEC contracts were not paid the relatively low wages of federal civil servants; most AEC-supported salaries were at the higher wage scales of professional engineers and scientists in private industry. This is because the AEC is only a skeleton bureaucracy: it has only seven thousand federal employees but spends well over $2 billion yearly. The big money goes to private industry, since the AEC does almost everything by contract to 538 companies, 223 colleges and universities and 125,000 contractor employees in all.[13] The top contractor (Union Carbide Corporation) gets almost *a third of a billion* dollars each year.

These large expenditures have a self-perpetuating aspect about them; after a time they become a necessary part of local economics. AEC support is so strong in some places that it's practically impossible to cancel a contract even when the AEC's customer no longer requires the hardware and says so before Congress. (See Chapter VI.)

The colleges and universities get their share, too. Some simply lend their names to AEC establishments in return for an annual fee. For example, the University of California at Berkeley receives $2.5

million annually as a fee for lending its name to the Lawrence Livermore Laboratory in Livermore, California, the Los Alamos Scientific Laboratory in New Mexico, and a smaller AEC biology unit at the University of California at Los Angeles. Remarkably, the University of California incurs almost no administrative expense, and therefore it can be legitimately said that for all practical purposes, the $2.5 million from the AEC is for the use of the university's name alone.

Other groups of universities work together in similar arrangements, and still other universities simply receive support for research directly. Princeton leads the list with over $17.5 million each year.[14] Besides annual payments, the AEC has littered the collegiate landscape with cyclotrons, accelerators and other research hardware. Two examples among many are the newest accelerators being built, one in Batavia, Illinois, and the other at Stanford University; their combined cost is over a half-billion dollars.

Though many scientists deny it (not all), such massive funding of basic research has a prostituting effect. It warps university research projects as well as the direction and shape of scientific inquiry itself. "He who pays the piper calls the tune": you deliver what the big customer wants or you don't come back and ask for more money. It seems more than a coincidence that men who have tapped deeply into atomic tills (several million dollars from the AEC for one scientist alone[15]) have at the same time been among the most consistent defenders of the AEC before public hearings and the federal courts. It's inevitable that when a promoter controls the purse strings, sooner or later everyone on the payroll agrees with the product line.

AEC grantsmanship has been so widespread that there is almost no chance to find an outside, objective review of the agency by men who know physics. Dr. Philip Handler, president of the National Academy of Sciences, admitted, "It is essentially impossible to find more than a small handful of such experts who have not, in relatively recent times, had significant support—either research grants or actual employment—from the U.S. Atomic Energy Commission."[16]

But occasionally even established "insiders" speak out despite their long history of support by the AEC. However, this is unusual and so far has had no effect on the AEC's plans in the end. (See the Pitzer Panel story later in this chapter.)

Though it is widely believed that all views are tolerated in the scientific community and that open publication of unorthodox opinions is encouraged (on the theory that ridicule by one's peers is the best cure for wrongheadedness), this is not so. It is not uncommon for legitimate research findings unfavorable to AEC policies to become squelched by establishment scientists during the pre-publication review process.[17] Very often this means that divergent views are put to rest without creating a stir. After all, education should not be equated with courage: scientists are not known for sticking their necks out.

And so the AEC and its contractors have set themselves in place firmly, difficult to dislodge, vulnerable only to the passage of time and to shifts in the political thought of the nation. Only recently does it seem that such a shift might be taking place.

4 · "BUILT-IN OBJECTIVITY"

ANOTHER PROFOUND CONTRIBUTION serving to insulate the AEC from the public was its mutually contradictory dual role of promoter and regulator of its own product, atomic energy. This grave mistake was made at the start and was written into the Atomic Energy Act itself. It was a built-in recipe for corruption, because aggressive promotion and honest regulation cannot coexist in the same authority for very long.

But self-regulation wasn't even a necessary arrangement. The aviation industry, where safety restrictions can be of great economic importance, managed to expand and serve the nation quite well with safety regulations taken care of by the Federal Aviation Agency and with its promotional and economic interests the responsibility of the Civil Aeronautics Board. Accordingly, even the Joint Committee eventually realized that "the very difficult job facing the Commissioners is compounded by the fact that the AEC . . . is subject to a strain on its objectivity for, in many instances, it is both the promoter and the regulator of the atomic energy project in question."[18] And so, in 1960, the Joint Committee and the AEC began separate studies in order to determine how best to resolve the dilemma.

In March of 1961, the Joint Committee summarized the various views: "At one extreme [the AEC's position], it has been suggested that the present organization be continued with only minor organizational and procedural changes. . . . At the other extreme [a University of Michigan study], it has been suggested that there be created a regulatory agency separate from the AEC." A compromise position was struck by the Joint Committee staff, who recommended that an Atomic Safety and Licensing Board be created inside the AEC.[19]

But the AEC wasn't about to wait for hearings, scheduled to take place three months later. It already knew what it wanted. In an unusually quick maneuver, only ten days after the Joint Committee's staff study of the question was handed over to the Joint Committee, AEC Chairman Glenn T. Seaborg announced, "The Commission has acted to separate its regulatory function from the operational and developmental [promotional] functions at General Manager level";[20] in other words, the "minor organizational and procedural change" described by the Joint Committee as "one extreme" was an accomplished fact.

When hearings into the matter finally took place, three months later,[21] Chairman Holifield acknowledged that "the AEC recommended, and has since adopted, certain organizational changes including creation of a Director of Regulation reporting directly to the Commission. These changes were adopted on the basis that they *would not prejudice a fair consideration of other proposals* for a revision of the regulating organization."* But that was the end of the matter. The AEC had weathered the attacks and kept control.

It is so typical of deliberations within the atomic bureaucracy: the one time in the twenty-five-year history of the AEC when its formal powers were to be pruned, it sat in judgment on itself. More precisely, it didn't even wait for a final determination, but gambled that presented with an accomplished fact, the Joint Committee would just accept it. It was a safe bet, because, like the AEC, the Joint Committee realized that regulation of a technology always leads to limitations, and the Joint Committee and the AEC were not interested in limitations. They were interested in expansion, so promotion naturally won. The AEC was to continue regulating itself, with the sole difference that the regulators within the commission would report directly to the commissioners instead of to the general manager, one administrative level down.

Other attempts at "built-in objectivity" were less contrived but just as futile. In the beginning, the AEC relied on a number of internal committees set up by the AEC, again to keep an eye on itself. The committees were to provide some semblance of outside, objective review. Included in the group is the General Advisory Committee, which Dr. J. Robert Oppenheimer headed after he stepped down as the wartime director of the Los Alamos Scientific Laboratory, the place where the atomic bomb was developed. The General Advisory Committee was designed to give technical advice to the supposedly nontechnical, civilian-oriented AEC. But excepting the very early days, until 1971 the AEC has been made up entirely of insiders who have been long connected with the atomic establishment and for whom technical advice would be an impertinence. So even the General Advisory Committee has become a useless and powerless appendage.

The first commissions were dominated by outsiders with a more objective view of the nation's nuclear efforts. The first commission was headed by David Lilienthal, from the Tennessee Valley Authority, and the other members were Sumner F. Pike, an investment

* Emphasis added.

banker; William Waymack, a Midwest newspaper editor; Robert Bacher, a physicist from the Manhattan Project, which developed the first atomic bombs; and Lewis Strauss, a rear-echelon Navy admiral and wealthy physics buff. However, in 1970 the commission was composed of James Ramey, former staff man to the Joint Committee; Chairman Glenn T. Seaborg and the late Theos J. Thompson, both scientists with a long history in the atomic establishment; Wilfrid E. Johnson from General Electric, the biggest corporation in the boiling-water-nuclear-reactor business; and Clarence E. Larson, former president of the Nuclear Division of Union Carbide Corporation, the largest single AEC contractor.

Commissioner Ramey told the Joint Committee on October 30, 1969, "Mr. Chairman, I would like to note that from the beginning the AEC has been fortunate in having wide experience in nuclear energy on the Commission. Each of the five of us presently serving on the Commission has more than twenty years of experience in the nuclear field . . ."[22] Thus, ironically, Ramey looks upon a commission of insiders as a great advantage. But by trading objectivity for technical expertise he strikes a poor bargain. After all, the commissioners can call up all the technical experts they need just for the asking, but objectivity is another matter. Either you have it or you don't.

Other so-called "independent" committees, such as the Advisory Committee on Reactor Safeguards, have developed such a close working arrangement with the AEC staff that all but a semblance of arm's-length dealing is lost. This committee, which former AEC Commissioner Dr. Thompson once headed, is appointed by the AEC on the recommendation of the existing committee and the AEC's director of regulations. The members come from the ranks of atomic industry or atomic sciences for which the AEC is the sole financial guardian angel. Still, the AEC stresses the independence and value of these committees, unable to see that such built-in administrative devices only guarantee perpetuation of nonobjectivity.

When presented with criticism of its committee system, the AEC points out the difficulty in obtaining talent for these committees which is devoid of the taint of self-interest. It maintains that its committees really are independent and free, but the facts tell another story: the committees are free until they "get out of hand."

5 · AMCHITKA: AN ADVISORY PANEL THAT ADVISED

ONLY ON RARE OCCASIONS will an AEC advisory committee issue a report containing conclusions criticizing AEC plans. Such reports are seldom weighed openly; more often they are suppressed and forgotten. An imaginative technique not generally known is often employed when a report contains a judgment offensive or unfavorable to the AEC: very few copies will be issued. The supply is quickly exhausted, sometimes in a single day, and purposely as well, by sending copies to individuals on the extensive *internal* distribution lists of the AEC. The report is then revised, often without benefit of consultation with the author, the objectionable passage (sometimes a single line) is removed, and it is then republished, this time in sufficient volume.

The Pitzer Panel is a classic but by no means singular case of another type of suppression which the AEC did not get away with completely.

For many years the AEC has fired off nuclear blasts at its Nevada test site, northwest of Las Vegas. These explosions have all taken place underground since the passage of the Nuclear Test Ban Treaty of 1963.[6] In the mid 1960s, pressured by billionaire Howard Hughes, who was worried about earthquakes,[23] and seeking new test areas for larger, megaton-sized weapons (a megaton is a measure of explosive force equivalent to one million tons of TNT), the AEC chose two new sites for its tests, one farther north in Nevada and another on Amchitka, in Alaska's Aleutian Islands. But by 1968 new public pressures were building, particularly in earthquake-conscious Alaska, where that same year Alaska's most serious earthquake took place. So in October 1968, at the request of the AEC, the President's Office of Science and Technology appointed a panel of scientists headed by Dr. Kenneth S. Pitzer, then president of Stanford University, to study the safety of underground testing of nuclear weapons.

Dr. Pitzer appeared at first to be a safe choice for the AEC, for he is a veteran of the atomic establishment. He served as director of research for the AEC from 1949 to 1951, was chairman of the General Advisory Committee and a member of the President's Science Advisory Committee, and was highly regarded throughout the atomic and academic field. Furthermore, the AEC could hardly question his loyalty, since he was one of the very few scientists (Dr. Edward Teller, the "father of the H-bomb" was another of the group) that the AEC could find in 1954 who would testify against J. Robert Oppenheimer during Oppenheimer's security trial before the AEC.[24, 25] Another member of the Pitzer Panel was Dr. James R. Killian, chairman of the Massachusetts Institute of Technology and former science adviser to President Eisenhower. It was, scientifically, a group of unimpeachable class.

The AEC had already selected Amchitka Island (in 1966) for its biggest underground tests and had already fired off test shots in the new central-Nevada site. "Faultless," an 800-kiloton explosion (a kiloton is a measure of explosive force equivalent to one thousand tons of TNT), had been set off in central Nevada on January 19, 1966, and had led to some of the controversy. Its effects were felt farther away than any previous underground shot. In Amchitka, beginning in 1967, the AEC had moved men and equipment to the test site, improving the harbor, building an airstrip and drilling the gigantic hole to be used for Project Milrow, the first big underground shot planned for Alaska. Easily half of the project's $130 million had already been spent when the Pitzer Panel was called in to review the geology and other safety considerations.

Dr. Pitzer's group met in November 1968 and did its work in a hurry—a report was ready in less than one month. It was critical of both the central-Nevada and Amchitka sites because of earthquakes associated with large tests:

> ... there does not now appear to be a basis for eliminating the possibility that a large test explosion might induce, either immediately or after a period of time, a severe earthquake of sufficiently large magnitude to cause serious damage well beyond the limits of the test site. . . . proposed tests at the central-Nevada site involve a greater risk of earthquake than those at the regular Nevada Test Site, since the more northerly portions of Nevada are more active seismically. Since the Amchitka area in Alaska is still more active seismically, the hazard of inducing an earthquake must be considered to be greater at that location than at either Nevada site. The recent evidence indicates that the risks of damaging side effects from megaton tests are larger than were estimated when the proposed test series was planned. However remote and uncertain these risks may be, in the Panel's judgment they still raise new and serious questions about such tests and about the selection of sites for such tests. . . . Consideration should also be given to the possibility of establishing a new high-yield test site in a non-seismic area. . . .[26]

The report, though it contained no military secrets, was made a government secret anyway. It was not the AEC's supersecret "Q" clearance system[27] which was used to suppress it, it was the AEC's use of executive privilege. As an arm of the President, the AEC has the right to withhold anything it determines to be purely an internal report for its own use.

So the AEC suppressed the Pitzer Panel report while it began, internally, to write other reports to refute it. (Several examples of this deceitful technique will be provided later.) Four anonymous papers were produced, all supporting the Amchitka and central-Nevada test sites and the safety of firing off big weapons there. Dr. Pitzer, Dr. Killian and others on the panel were not afraid to have their names on their report, but the AEC people ducked. The AEC staff said that since the four anonymous studies were made by "many members of the staffs within the AEC, AEC contract laboratories and the Batelle Memorial Institutes [also AEC] . . . it would be difficult to attribute any specific statement to any single individual." But in actual practice such reports are routinely produced by very few people, sometimes a single individual, and then sent around to as many as a score of others for reading and initialing before publication. Unsigned reports have the dual advantage of suggesting (incorrectly) that the report is the result of the collective wisdom of many individuals and of protecting the real author from cross-examination. But in fairness it must be pointed out that not all the anonymous authors refused to sign their reports because they were afraid of cross-examination. At least one AEC scientist refused because he could not accept the changes made in his report "after it had been through four levels of bureaucracy."[28]

The whole matter came to the attention of Congress in late 1969, just a few days before the AEC was to push the button on its first test in Amchitka. Alaska Senator Mike Gravel was pulling out all stops in an effort to stop Project Milrow, the megaton-sized hydrogen bomb already buried four thousand feet down. Senator Gravel steered a number of bills and resolutions around the Joint Committee, convinced by now, and with good reason, that it was useless to talk to them.

The issue was finally discussed publicly before the Senate Foreign Relations Committee.[26] Chairman J. William Fulbright questioned AEC Commissioner Wilfrid Johnson about the Pitzer report: "Is there any substantive reason why this report should be classified?"

"The substantive reason would have to come from the White House, of course," Johnson replied, evading the question, since the President obviously did not classify the report.

"It should have been released last November when the report was made," Senator Fulbright insisted.

AEC Commissioner Johnson replied that "there was a great deal more information desired" by the AEC staff before publishing it.

"That is another thing that does not appeal to me," Chairman Fulbright continued. "You put three or four statements in this booklet *ahead* of the Pitzer report, all of them denigrating the Pitzer report, which seems to me a very strange way to present a report; it should stand on its own. You put it in the back. Why didn't you put the Pitzer report in front and then follow it with your report?"

"We thought the sequence was appropriate," the commissioner replied, again without giving his reasons.

"This sounds like Madison Avenue propaganda," the chairman said. "I do not think it is worthy of the AEC. We are looking for truth now, trying to seek the truth. These people's lives and property are involved. It is a very serious matter," said Fulbright.

Commissioner Johnson replied, "I believe, Mr. Chairman, that truth permeates the entire report, not just the Pitzer report."

Chairman Fulbright persisted: "I am talking about the form of it. It seems very odd to me. A copy was given to me only twenty minutes before I came up here. I have not read it, obviously, but the staff calls attention to the fact that the Pitzer Panel report is the last one in the series. The first three or four all undertake to make the Pitzer report seem innocuous and unimportant."

"Mr. Chairman, that's not my reading of it," Commissioner Johnson replied.

"It's never anybody's responsibility," the chairman observed philosophically. "It is always someone else's responsibility."

Commissioner Johnson had explained that the report, though done at the request of the AEC, was "an in-house report" for the benefit of the executive branch of government and that the AEC had no right to release it. It had been marked "OFFICIAL USE ONLY" and "PRIVILEGED." Senator Gravel, who had repeatedly requested the report, got it like everyone else, three days before Milrow's detonation, in the same booklet with the anonymous AEC staff reports.

Senator Fulbright pointed out that if an outside report agrees with any government agency's position, it is printed in a matter of days or weeks. If it doesn't, it is difficult and often impossible to obtain. Had it been a favorable report, there is no doubt that it would have been issued immediately after completion, together with the usual AEC press releases and unlimited, freely available copies to all interested persons, and then some.

The entire question died down when Milrow exploded and no great earthquakes or tidal waves or leaks of radioactivity followed.

The success of this and of the second Alaskan shot, Cannikin, still does not mean that it is safe to fire off major shots in Amchitka. It only means it was all right twice. And mistakes did happen. On December 18, 1970, Project Baneberry, designed to be a completely contained underground test, broke through the ground surface and sent a cloud of radioactive fallout over eight thousand feet into the air, contaminating at least twelve states and Canada.[29] While it is true that Baneberry was detonated one thousand feet underground (compared to Milrow's four-thousand-foot depth), it was fifty times smaller in explosive yield and therefore might be expected to be less likely to vent.

The whole Pitzer Panel affair points up several lessons, but one thing is dramatically clear: once the Atomic Energy Commission makes up its mind to do something, it shoves even rational objections out of its way. The AEC was obviously surprised when its own Pitzer Panel failed to rubber-stamp the whole project. But it coped with the situation by confronting the Senate Foreign Relations Committee, and everyone else concerned, with action that had already been taken and was too late to call back. The Pitzer Panel incident is a further demonstration that built-in objectivity is an illusion. True control, as always, must come from the outside.

6 · THE REACTORS ARRIVE

THERE HAS NEVER BEEN an atomic marketplace in this country, though the Joint Committee has striven hard to create one. Certainly nuclear bombs never found themselves in competition with other weapons. The situation, in fact, has been just the opposite. The Department of Defense has always had its nuclear warheads provided free of charge from the AEC's separate budget, so it never had to choose between a nuclear warhead and a tank, or between a nuclear warhead and an airplane. This fact alone accounts in large measure for the excessive size of our massive nuclear arsenal, although other forces were at play as well.

In civilian affairs there is a great deal of pretending about competition between nuclear and fossil-fuel plants for generating electric power. But it's a rigged competition which, although heavily biased against the fossil-fuel plants, has not yet resulted in self-supporting nuclear plants. Though propped and boosted by government crutches and subsidies, and already accounting for over $40 billion of the combined efforts of government and private industry, nuclear plants are still more expensive to build and maintain than coal-fired plants if *all* of the costs are taken into account. But, even so, their future looks bright in the long run if the AEC and the Joint Committee, through their insensitivity and incompetence, don't succeed in further alienating public opinion to the point of no return.

Nuclear electric-generating plants were little noticed until they had spread through thirty of the fifty states. They had been quietly peddled to a power-conscious public in a manner that never hinted that a major accident at just one plant could bring death and destruction on a scale that could outrank any of the nation's major natural disasters. The one-sided story, the trademark of the peddler, became the trademark of the AEC in the nuclear-power business, as never before.

When Americans began to notice these plants and look into them, they discovered the breakdown in checks and balances, not only in government but also in the AEC's agency review process for siting and building these plants. Now a growing group—scientists and laymen, politicians and environmentalists—have mounted an increasingly shrill campaign against the conduct of this nation's atomic affairs, all agreeing basically that the mechanisms for public control have broken down. They feel that because the Joint Committee has taken sides and because the AEC is both the regulator and the promoter of atomic energy, there is no longer a dispassionate voice in government to weigh the facts and protect the public interest.

As happens when checks and balances break down and power is

thus undivided and unquestioned, the men who hold that power become isolated from public opinion, contemptuous of outsiders and even immune to internal technical criticism.

Asked why criticism has boiled up, one of the Joint Committee staff members wrote it off, as Chairman Holifield has done, to "kooks." Said the aide, "We've got a relentless group in this country with a masochistic psychological guilt complex that says we've got to get rid of all nuclear weapons."[30]

Commissioner Ramey and Chairman Holifield discussed the problem during hearings in 1969.[31] Ramey, who that year had attended public meetings in both Minnesota and Vermont, testified, "At each of these meetings that I have gone through—the Vermont and Minnesota ones—there are some professional 'stirrer-uppers' involved . . ."

"That is a good name, 'stirrer-uppers,' " Chairman Holifield agreed.

Commissioner Ramey continued, ". . . gentlemen from some 'paper' conservation organizations that you can hardly find an address for, to persons associated with the coal industry . . ." The commissioner has long been convinced that "coal dust" is involved in opposition to nuclear plants, since nuclear heat is used to generate steam rather than coal heat. Early on in the game he was right, since the United Mine Workers at first strongly opposed the construction of nuclear plants. But he sees other devils, too.

"Second," he continued, "there is a group of younger scientists, some of whom might be a little bit on the extremist side, who seem to always be talking on matters beyond their own professional competence. They discuss and comment on areas in which they have not performed their scientific work."

"Well, we have a certain number of book writers too, of sensational books," Chairman Holifield offered.

"They are usually journalists and public-relations men," the commissioner said.

"That is right," Chairman Holifield agreed, "with no scientific background or competence."

"None whatsoever," Ramey answered, "that is right."

Thus the most powerful single man in the AEC and the most powerful member of Congress in atomic matters (neither man, by the way, having any of the scientific training they seem to require in others) consoled each other that the fault was not theirs, if fault existed at all—it was all simply due to outside agitators.

The chairman acknowledged that there were some responsible critics. AEC Commissioner Ramey agreed and quickly changed the subject, saying, "One of the things that has struck me, though, on these is the number of really phony arguments that have been submitted in these meetings. . . . As you know, Mr. Chairman, I am not a scientist, but I have been in this game for a long time. I went through the whole fallout controversy and other controversies *when I was staff director of the Joint Committee.** I may have gotten a pretty good ear for detecting phonies and phony arguments."

With such disdain have the two most powerful men in the nation's atomic establishment disposed of their critics. They couldn't be more wrong. There are many responsible scientists who honestly feel that there are real arguments against the way the AEC and the Joint Committee have brought nuclear power into existence. It is a disservice to both the atomic industry and the public whose money they so lavishly spend to treat these arguments with sneering impatience.

But these two men control America's atomic establishment, a multibillion-dollar complex with military, industrial and governmental members, and they still live in the sheltered world of each other's opinions. For if nuclear power falters or even fails, it will be no one's fault but Holifield's, Ramey's and that of the other insensitive directors of the atomic establishment who respond to legitimate public criticism by name-calling instead of realizing that the dispute is their own creation, a Frankenstein's monster created from their own ineptness.

* Emphasis added.

7 · THE ATOM TODAY

WE ALL HOPED the atom would become the means to a better life for this nation, and the means to a world of peace if we stockpiled atomic weapons high enough to frighten our enemies. But the atom has brought neither peace nor affluence.

As for world peace, the atom's main contribution has been as a weapon, a weapon alone and a weapon we dare not use. Each decade had its war, Korea for the 1950s, Vietnam for the 1960s, and the nuclear weapons that were to keep us at peace wait on the shelf, as useless as mustard gas, appearing increasingly aggressive and absurd to the rest of the world. In this, of course, we are not alone.

And as for national affluence, the $50 billion spent so far by the AEC has done little. Missiles and bombs surely provide wages for American workers who make them, but the economics of defense spending are weak. There are few "economic multipliers" in a bomb.[32] Bombs are designed to be dropped, lost, discarded or stockpiled, but bombs have no lasting impact on a nation's economy as does a new house, for example, which not only provides immediate jobs and consumption but serves continually for many decades, requiring and producing further services. All the war goods could be dumped into the ocean tomorrow and have no effect on the nation's economy; you can hardly say that for anything else. War goods have no lasting impact because they are not reusable. But money spent on housing, on the decaying American cities, on courts, prisons and police, on sewers and smoke abatement, on mass transit and wilderness areas, on training the jobless and healing the desperate among us, all have an end product with a lasting impact. Their effect bounces again and again through the economics of the nation.

However, that $50 billion has provided a way of life for American physicists and associated scientists. For some of these people the arms race has become an end in itself, an only slightly productive end, with no promise of self-support, around which have gathered special economic and political interests whose main effort lately is to protect it from attack and keep it going. For if the arms race does nothing else, it supports those most intimately involved with keeping it going.

But about $20 billion of that $50 billion has given the nation some hope of atomic affluence after all, and that hope lies with the nuclear-power reactors. Although electricity from atomic plants can never become as cheap as early AEC propaganda would have it, using the heat from nuclear fission to generate electricity can, on a technical basis at least, prove more desirable than employing conventional fossil fuels.

But there are serious problems standing in the way of public acceptance of nuclear energy, and they are all caused by the arrogant insensitivity and ineptness of the stewards of the atomic establishment themselves. For by their intransigent refusal to yield even to the legitimate demands of responsible technical and political critics, they have lost their credibility to contradict the increasing attacks made upon them by irresponsible critics. Accordingly, the public of the 1970s has come to believe that nuclear energy is even more dangerous than it actually is. This is a far cry from the 1950s, when it was widely accepted that nuclear energy not only was perfectly safe but would provide electricity so cheap that electric meters would soon be obsolete.

And so the very men who brought nuclear energy into existence have, unburdened by self-doubt, become its greatest enemies today, and, to complete the paradox, they will be the last to know.

II
THE HEART
OF THE MATTER:
WEAPONS

*I have examined man's wonderful inventions. And I
tell you in the arts of life, man invents nothing: but
in the arts of death he outdoes nature herself. . . .
There is nothing in man's industrial machinery but
his greed and his sloth: his heart is in his weapons.*
—GEORGE BERNARD SHAW[33]

1 · MILITARY THINKING:
POSSIBILITIES, WORST-CASE ANALYSIS,
AND SECOND STRIKE

OF ALL THE EFFORTS that the atomic scientist has turned his attention to in the last twenty-five years, weapons are his most outstanding product. We have been testing them at the rate of about thirty each year, and they work remarkably well. Though there were early fizzles, they hardly ever fail to go off.[34]

To understand these weapons, why they were built and tested and how this nation came to have such a mighty stockpile of them, a few basic points must be made about the thinking of some of our military and political leaders.

In the spring of 1966, two visitors stopped to see General Lyman L. Lemnitzer, then Supreme Allied Commander in Europe, at his headquarters in Versailles, France.[35] All of Western Europe was under a Pax Americana, without a war in twenty years, perhaps maintained by the presence of more than 300,000 American troops.

The general was asked what would happen if all the American troops were withdrawn from Europe the next day. Did the general think Russian tanks would come rumbling across the borders and take over?

No, General Lemnitzer replied, of course not. But he explained that in the military, preparation is always made for an enemy's capabilities rather than his intentions, and the Russians clearly had the capability to invade Western Europe. Thus, he reflected a type of thinking which has become increasingly common even outside the military, especially since the advent of nuclear weapons: that the responsibility of the military is to consider the worst possible actions of an enemy and prepare for them—that the possibilities are the important things, and the probabilities of those actions actually occurring are irrelevant. But there is a very important distinction between the two words: probabilities have limits, but possibilities can trail on forever.

Neither a man nor a nation can live sanely in a world of possibilities, because there is danger everywhere if you look hard enough. So although it would seem proper to strike a balance between possibility and probability, no such balance has been evident in the military posture of the United States until recently. General Lemnitzer's concern with enemy capabilities reflects one of the key ideas which permeates not only the military but also our diplomatic dealings with foreign powers. And the difference between our military policy and our foreign policy has at times in the past been hard to discern.

Adam Yarmolinsky, former Deputy Assistant Secretary of Defense, stated that "in substance and in character, United States foreign policy has become substantially militarized." He noted that "policy makers adopted military staff habits of reckoning contingencies in terms of capabilities rather than the intentions of potential enemies and . . . emphasizing readiness for the worst contingencies that might arise."[36] Even very recently, President Nixon, in promoting the Safeguard anti–ballistic-missile (ABM) program, said it would provide a "credible foreign policy in the Pacific Areas."[37]

General Bruce K. Holloway, commander in chief of the Strategic Air Command and overseer of much of the nation's mighty nuclear strategic weapons forces said, ". . . the central fact of our time . . . is the present relative equality of the U.S. and Soviet strategic military power. Since this power is the *foundation of all diplomacy as well as war,* and since the Soviet Union demonstrates so clearly a desperation to achieve strategic supremacy, then the United States faces the greatest jeopardy to its existence since that war against fascism a quarter century ago, if not for all time."[38]* Thus, while General Holloway's opinion is represented as a balanced view, he is really presenting a worst-case analysis.

Thus, preoccupation with possibilities instead of probabilities leads to worst-case planning and is the keystone to understanding how this nation has dealt with its nuclear power. Two other military concepts, which are interconnected, are equally vital.

The first is "sneak attack." When the Japanese struck Pearl Harbor on December 7, 1941, bringing this country directly into World War II, they caught the United States armed forces by surprise. Although the incoming Japanese attacking force was detected by our Army's primitive radar on Hawaii, the planes were assumed to be our own. Much of the American naval and air power in the Pacific was destroyed that morning, but because of our remoteness and the failure of the Japanese to appreciate the success of their attack, our nation had time to gather its strength and begin the fight back. Some of our military leaders in Hawaii were punished because of their lack of preparedness for the attack.[39] It would be too cynical to suggest that their reprimand was the only reason why military leaders have been preoccupied with blunting surprise attacks since that time, but military men did indeed resolve never to let it happen again.

But the real turning point was nuclear arms. A surprise attack by conventional forces is one thing. But a surprise attack by nuclear weapons, capable of wiping out major sections of an entire nation, is quite another. So the determination to avoid another Pearl Harbor was only increased by the development of the atomic bomb.

* Emphasis added.

The result has been flights of spy planes and spy satellites around the world, banks of mighty radar systems costing billions, thousands of fighter planes, bombers and radar picket planes in the air all the time. All of these warning and protection systems are tied together in the American-Canadian joint North American Air Defense Command, which is located in a $142-million warning and command center, mounted on springs, in a hollowed-out granite mountain in Colorado. "The Ballistic Missile Early Warning System is the checkmate to a sneak intercontinental ballistic missile attack against this continent," reads a booklet for visitors to the mountain headquarters.

The second major concept is "second strike." It has been the historic policy of the United States to avoid aggressive war. "We have not forsworn our national character because of the bomb," wrote the military critic Brigadier General (Ret.) S. L. A. Marshall. "We will not wage aggressive war upon our neighbors. Therefore we can never count on striking the first blow."[40] But once attacked by others, we can launch a second strike.

Though many may argue that we have violated this principle occasionally (the Mexican War, the Spanish–American War, the Vietnamese War), the fact remains that second strike has become firmly imbedded in American military policy as one of its guiding principles.

Out of the military concept of second strike came two more catchwords: "deterrent" and "survivability." The force available for a second strike must be so great that all enemies will be deterred from launching a sneak attack. But since a deterrent is no good unless it can survive an enemy's first strike, it must possess survivability as well, since if it won't survive an attack, it's worthless.

According to military thinking, survivability depends upon four factors, and military tacticians try to build as many of them as possible into any nuclear-weapons system:

1. *Dispersion:* Spread out weapons system thinly, to decrease the possibility that all of our retaliatory capability could be destroyed by the enemy's first strike.

2. *Redundancy:* Build a great number of weapons and systems,

all capable of responding after the enemy's first strike, again so that one enemy attack can't cancel out our retaliatory potential.

3. *Hardness:* Keep weapons well protected physically by burying them in concrete silos or putting them inside mountains or on board submarines.

4. *Mobility:* When possible, make weapons mobile, since it is harder to locate and hit a moving target.

According to the military, the *intentions* of the enemy have always been irrelevant. Consider the words of Air Force Secretary Robert C. Seamans in an interview with the editors of *Skyline,* the company magazine put out by the North American Rockwell Corporation, one of the nation's ten largest defense contractors. It is a mixture of worst-case analysis, second-strike philosophy, and the possibilities ("capabilities") argument:

> We must study as best we can the capabilities of potential enemies—not as a scare tactic, not to produce panic reaction, but because the capabilities of potential enemies are, after all, the true measure of the forces we really need. . . . The best way to prevent nuclear war is to ensure that there is no doubt at all in anyone's mind about our capability to withstand an attack and still strike back effectively. We predicate our policy on a second strike or retaliatory capability. This must be credible to anyone who would threaten to attack.

Nowhere in these words is the reality of an enemy's intentions. Instead we liberally assess the quantity of his weapons and men, and then, judging from afar his worst possible intentions, we prepare ourselves to meet them. But since possibilities have no practical limit, neither does our preparation for them. To be ready sensibly for danger is one thing, but to make military and diplomatic judgments from the paranoid extreme of worst-case analysis is to lose completely a sense of balance.

What we have been seeking is riskless security. It does not exist.

2 · NUCLEAR SHIELD

THE EXISTENCE of the nuclear superweapon, the elusive chase for low-risk military security, some frankly bad military thinking, and the fact that we felt that we could afford the price we had to pay for it bought us the "nuclear shield." The concept of the nuclear shield, which, interestingly, is similar to the title of the official AEC history of that period, *Atomic Shield*,[41] simply means that an enemy striking us first had better remember that we are determined that our *weapons* will survive that first attack and we will hit back with so much power that our enemy will find that he has lost more than we did.

On March 14, 1969, President Richard M. Nixon stated during the debate over the anti–ballistic-missile system (ABM), "The imperative that our *nuclear deterrent remain secure beyond any possible doubt* requires that the U.S. must take steps now to insure that our strategic retaliatory forces will not become vulnerable to Soviet attack."* In his State of the World message in 1970 the President said, "We must insure that all potential aggressors see unacceptable risks in contemplating a nuclear attack."

Of course, this thinking is not original with Nixon. Its beginnings go back to the early days of the Joint Committee and the AEC. One of the early nuclear-shield promoters was William L. Borden, who was appointed executive director of the Joint Committee in 1949. In addition to being the prime instigator of the AEC security trial of J. Robert Oppenheimer (Borden's letter to former FBI Director J. Edgar Hoover stating "J. Robert Oppenheimer is an agent of the Soviet Union" is regarded as the stimulus of the trial itself),[25] Borden

---

* Emphasis added.

was also the author of a 1946 book, *There Will Be No Time,* in which he recommended giving national defense top priority. He saw instant wars of the future with atomic arms—wars which would make conventional arms obsolete. Borden felt the nation should be ready for instant retaliation in case of a sneak attack.[42]

Borden and Senator McMahon, with whom he worked, were of such like mind in this matter that it was hard to tell from whom the initiative came, the Senator or his staff man. They urged increased atomic-bomb production in a letter to Secretary of Defense Louis A. Johnson on July 14, 1949. They argued that strategic bombing with atomic weapons (that is, in crushing an enemy's will and capacity to fight) was "the keystone of our military policy and a foundation pillar of our foreign policy as well." They saw a need for unlimited numbers of atomic bombs.[43]

The mood of the times was best expressed in a statement made by Congressman (now Senator) Henry M. Jackson in 1951: "How can we conceivably not want to make every possible atomic weapon we can? I cannot imagine any member of this House going before his constituency and saying he is not in favor of making every single atomic weapon it is within our power to produce." He also called for a *tenfold* increase in the AEC's budget.[44] Jackson's hawkishness has not diminished significantly to this day.

Much of this state of mind carried forward well into the future when Senator Richard B. Russell of Georgia, speaking in favor of the unpopular national fallout-shelter programs, said, "If we have to start all over again with another Adam and Eve, I want them to be Americans and I want them on this continent and not in Europe."[45]

By 1951 the Joint Chiefs of Staff were demanding a $5-billion expansion of uranium and plutonium production, at the same time refusing to say how many weapons they would eventually need to guarantee national defense. The AEC was still struggling to keep some sort of civilian control over atomic weapons, but was losing the fight. The Joint Chiefs were strongly opposed to any civilian agency placing itself between themselves and the President on military matters. Little by little, control of the nuclear stockpile was going over to the generals and the admirals. It wasn't until twenty years later that a chairman of the AEC would admit publicly that control had in fact slipped away from the AEC.[5]

The military men made it clear that they regarded the AEC as little more than a supplier; just fill the orders and deliver the bombs and let others worry about national goals, priorities and strategies. President Truman approved the Joint Chiefs' request for the $5-billion expansion of uranium and plutonium production, thereby setting in motion a series of repercussions that went far beyond the victory of the military over the reluctant civilian managers of the AEC. Now there would be enough of the rare radioactive metals for a huge expansion of strategic weapons, enough for every other atomic scheme and dream that politicians, weapons scientists and military men could invent.

When John Foster Dulles became Secretary of State under President Eisenhower, he based his foreign policy upon the foundations laid by Borden and McMahon. It promised "massive retaliation" by nuclear weapons against any Communist aggression anywhere around the globe—a stiff and frightening nuclear answer to the apparently softening attitude of the Soviet Union following the death of Stalin. Dulles flew around the world signing up nations in defense arrangements against the Communist menace.

Arthur M. Schlesinger, Jr., wrote of Mr. Dulles' world caustically:

The Dulles world rested on unitary conceptions of the opposing blocks: on the one hand, the "free world," capriciously defined to include such places as Spain, Paraguay, Batista's Cuba and Mississippi, . . . and, on the other, the "communist camp," a monolithic conspiracy with headquarters in Moscow, enslaving captive peoples and orchestrating global crises according to a comprehensive master plan.[46]

The Dulles approach could pass for a far-right-wing political tract today and even in the mid-1950s was thought to be rigid.[47] But the specter of Communism was so abiding that it aroused anti-Communist feelings across the political spectrum. Liberals were Cold Warriors, too, as the British scientist-author-critic C. P. Snow noted:

"I fancy a number of people all over the Western World still think of themselves as liberals, but are in essence no such thing. In their hearts they believe that their society won't (and shouldn't) change much, that Communism is the enemy absolute, and that the only tasks open to men of good will are to fight the Cold War with one hand and perform minor benevolent activities with the other."[48]

But what, actually, is the nuclear shield? *Americans are invariably appalled to learn that it is the cities; they are the targets because they must remain exposed. They can't go underground, scatter or dig into the mountains as the military has done. So the monstrous paradox of modern military philosophy is that the civilian population is in fact the shield for the nuclear weapons—the civilians are protecting the military.*

"We see here, already in process," General Marshall wrote in 1947, "a curious transposition whereby the civil mass becomes the shield covering the body of the military, and wherein the prospect for final military success lies in the chance that the shield will be able to sustain the shock . . . until the military body can make decisive use of its weapons."[40]

The Kennedy Administration inherited the nuclear shield and did not dismantle it, though the President began to tone down the harsh Cold War rhetoric and even moved some of our threatening missiles from close to Russia's borders.

But the nuclear shield is, of course, only designed to frighten an enemy. Whether it would actually be used is an entirely different question. But there is no room for a President who would not retaliate, because our nuclear deterrent must be "credible," as the military thinkers say. That means the enemy must believe you would actually use it. You cannot allow him any real doubt or the nuclear-shield idea is worthless. The Soviets have to maintain their credibility, too. Their weapons must look very deadly and threatening, and they do, and it frightens Americans into reacting. And when American missiles look the same way to the Russians, they react. This is the built-in escalator—the stuff from which arms races are made.

3 · COLD WAR

BUT IT IS UNFAIR to judge the policies of the 1950s without realizing that they were set against the background of the Cold War. Perhaps the mood for the day is best expressed in Henry Chamberlin's book *Blueprint for World Conquest,* in which he darkly held that in Stalin's mind there was "irreconcilable hostility between the Soviet Union and the 'capitalist' world" and that "Russia can never know security so long as the 'capitalist' states continue to exist."

Professor Robert A. Skotheim, reviewing those days (and Chamberlin's book), wrote that "an enemy existed which not only held an unwavering goal of international revolution, but which conceived of its national security in terms so broad as to require the destruction of all different forms of government."[49]

The big red scare of the 1950s had begun. There were revelations that a few government officials had been members of the Communist Party, actual spies were arrested, Russia exploded an atomic bomb, the Republican Party, out of power twenty years, hurled soft-on-Communism charges against the Democratic Party, the Russian grip tightened on Eastern Europe with the takeover of Czechoslovakia, China fell to the Communists, and one thing after another rattled the political nerves of this country.

In 1950, the still classified NSC-68 report[36] of the National Security Council predicted that the Soviets would have the capability to attack us with atomic weapons by 1954. (The National Security Council, created by the National Security Act of 1947, is a major policy advisory group which includes the President himself, the Secretaries of State, Defense and the three armed services, and the heads of the other defense-related departments and agencies).

Consider some other events of a single year, 1950:

JANUARY: State Department official Alger Hiss was convicted of perjury for denying that he had passed secret documents to admitted former Communist Whittaker Chambers.

FEBRUARY: Dr. Klaus Fuchs confessed passing atomic secrets to the Russians.

Senator Joseph McCarthy waved a piece of paper at the Women's Republican Club in Wheeling, West Virginia, saying it was a list of 205 known Communists in the State Department, thus beginning the era of "McCarthyism."

MARCH: Fuchs was convicted.

MAY: Harry Gold, a Philadelphia chemist, admitted passing papers between Fuchs and a Russian vice-consul.

JUNE: South Korea was invaded by Communist North Korea.

David Greenglass, a Los Alamos machinist, was arrested as an accomplice of Gold.

JULY: Julius Rosenberg, brother-in-law of Greenglass, was arrested as part of the same espionage ring.

AUGUST: Ethel Rosenberg, his wife, was arrested on the same charges.

SEPTEMBER: Over President Truman's veto, the Internal Security Act was passed requiring Communists to register with the government, denying them passports and access to defense plants, and setting up a Subversive Activities Control Board.

It is little wonder that our foreign military assistance budget jumped by almost $4 billion in that single year alone and that America began the all-out race for the hydrogen bomb.

But this attitude is not something that America has completely outgrown. Even today many of the most powerful men inside the AEC are still fierce Cold Warriors. Simplistically hawkish, but fortunately under restraint, they advocate the use of nuclear weapons even today. Dr. Harold M. Agnew, the new director of the Los Alamos Scientific Laboratory, said in 1970 (as if we still had a nuclear monopoly), "It is my belief that if people would prepare the right spectrum of tactical weapons [small nuclear weapons for use in conventional battle by foot soldiers], we might be able to knock off this sort of foolishness we now have in Vietnam and the Middle East or anyplace else."[50] Agnew's breezy remarks are serious enough, though. It would seem that when the American participation in the defense of Western Europe winds down, as it must sooner or later, the Atlantic Pact nations will indeed increase their commitment to build their own nuclear deterrents, including tactical atomic weapons.[51]

Dr. Edward Teller, the leader of the group of physicists who developed the hydrogen bomb and still a driving force within the AEC, joined with General Curtis LeMay, Patrick J. Frawley, Jr., the long-time supporter of right-wing causes, former AEC Commissioner Willard F. Libby and Dr. Agnew as part of the National Strategy Committee of the far-right-wing American Security Council. Not be confused with the National Security Council (above), the American Security Council is a private right-wing organization whose main effort has been to convince the American public, through newspaper ads, that we lag behind the Soviet Union in our nuclear-weapons stockpile and we had better get busy and close that gap.[52] Such a comparison was labeled "scare tactics" by the Federation of American Scientists, who pointed out that, although true, except for its psychological value it had no real meaning, since it was based on the difference between the *total explosive power* in the two nations' nuclear stockpiles. A more meaningful comparison, the critics argued, and the basis upon which our Department of Defense has designed our nuclear arsenal, is between the nations' ability to *deliver* their weapons to targets, and in this comparison the gap favors the United States.[53]

4 · OUR NUCLEAR ARSENAL

BY 1960, the United States not only had atomic-fission bombs in great numbers but also had many fusion devices. While fission bombs (A-bombs) obtain their power from splitting uranium or plutonium atoms, fusion bombs (H-bombs) obtain their power by fusing hydrogen atoms to form helium. But because of the easier availability of H-bomb fuel, very much larger fusion weapons can be conveniently built. H-bombs use small A-bombs as their triggering devices, for fusion takes place only under conditions of intense heat and pressure. An even more dramatic effect has been produced by coating a hydrogen bomb with uranium, producing a fission-fusion-fission reaction of incredible proportions, especially when viewed from its ability to produce radioactive fallout. This was the infamous Castle-Bravo experiment, which, as the result of AEC mishandling, seriously contaminated the natives of Rongelap Atoll in the Pacific as well as the crew of the Japanese fishing trawler *The Lucky Dragon*[54] (see Chapter III).

Dr. Herbert York, who headed the AEC's weapons laboratory at Livermore, California, and later served as Director of Defense Research and Engineering under President Kennedy, estimates that by 1960 the United States alone had strategic nuclear weapons with the power of twenty to forty billion tons of TNT, "most of which could be released in a matter of hours"—many times more bombs than there were reasonable targets to hit in Russia.[34] We possess far more destructive power today, amounting to well over ten thousand warheads, some of which have been designed for delivery systems which are no longer operational. As a consequence, in 1971 the AEC conducted its first comprehensive review of its warhead stockpile, and as much as twenty percent of that stockpile may be pruned out of our atomic arsenal.[55]

Perhaps even more ominous than the explosive power of these warheads is the radioactive fallout they could produce. "By 1960, the two major nuclear powers together possessed stockpiles which could bathe tens of millions of square miles in lethal levels of radioactivity, an area larger than the total land area of the two principals themselves," Dr. York said.

The crash program for missiles in the early 1950s accelerated with the Russian launching of Sputnik in 1957, which demonstrated that the Soviet Union had conquered the engineering problems of big intercontinental rockets even before the United States had. We began storing fragile, liquid-fueled Atlas missiles across the nation, many in $11-million concrete underground sites, all of which have since been abandoned. In December 1962 the first Minuteman solid-fuel intercontinental missile was delivered, followed in 1963 by the Titan II missiles. Today the nation has fifty-four Titans and one thousand Minuteman missiles buried in underground concrete silos and ready for instant launching.[56]

President Lyndon B. Johnson's Administration originated the ABM program, which was designed to halt incoming enemy missiles by exploding a hydrogen bomb in their paths. Mr. Johnson proposed to install ABM sites around several of America's big cities but was defeated, mostly by public protest. It is not generally realized, but some of the military were against the original ABM concept as well, for reasons not immediately apparent. Since the cities are pawns in the nuclear deterrent game, many nuclear strategists feared losing the leverage the unprotected cities gave them. Under President Nixon the emphasis switched, nuclear-shield fashion, to guarding our weapons, the Minuteman sites in North Dakota and Montana. At the same time, we began installing multiple warheads on our missiles.

Much like the Minuteman and Titan missiles in their silos, the Navy Polaris missile submarines wait constantly undersea for instructions from Washington, each of the forty-one ready to fire its sixteen ICBMs. The Polaris missiles are already tipped with triple warheads, and the new Poseidon missiles will be installed on thirty-one sub-marines, each missile carrying ten to fourteen MIRV (multiple independently targetable reentry vehicles) warheads.

In addition there are three hundred B-52 heavy bombers and another seventy F-111 medium bombers proposed, if that swing-wing aircraft can ever get over its plague of troubles. On top of that mound of weaponry are the tactical nuclear weapons, those smaller devices designed for battlefield use but most of them with as great a power as the bombs which destroyed the Japanese cities in World War II. They exist by the tens of thousands and include missiles, rocket bombs, howitzer shells, even nuclear torpedoes.[57]

Although less dramatic than the atomic bomb, the nuclear power reactor has changed the Navy more than anything since the steam engine. Nuclear engines have brought a freedom to naval vessels unknown since man first sailed the seas. Ships can cruise at top speeds for many months without refueling, without the trail of sup-porting ships and without the covey of oilers following and holding back the faster ships. Under water, the submarines can cruise for long periods, avoiding the constant surfacing ordinarily required in order to recharge their electric batteries from on-board diesel engines. Since they are most vulnerable when they are on the surface, the advantage of a nuclear propulsion system is even greater to the sub-marine than to the surface ship.

The engines inside these ships and submarines are still steam-driven; the only difference is that they use a nuclear reactor as the heat source instead of an ordinary firebox. Where once the reactors had to be refueled every two or three years, the Navy is now working on reactors which last ten to thirteen years without refueling. Where eight reactors provided power for the first nuclear aircraft carrier (*Enterprise*), only two huge reactors each are planned for the *Nimitz,* the *Eisenhower* and the as yet unnamed CVAN-70.

They are, however, the most expensive war machines ever built. Adding nuclear power almost doubles the normal costs, and the overall costs are about ten times that of their World War II equiva-lents. The average price for a World War II submarine was $11.3

million; the cost of a nuclear attack submarine is $105 million, and that of a Polaris submarine is $155 million, not counting its sixteen missiles. Aircraft-carrier costs are even more dramatic: the *Franklin D. Roosevelt,* built during World War II, cost $39.5 million; the *Constellation,* completed in 1961, had jumped in price to $188 million. That same year the first nuclear carrier, the *Enterprise,* was completed for $451 million. By comparison, the *John F. Kennedy,* commissioned seven years later, with oil-fired engines, cost only $281 million. Two new nuclear carriers, the *Nimitz* and the *Dwight D. Eisenhower,* both under construction, are expected to cost $594 million and $616 million respectively. The CVAN-70, the next carrier sought by the Navy but postponed indefinitely by the Department of Defense, is projected to cost $640 million if begun in 1971. Admiral Elmo R. Zumwalt, Jr., Chief of Naval Operations, said each year's delay would add another $125 million to the proposed cost of the CVAN-70. But that is not all of the money involved. Add to the total a flight of ninety planes ($205 million) and annual operating costs ($95 million), and the investment edges close to a billion dollars to keep just one giant carrier going.[58]

These expensive weapons have been difficult to win from the Department of Defense. Vice-Admiral Hyman G. Rickover fought hard and won the submarine fight, but in recent years, because of the appalling price, the Joint Committee and Admiral Rickover and the Navy have had their difficulties with Congress. The two newest carriers in the fleet, the *America* and the *Kennedy,* both are oil-fired despite a long fight.

Admiral Rickover, who also works for the AEC's Division of Naval Reactors, plainly sees opponents of military preparedness as those who would appease rather than confront our potential enemies. It is another of the undercurrents in American military thinking and grows from Prime Minister Neville Chamberlain's meeting in Munich in September 1938 with Edouard Daladier of France, Adolf Hitler and Benito Mussolini. Chamberlain signed the Munich Pact and came home to England to tell the British people, "For the second time in our history, a British Prime Minister has returned from Germany bringing peace with honor. I believe it is a peace for our time. . . . Go home and get a nice quiet sleep." Germany had been given the Sudetenland, the western portion of Czechoslovakia, but within a year would swallow up the rest of the nation and attack Poland, bringing on World War II.

In a letter to Senator John Stennis, chairman of the Senate Armed Services Committee, on September 5, 1969, Admiral Rickover asked for support for the Navy nuclear aircraft carriers and noted at the end of a long letter:

A statement by Anthony Eden, Foreign Secretary under Prime Minister Neville Chamberlain, on Britain's entry into World War II is worth pondering. He said: "The Prime Minister would tolerate no interference in his policy toward the dictators. He believed he could negotiate agreements with Hitler and Mussolini which they would keep. We know the results of that policy. Yet those who today oppose military preparedness take the identical position. . . ."[59]

Military men, by their training and background, present simple military answers to such vital and complicated questions as foreign policy and domestic priorities. Perhaps it would be expecting too much for them to be otherwise. But to have let them make so many important decisions for so long without public scrutiny has been one of our more serious national mistakes. The public should know more fully how the choices are made and what information is considered. It does not.

Though the matters are discussed before the Joint Committee, the National Security Council, the armed-services committees and the appropriations committees in the Congress, a position rather than a discussion is presented to the public, a fact rather than a question. And those who would look to find what questions were asked when the fact was decided, what compromises were made, what conflicting reports there were, find it impossible to study meaningfully the official documents. Positions are worked out in executive session, and the printed record of these hearings swarms with deletions so extensive as to make it almost useless. It has only one real advantage: it maintains the fiction that there is still a free flow of information and thereby forestalls public criticism.

As an example, in the official "open" record of Joint Committee hearings at which Admiral Rickover discussed the Soviet submarine threat to the United States, ninety-one items were censored from his eight-page testimony, an excerpt from which follows.

ADMIRAL RICKOVER: . . . Last year the United States had a net advantage of [classified matter deleted] more nuclear submarines than the Russians. Today this advantage has shrunk to possibly [classified matter deleted]. Unfortunately [classified matter deleted] I cannot be exact in these comparisons.

We know, however, there are many more nuclear units under construction. For this reason it is clear that any advantage we may possess in operational submarines will vanish shortly. For example, even though we credit the Soviets with only [classified matter deleted] Yankee class submarines being operational by mid-1970, [classified matter deleted]. We know they have [classified matter deleted] but they have started work on their [classified matter deleted]. Just how far they are going in this particular class, we do not know. . . .[60]

From whom is our government withholding information? Surely the Soviets know how many submarines they have and they can fill in those blanks for themselves. Furthermore, Congressmen leak these "secrets" with impunity. It's the American people that our security people aim to keep in the dark lest the public, after independently evaluating the data, come to a different conclusion than do the military.

In discussing intelligence estimates, the printed record includes this:

CHAIRMAN HOLIFIELD: [classified matter deleted] gave us a little different story on that. He told us, I believe, [classified matter deleted].

ADMIRAL RICKOVER: This information comes from the [classified matter deleted].

MR. WAGNER [William Wagner, Rickover's deputy]: The information Admiral Rickover is presenting on the Soviet submarine program is based on the latest intelligence information we have received from the [classified matter deleted].

MR. MURPHY [George F. Murphy, Jr., deputy director of the Joint Committee staff]: I think [classified matter deleted] was talking about the Polaris.

ADMIRAL RICKOVER: I am talking about the total number of Soviet nuclear-powered submarines.

CHAIRMAN HOLIFIELD: I am glad we got that clarified.

If an exchange like this did not involve the arms race and did not put the survival of nations in the balance, it would be amusing, but it is precisely because of this kind of misuse of secrecy that the abuses and excesses of the arms race have been permitted to occur.

Asked if he thought public control had broken down in atomic-energy affairs, Herbert York said, "The mechanisms are all there for public control. The trouble really is that security has kept people out of it. It has kept the press and critics at arm's length so public control is not effective."[61]

5 · FAILURE OF THE NUCLEAR SHIELD

IT IS OFTEN SAID that the military always fights the last war, and the Cold War was no different. Obsessed with the concepts of airpower and saturation bombing of cities of World War II days, the military regarded the nuclear bomb as just another blockbuster, only bigger and better. And so, with total reliance on the nuclear superweapons, we not only allowed our capability to wage conventional warfare to deteriorate, but we found ourselves frozen into only one form of retaliation in the event we were attacked. The massive nuclear response was just not suited to all situations. Ironically, the nuclear shield weakened America rather than strengthened us, as the lesson of Vietnam clearly illustrates.

President Kennedy managed to add to our defense thinking the idea of a "flexible response," hopefully to enable this country to deal with small "brushfire" wars instead of having only the nuclear answer.

Our massive arsenal of nuclear weapons and nuclear counter-weapons is troublesome even to the Joint Committee. In March of 1970, during hearings on the Navy's nuclear program, Chairman Holifield remarked, "In spite of our vaunted superiority we have had these terrific losses in Vietnam even with our modern war implements against a nation that hasn't got anything but a canoe to go against us . . ."[62]

But there is danger just in having so many nuclear weapons poised and waiting for their special electronic signal to send them off to Russia, and that is the danger of an accident. Wolfgang K. H. Panofsky, one of our negotiators at the Nuclear Test Ban Treaty talks in 1962 and the director of the AEC's Linear Accelerator Center at Stanford University, said, "The various arguments in which contrived situations are created to justify even further expansion of this enormous arsenal in the name of 'security' must be weighed against the resulting ever-increasing danger of accident and inadvertent escalation into nuclear war."[63]

So, with worst-case analysis, sneak-attack psychology, second-strike dedication, and survivability ideas, it is easy to fall into such a trap as the nuclear shield. And yet it goes on and on, with only the results of the Strategic Arms Limitation Talks (SALT) in Helsinki as a hopeful sign that we may somehow put an end to that spiral.

6 · THE MINI ARMS RACE: COMPETITION BETWEEN THE WEAPONS LABORATORIES

WEAPONS SCIENTISTS split into two camps following World War II. Although they agreed on most scientific matters, the breakdown came over a political question. On one side was J. Robert Oppenheimer, the informal leader of those scientists seeking to go slow on the development of the hydrogen bomb, and on the other side were the forces of Edward Teller and Ernest O. Lawrence, which, although numerically smaller, eventually won the ear of the politicians. They not only won a crash program for an H-bomb, they also got their own weapons laboratory in Livermore, California, and even a cruel measure of revenge in the 1954 AEC security hearings at which Oppenheimer's initial efforts to go slow on developing the H-bomb were equated with disloyalty to the nation in "the closest thing to a heresy trial that modern American politics has provided."[7, 25]

Many at Los Alamos to this day have little use for Teller, who not only provided key testimony against Oppenheimer but also managed to cast doubt on the technical competence of the Los Alamos scientists themselves[64]—an irony in that all of the major advances (the atom bomb, the hydrogen bomb itself, and controlled fusion) were made not at Livermore but at Los Alamos.

So when the second laboratory, named after Lawrence, was founded at Livermore in 1952, there were already in motion intense feelings of competition between Livermore and Los Alamos. As if the nuclear-arms race between America and the Russians wasn't enough, the competition between the two AEC laboratories created a home-grown arms race within the system. York, who headed the Lawrence Livermore Laboratory from 1952 until 1957, said that it was the competition with Los Alamos that spurred them on.

Discussing that point in his home at La Jolla, California,[61] Dr. Herbert York said, "We had no requirement for a warhead that fit an ICBM. The laboratories were in competition to see how small they could make nuclear weapons. This led to the feasibility of the ICBM. The Polaris was the same. There was no official requirement. Myself, Teller and the others—we knew what was coming along in missiles." They kept close watch on missile developments and went outside normal military channels, designing weapons *in advance* to fit missiles they were certain could be developed. "The dynamism of the American nuclear-weapons program is because normal channels were avoided," York observed.

(Dr. York went on to become Director of Defense Research and

Engineering for the Department of Defense and was succeeded at Livermore by Dr. Harold Brown, who also later replaced York at the Department of Defense. The third man to follow the exact same pattern was Dr. John S. Foster, Jr., who succeeded Brown at Livermore and is now at the Department of Defense.)

But without natural mechanisms such as exist in the outside world for eliminating unproductive ideas, competition within the overly funded defense atomic establishment only led to duplication and excesses. Weapons, too many and too varied even for the military, were aggressively promoted by the Joint Committee, and especially by Senator Brien McMahon, whose intoxicated views of atomic wars of the future included an Army, a Navy and an Air Force completely outfitted not only with strategic nuclear weapons but with the smaller tactical nuclear weapons as well. The Joint Committee badgered the Joint Chiefs, the AEC and the Administration to come up with long-range plans for a whole family of atomic weapons. They got what they wanted from a reluctant executive department and pushed the program through Congress. They also pushed through an expansion of plutonium production over the objection of the Eisenhower Administration and jammed through the crash program for the hydrogen bomb although the Atomic Energy Commissioners themselves had voted three to two *against* it.[8]

"The AEC probably built more warheads than would have been built if the D.O.D. [Department of Defense] had it," was Dr. York's view. The AEC in the early years came up with new designs and ideas which it had to "press on the military," which, York observed, was traditionally reluctant to change a weapons system once one was established.[61]

Unlike scientists, military leaders are not oriented toward change. And rightly so, perhaps, for it is not as easy for them to return to the drawing board after a failure. The military has always wanted reliable and simple tools, but the atomic-weapons scientists were teaching them new things all the time.

7 · THE BAROQUE PERIOD

THERE IS NOTHING to excite men like the challenge of the unknown. If that challenge is combined with a noble purpose, it attracts great men and drives them on. Thus it was with the invention of the first atomic bomb, the Manhattan Project of World War II. But when the great challenge was met and conquered, the excitement faded away; it is a law as old as man himself. And so the great men returned to their universities and left the others behind. Not long after the explosion of the first atomic device at Alamagordo, New Mexico, in 1945, Oppenheimer is said to have remarked wearily, "Now let the second team take over."[24]

In the AEC, particularly in the weapons laboratories, the attrition of scientific talent was bound to take place when the big challenges were gone and only small ones remained. But it took a while. Dr. Hugh E. De Witt, a theoretical physicist who shared his time for thirteen years between the University of California at Berkeley and the AEC's Lawrence Livermore Laboratory, speaking of the situation at Livermore, said there was "a high level mediocrity. The kind of scientific originality which led to the first atomic bomb simply does not exist at Livermore."[65]

The first atomic bomb was built in 1945; the first hydrogen-device explosion went off in 1951. By 1960, as one physicist put it, weapons building was "a completed technology in the sense of maximum and minimum sizes." Because of the military secrecy surrounding weapons development (despite the fact that the British, the Soviets, the Chinese, the French and probably the Israelis and others all know the "secrets" of fission and fusion), scientists are reluctant to discuss the state of the art publicly. Those who will talk in private say that the weapons scientists at Los Alamos and Livermore concentrate only on details and refinements such as trying to predict with precision the exact energy yields of a given weapon, trying to get a larger explosion from less material, trying to change the mix of radioactivity effects such as more X rays or more neutrons, trying out different mechanical forms and materials such as hardening or multiple warheads, and trying to reduce the amount of fission needed to produce a fusion reaction. Herbert York said, *"Weapons development has entered the baroque period: it does little, costs a lot and keeps a lot of people busy."*[66]*

If the weapons scientists and engineers have been on a sort of treadmill to nowhere since 1960, then interested citizens are bound to ask why the nation has not dismantled the laboratories long ago, or at least closed one of them down.[67] In an interview in 1970 Dr. Frederick R. Tesche, the AEC's assistant director for military applications, said, "The specific goal of LASL [Los Alamos] and LRL [Lawrence Radiation Laboratory, the old name for the Lawrence Livermore Laboratory] is to keep employment constant beyond the usual swings of D.O.D. contracts." Adding that the "baroque" description by Herbert York "in very large measure" is not true, Tesche continued: "Quite obviously many early notions of fission are being employed. But I don't think the changes made can be categorized as nut-and-bolt changes. In addition, there have been other advances of considerable consequence in our ability to modernize the forces. If you agree with the postulate that the laboratories are filled with pretty topflight people, then it follows that you're not going to keep a Los Alamos and a Livermore going with the job of chrome-plating the bolts made in 1945."[66, 68]

Tesche's words in defense of the atomic establishment seem logical, but they also seem everywhere to underscore the treadmill, bureaucratic, make-work aspect of the situation, justified by a silent patriotism. "I never met a more dedicated group of men," he said. "Their level of patriotism is goddamned high . . . they are trying to do their best in an area that is very controversial. It's pretty hard

* Emphasis added.

to work as hard as we do and then walk out of here and have people accuse you of wanting to blow Amchitka up or poison the environment. There's an awful lot of dedicated people trying their best and very competent. It's done out of sheer patriotism, not paychecks."

Such a defense of the laboratories working at full steam as they are is a poor one. There are endless refinements, changes and minor advances that can be made in any technology. There will never be a "perfect" atomic bomb any more than there will ever be a "perfect" automobile. But the real question is overlooked or deferred to others: each technological advance that makes American missiles work better only unbalances the nuclear-arms race. In an arms race like the present one, new developments only pour oil on the fire. If the Soviets have a new development, the Department of Defense rushes to Congress with dark predictions to get more money to meet the new threats. And if Americans develop something new, the Russians begin to search frantically for an answer, too.

In the arms race, everything is upside down. Forward is really backward, because progress only drags you in deeper.

8 · THE ARMS RACE AS UNEMPLOYMENT INSURANCE

MORE THAN two thirds of the $51 billion committed by this nation to atomic energy since 1940 has gone for the raw materials, research, development, production and testing of military arms. These were not paid for by the Department of Defense after 1946, but instead were provided "free of charge" from the AEC's separate budget.

"The special arrangements for the control of atomic energy which a frightened Congress enacted in 1946 have turned into a system not for its restraint but for its promotion," wrote Don K. Price.

In no field, ironically, has this been more true than in military affairs. The great purpose of the Atomic Energy Act was to take the atom away from the soldiers and devote it to peaceful purposes. But the result . . . has been just the opposite. For more than a decade every military staff planner, as he computed the alternative advantages and costs of using different types of weapons to accomplish any particular objective, was given a powerful incentive to choose nuclear weapons because they were free. That is to say, the warheads were provided not out of the budget of the military service, as were conventional weapons, but by the Atomic Energy Commission.[7]

But beyond even these arguments, the scientists and engineers at Los Alamos and Livermore hold on to their jobs through politics— not through their personal connections but through a political deal made by President Kennedy to secure passage of the Nuclear Test Ban Treaty of 1963. In case anyone at Los Alamos may have forgotten about the deal, the terms are displayed on the wall of the scientific museum at the laboratory.[69]

Gerald F. Tape, former AEC commissioner, explained it in a 1969 speech to a group of governors touring the Nevada test site: "When the Senate ratified the Treaty Banning Nuclear Weapons Tests in the Atmosphere, in Outer Space and Under Water, it insisted on assurances that four safeguards would be implemented under the joint responsibility of the Atomic Energy Commission and the Department of Defense." He went on to say that as preconditions to ratification the Senate demanded "aggressive and continuing" underground testing of weapons, the maintenance of the weapons laboratories and the weapons programs, readiness to resume atmospheric testing at once if the Russians resumed, and improving our capability to detect violations of the treaty as well as keeping a generally close watch on Soviet and Chinese nuclear activity.[70]

Though the Senate technically insisted, it was not the senators but the Joint Chiefs of Staff who extracted the promises, even though they should have stayed out of the nuclear political game in deference to the President who appointed them. Instead, a parade of generals and admirals testified against the treaty before the Senate, backed up by the former AEC Chairman, Lewis L. Strauss, and Dr. Edward

Teller, who told the senators remarkably, "If you ratify this treaty . . . *you will have given away the future safety of this country.*"[46]* General Thomas S. Power, chief of the Strategic Air Command, who, Air Force public-relations men say, became known as "Kremlin's Enemy No. 1,"[71] and who is, like Teller, a member of the private, right-wing American Security Council, testified in secret against the treaty.

Arthur M. Schlesinger, Jr., wrote later:

> The President, determined that the treaty should be ratified, gave his unqualified and unequivocal assurances that the conditions would be met. Secretary Robert McNamara, while questioning whether the vast increases in our nuclear forces had produced a comparable enhancement in our security, nevertheless assured the Senate that he would move in the next years further to raise the megatonnage of our strategic alert forces. Senators, reluctant to be associated with what critics might regard as disarmament, seized with delight on the chance of interpreting the renunciation of atmospheric tests as a green light for underground tests. The effect for a moment, as Richard Rovere put it, was to turn an agreement intended to limit nuclear testing into a limited warrant for increasing nuclear testing. The President was prepared to pay this price to commit the nation to a treaty outlawing atmospheric tests.[46]

Because of these agreements, Los Alamos and Livermore were maintained at full strength, the testing program went forward aggressively, averaging thirty announced shots a year, Johnstown Island and Hawaiian test facilities were developed, three specially outfitted "diagnostic aircraft" were kept ready at Kirtland Air Force Base in New Mexico, joint AEC-DOD readiness exercises were held, a dozen Vela satellites were launched to watch the Soviets, and both nuclear and conventional explosives were detonated in Nevada and Mississippi to test seismic equipment for measuring underground shock waves accurately.[13]

This political deal stood unquestioned until President Nixon ordered across-the-board cuts in the AEC budget. The readiness program was cut back, the last of the Vela satellites was launched and Johnstown Island was placed on standby status. But despite a strike of construction workers at the Nevada test site that lasted

* Emphasis added.

almost four months, the AEC still managed to work in twenty-nine announced underground shots in 1970, bringing the total by year's end to 517 announced nuclear explosions since the first shot on the Jornada del Muerto desert near Alamagordo, New Mexico, in 1945.

Every announced test in recent years has worked; the weapons have all gone off. A number of other tests have also been held, but their number is a military secret. "It's a little too gratuitous to the opposition to announce them all," said Frederick R. Tesche, assistant director of the AEC's Division of Military Applications."[68] He said that Enrico Fermi, the atomic scientist, had once held that an experiment with more than a fifty percent chance of success is not worth doing, but the AEC found its present testing "extremely necessary." Perhaps if scientists of Fermi's caliber still influenced weapons development, things would be different today.

The high degree of success of the tests, Tesche said, was almost a necessity, since it costs so much money to dig the holes and make other preparations. "We spent fifteen to twenty million for the hole in Amchitka" (for the Milrow test which was fired on Amchitka Island, Alaska, in October 1969). Because tests are so expensive, he said, "the degree to which you gamble is different."

And so the busy men, large minds and small, debate in private the crucial issues of our day, while in the laboratories the men of science and engineering polish up the latest technical marvel that will astound the Russians. Scattered out across the nation, the eight weapons-production plants retool—a $314-million expansion[66, 72] as the President's emissaries sit down in Helsinki to talk about arms limitation. In Nevada and Alaska, they test their warheads to make sure the mighty stockpiles still work, to try out new ideas or to see what effect the explosions will have. And in the evenings men come home to their families. The atomic scientists and engineers have made their beds with the military leaders and the politicians of the Joint Committee in the tight secluded world where there are only friendly faces, job security and the encouragement of a common purpose.

But make no mistake about it: their works are mighty to behold.

9 · THE OLD WEAPONS SCIENTISTS

FOR REASONS difficult to understand, some of the scientists who helped produce the first atomic bomb are widely believed today to have actually been men of peace. There is no question that some of them recognized the awesome portent of their creation and agonized over their participation in its development. But if today we are to choose whether these misgivings arose from guilt or were simply rooted in the scientist's habit of exhaustive analysis of the view opposite to his own, we cannot decide; it was probably a little bit of both.

J. Robert Oppenheimer epitomizes in one man the contradictions present in them all. In 1946, apparently remorseful about his role in the production of the atomic bomb, he startled President Truman during a meeting by blurting out, "Mr. President, I have blood on my hands."[25] Only five years later, he described the new superweapon, the hydrogen bomb developed by Stanislaw Ulam and Edward Teller at Los Alamos, as "sweet and lovely and beautiful."[24] So words are scant help in judging the protestations of some of the weapons scientists; we must let their decisions speak for them.

Perhaps it seems unfair today to judge their motives. After all, wasn't every allied scientist who had any special knowledge which could be of value to the atomic-bomb program expected to participate? There were exceptions. The most notable was Albert Einstein. After warning President Roosevelt in August 1939 of the possibility that Germany could develop an atomic bomb, he was conspicuously absent from all atomic research from that time on. Probably, according to Vannevar Bush, head of the National Defense Research Committee, "in view of the attitude of people here in Washington who had studied his whole history." What Bush was referring to was that Einstein was well known, even then, as a pacifist.[73]

The very real threat that the Nazis were working on their own atomic bomb[74] was surely sufficient justification for participation in the program. But that reason didn't last out the war. In November of 1944, the Alsos mission, a team of soldier-scientists, discovered among captured scientific papers at the Strasbourg Institute of Physics conclusive evidence that Germany made no serious attempt to develop an atomic bomb.[75] But our work went on at a feverish pace nevertheless.

After the defeat of Germany and our completion of the atomic-bomb development, some held the view that an atomic bomb ought first to be demonstrated to the Japanese by dropping one on an uninhabited area. On April 25, 1945, President Truman appointed an "Interim Committee" to help formulate plans for the long-term use of nuclear energy, as well as to help decide what to do with the first atomic bombs. At a meeting with its Scientific Advisory Panel, composed of Ernest O. Lawrence, Arthur Compton, Enrico Fermi and J. Robert Oppenheimer, "Oppenheimer argued against the notion of a demonstration test of the A-bomb [as distinct from its actual military use against Japan] as a means of first introducing it into the world. No such demonstration, he said, could be sufficiently spectacular to convince the Japanese to end the war."[25] On the basis of this argument and the concurrence of the other panel members, the Interim Committee recommended the use of the atom bomb, without warning, against a Japanese military target surrounded by a civilian population.[76, 77]

As it turned out, Oppenheimer and the others were wrong. Japan was having her internal troubles, and a "demonstration drop" would almost certainly have turned the tide there in favor of those forces inside Japan that favored accepting the Potsdam Declaration of Unconditional Surrender of July 26, 1945.[78]

In any case, the destruction on August 6 of the city of Hiroshima, where 100,000 people lost their lives in an instant, was a pretty convincing demonstration of the power of America's new superweapon. But Japan no longer possessed the capacity for quick and decisive action (the attack severed communications between Hiroshima and Tokyo). It was not until the next day that Tokyo knew that it was a single bomb that had destroyed Hiroshima. On August 8, sixteen million leaflets were dropped over Japan addressed "To the Japanese People." The leaflets described the new weapon, its power and our plans to use more of it until military resistance ceased.[79] Surely it would be only a matter of a week or so, despite disrupted communications, before a consensus could be reached and Japan would surrender.

But we weren't prepared to wait at all. The remarkable fact is that our forces were ordered "to deliver additional bombs on these cities *as soon as they became available.*"[80]* Three days after Hiroshima, a single atomic bomb destroyed the city of Nagasaki and another 75,000 lives.

The question of the necessity for the August 9 Nagasaki raid has never been answered. Surely it didn't serve to shorten the war, for if Hiroshima wasn't enough three days before, the Russians declared war on Japan that same day. Remarkably, the memory of the Nagasaki bombing has already faded. The official AEC history of the period describes the raid in a single sentence,[81] and some books which discuss Hiroshima in detail fail to mention Nagasaki at all.[25]

Moments after the detonation of the first atomic bomb in the New Mexico desert on the morning of July 16, 1945, a thought flashed into Oppenheimer's mind, a quote from the *Bhagavad-Gita:* "I am become Death, the shatterer of worlds!" But another thought occurred to Kenneth T. Bainbridge, the official test leader; it was a far less pretentious thought, but just as accurate: "Now we are all sons-of-bitches."[82]

* Emphasis added.

10 · THE NEW WEAPONS SCIENTISTS

BUT SINCE those days a whole generation of scientists, engineers, technicians and bureaucrats built a world apart, a world which few of them realized was held together by their vested interest in the arms race. For the most part, they were silent about the implications of what they were doing. In the leftover rhetoric of World War II, they were contributing to the defense effort and were anti-Communist along with the rest of the nation.

To suggest that the scientists and engineers involved in the twenty-five years of atomic energy in this country were oblivious to all but their immediate tasks would be to dishonor some men unjustly. Ralph Lapp, Leo Szilard, Niels Bohr, Eugene Rabinowitch, Hans Bethe, Edward U. Condon and others all questioned the direction of American policy and worked to change it. But many more can be found on the other side. Some of the more vocal were Edward Teller, Willard F. Libby, Ernest O. Lawrence and Harold Agnew; all called for a hard-nosed stance.

So one must judge the vast middle ground where most of the scientists and engineers operate. This group has chosen, for its own reasons, to be above politics. It has taken the position not of the scientist but of the engineer who works within the narrow dimensions of a problem to find a practical solution and, like the true functionary, never asks whether the solution might be better left unfound.[83]

A few find this approach appalling: after thirteen years there, Hugh De Witt said that the scientist involved in weapons work at the Lawrence Livermore Laboratory lived in "an intense social and political isolation." He said there was a general acceptance of a nobility of purpose of the United States government. "The political, social and moral implications of the weapons are never discussed out there," he said.[65] In speaking to a young woman reporter whom the *Daily Californian* sent to interview him, Dr. De Witt called some of his fellow scientists at Livermore "deadheads." He immediately regretted it and asked the reporter not to print the word, but she used it anyway.[84] It triggered a memo from his superior, part of which read:

I am saddened by your identification of some of the scientists at Livermore as "deadheads." This does a grave disservice to the members of this Laboratory who have agonized over questions of national import more than you could guess and through exercise of self-discipline have sought to contribute their utmost to the furtherance of this nation's strength. Their general silence may also be construed as a manifestation of quiet loyalty and faith in the orderly process of government.[85]

But their silence has a less self-serving explanation too. "Science is neither democratic nor responsible in the political senses of those two terms," wrote Don K. Price, dean of the Harvard University Business School. "The notion of democracy, or ultimate rule by votes of the people, is simply irrelevant to science. . . . Most scientists are prepared to work most of the time within the framework of ideas developed by their acknowledged leaders. In that sense, within any discipline, science is ruled by oligarchs who hold influence as long as their concepts and systems are accepted as the most successful strategy."[7]

It is not surprising, therefore, that it has been easy for the weapons scientists and engineers to accept the Cold War unquestioned, to accept the uncounterbalanced authority of the Joint Committee, to accept the absurdity of the nuclear-arms race, to accept the paranoid thinking of the military, to accept their placid bureaucratic life. After all, except for that last point, the rest was none of their business.

No greater symbol of this abstract, docile, apolitical and yet at the same time arrogant stance exists than the last chairman of the AEC, Dr. Glenn T. Seaborg. His voice is gentle, his actions noncontroversial, and he plodded quietly on, from speech to speech, promoting atomic energy, the AEC and his own pet interests. In 1969 Seaborg delivered twenty-five speeches, both here and abroad (Sweden and Austria).[86] In 1970 he gave another twenty-five speeches, five outside the country this time, from Vienna to Tokyo.[87] He had been chairman of the AEC through Presidents as diverse as Kennedy, Johnson and Nixon. "President Nixon's not much different," he said in a 1970 interview.[66] "The overall thrust continues."

And that thrust, according to law, was to achieve two ends: to provide the military with the most up-to-date nuclear weaponry and to discover and promote the benefits of nuclear energy for the civilian sector. But how many weapons to produce, or how deeply to commit this country to multibillion-dollar civilian nuclear programs, or how and when to turn the money faucet off was a decision for insiders alone.

At his retirement, some middle-level AEC official said in private that Dr. Seaborg, who headed the commission for a decade, believed that policy decisions should best be made by the experts without the benefit of public debate. "He sincerely believed that the AEC was serving the public interest," said one AEC staffer about Dr. Seaborg. "The hitch was that he thought his word should be taken as gospel without public discussion."[88]

Thus, in the largest sense, Seaborg typifies the weapons scientist: sure of his course, he can be depended upon to produce whatever is asked of him, providing it does not violate the laws of science. But the public operates under different laws, and when they complain, they are treated with the impatience and arrogant disdain which has become so inseparably identified with the atomic establishment in this country.

And so the Atomic Energy Commission and its scientists, engineers and technicians have done more than placidly live out their lives accepting what came along. They are, in fact, the shock troops of the arms race. They live on comfortable, government-fed payrolls thinking up minor refinements to weapons we dare not use.

It is the most dangerous of games, played out for the petty stakes of this month's paycheck, a new form of government welfare.

11 · BUILT-IN CONTROLS OF THE ARMS RACE

ARMS RACES have some of the most persuasive reasons for existence of any national effort throughout man's history. They are based upon survival itself, not to mention the effective lobbying of those who benefit most directly: the armament makers. Those who argue against the arms race by advocating that we must trust those we have been taught over the years to distrust base their case on hoped-for behavior patterns never observed in recorded history. Man's history is an unbroken testament to the fact that mutual fear is the only force that keeps potential antagonists apart.

But nothing in nature increases without limit (save entropy). Arms races have built-in limits, too. Once the cost of an arms buildup begins to drain a national economy, the dissatisfaction thus generated is most often directed against the enemy, thereby strengthening the position of those leaders who want war (the very same people who started the arms race in the first place). And so the normal solution to an arms race always has been war. But until now man has never regarded that as an unacceptable solution. After all, having drained his treasury to pay for the arms race, the victor can replenish his loss from booty gained by his conquest.

But that's all changed now. Because of the fantastic destructive power of nuclear explosives and their unprecedented ease of delivery anywhere on earth, all-out thermonuclear war involves two new inevitabilities. Firstly, the victor must absorb unacceptable punishment himself, and, secondly, there will be no spoils of war left in the enemy's land to replenish his own country. And so we haven't gone to nuclear war—yet.

But deprived of its usual solution, the arms race is still not free to increase without limit. It just means that less efficient controls eventually take over, and they have already begun to work. On the one hand, our enemies have become less fearful to us, and on the other hand, the cost of the arms race is becoming increasingly intolerable.

In 1947 General S. L. A. Marshall wrote: "No nation on earth possesses such limitless resources that it can maintain itself in a state of perfect readiness to engage in war immediately and decisively and win a total victory soon after the outbreak *without destroying its own economy, pauperizing its own people, and promoting interior disorder.*"[40]* We can see this taking place already: we have accomplished much of the destruction of our own country that Marshall said we must in order to maintain our defense posture, and our nation has begun to appreciate that. The billion-dollar aircraft carrier, the CVAN-70, would have been approved easily ten years ago, but it was turned down in 1971.

And so the new mechanism for arms-race control, *to pauperize the participants,* is becoming more obvious to all. It has to get a lot worse before it gets better, and it's dangerous as can be for a lot of reasons, but it's the only force operating to check the arms race, and, considering the alternative, it will have to do for now.

* Emphasis added.

III
THE TURNING POINT: ATOMIC FALLOUT

... the attack on nuclear power that we find least responsible is that which isolates a few shortcomings, difficulties and failures over a twenty-five-year history.
—Dr. Glenn T. Seaborg, former chairman, U. S. Atomic Energy Commission[89]

1 · WHY THE TRACK RECORD IS IMPORTANT

The future will see a great expansion of atomic technology. According to the AEC's director of military applications, General Edward B. Giller, the AEC is "heading into the biggest weapons production program in our history," a fact brought to light recently during his testimony in support of a $355-million additional appropriation for the upgrading of the AEC's weapons production facilities across the country.[72] But the greatest increase by far will come in the civilian sector, with the spread of nuclear electric-generating stations[90] and other applications of the peaceful atom.[91]

Throughout this expansion, the Atomic Energy Commission will be doing its best, within the constraints of its promotional bias, to assure that public health is maintained, even though an increase in atomic technology inevitably increases the public's risk of exposure to atomic radiation. Accordingly, extravagant assurances as to the safety of every new advance are routinely provided by the AEC.

It is difficult to gauge the reliability of these public-health assurances, because, unlike smog, the spread of radioactive pollution is not perceived by our senses, and also because of the insidious nature of radiation damage itself. Physical damage from other forms of radiation, such as heat or sound, are immediate and obvious. Radiation damage, on the other hand, is not immediately noticeable except when it is caused by very large doses. Cancer, the most feared outcome, appears only decades after exposure to the damage-causing radiation, and the appearance of mutations takes several generations or longer. So a true assessment of the damage caused by a given atomic enterprise, such as the atmospheric weapons-testing program or the uranium-mining boom of the fifties, may not be possible for a very long time after it is terminated.

Faced as we are with a great expansion of atomic technology, it is important somehow to calibrate quickly the competence of the Atomic Energy Commission and the Joint Committee on Atomic Energy to make the sweeping assurances of public safety they do. The only reliable way to accomplish this is to look at the past; only there can we compare AEC advance assurances of public health with what actually took place in the end, because only with atomic enterprises long since terminated has enough time passed for the delayed effects of radioactive pollution to show themselves.

In the field of public health, the AEC and the Joint Committee have had three great failures, all resulting from the same weakness. Over the twenty-five years of their existence they seem never to have been able to free themselves of their promotional bias when they found themselves in conflict with public-health judgments which would seek to limit the free expansion of their technology. It's not surprising, therefore, that the AEC soon found itself minimizing and even ignoring radiation dangers, and this was to be the root of its most costly and consistent mistakes.

The AEC's and the Joint Committee's three great failures have been in not foreseeing sufficiently, even when it was pointed out to them for years, firstly, the dangers associated with radioactive fallout from atmospheric nuclear testing; secondly, the hazards of breathing uranium-mine atmospheres where no effort was made to reduce the airborne radioactivity therein (despite the fact that the AEC knew *before* it began its massive uranium-procurement program that a thousand European uranium miners had already died under conditions identical to those the AEC was to create on the Colorado Plateau in the 1950s); and, thirdly, the dangers in permitting the free distribution of radioactive uranium mill tailings from AEC licensed mills, whose misuse has caused many thousands of private homes to be made unsafe for occupancy.

2 · SETTING THE STAGE FOR ERROR

UNTIL the late 1950s, few raised serious questions concerning the competence of the AEC. As it was the glamour agency of the day, the chairman of the AEC at that time was as high as number four on the State Department's protocol list, the best guide to the "in crowd" of official Washington. This entitled him to appear at state functions just after the Vice-President, the Secretary of State, and the Speaker of the House.

Understandably proud, the AEC and the Joint Committee fell heir, however, to that occupational hazard of all those who achieve success: they began to believe in their own propaganda. Not only did the AEC inflate beyond all reason the ways in which the atom could serve man, but in its enthusiasm for atomic energy it developed a tragically strong tendency to ignore its many harmful effects. Furthermore, as we shall see when the AEC meets its first criticism, the AEC and the Joint Committee began to believe in their own omnicompetence and the infallibility of their own judgments. This is not to say that the AEC was incompetent, only that its competence, like that of all men and institutions, had natural limits and it simply did not recognize these limits.

Still another reason why the AEC became so error-prone was that it misjudged its role after the 1954 revision of the Atomic Energy Act.[6] "Industrial partners" (as the AEC calls them) were invited in to share the benefits of atomic energy. Instead of remaining neutral and merely helping the infant nuclear industry along with technical assistance, the AEC became an even more aggressive promoter and was the nuclear industry's protector and representative, to the exclusion of the public, ushering in the nuclear age like a used-car salesman.

Though Americans' distaste for used-car salesmen is legendary, we overlook the fast-buck tactic because we're more interested in the product. And so it was with atomic energy in the early days: the same men who brought us the miraculous atomic bomb were about to revolutionize our peacetime world with the mighty atom; our sales resistance was at an all-time low.

As if having the complete faith and confidence of the public wasn't enough, the AEC had something else going for it, and that was secrecy. Even members of the Joint Committee (unwillingly, in the early days) made it clear that the Congress would just have to accept their recommendations on faith. Members of the House Appropriations Committee in the early 1950s regularly cut the AEC's budget, charging that the agency was "lax in presentation of detailed estimates" and that it cloaked itself in the "aura of a scientific subject." The predominant attitude of the Senate was to "rely more on you gentlemen to tell us the truth and keep costs down."[8]

Secrecy also meant that important decisions could be made without the usual outside critical review and that mistakes could be more easily concealed. And perhaps it was secrecy, more than any other single factor, that led to the problems which beset atomic energy today. With organizations as with individuals it is outside objective criticism which keeps us honest, if not sane, for objectivity is impossible if we have only subjective internal standards to go by.

But unburdened by self-doubt as it was, and charged by Congress with policing itself, it was thus preordained that the AEC could not maintain that number-four position on the State Department's protocol list for very long. Arrogance and humility cannot coexist; some humility is required in order to admit to error and react to it constructively. So it would seem that the very first major error made by the AEC would spell the end of that agency as a servant of the public—and so it did.

3 · THE TURNING POINT

THE AEC's first major error concerned its reading of the dangers of radioactive fallout from atmospheric nuclear-weapons tests. In 1953, as today, there was a debate going on among scientists regarding the dangers of atomic radiation. In situations of technical uncertainty, the traditional position of public-health agencies has always been to take the most conservative view—that is, to err on the side of safety. But then, as now, the official position of the AEC was the opposite, despite the fact that included in its charge by Congress was the responsibility to protect public health.

The AEC's view, described before the Joint Committee as the "body-in-the-morgue approach,"[92] is common among engineering organizations. Danger is taken seriously only when it can be "readily noticeable," and there's the rub. Normally there are 307 new cases of cancer each year for every 100,000 individuals in the general population.[93] This doesn't mean that a city of 100,000 people will produce *precisely* 307 new cases every year; it is a simple average; the actual number is less one year and more another. But suppose some new poison is released into the environment which causes a true increase in the incidence of cancer; how can that be proven? If, as a consequence, the cancer rate is increased by ten percent, the extra thirty-one cases per year in a city of 100,000 surely would not be "noticed" for some time (and wasn't—see Chapter V). This is because the normal yearly variation in cancer incidence prior to any true ten percent increase might easily have been ten percent higher than the average in occasional years (a false increase); but that false rise would have been balanced off by a decrease in cancer incidence during other years. A *true* ten percent increase in the cancer rate is, of course, not balanced by a corresponding decrease. The problem is that many years must pass before a *trend* toward a higher rate of cancer can be proven to be a reflection of a *true increase* in the yearly rate. Therefore, a large population of affected individuals, sophisticated statistical techniques, and long time periods are needed to prove conclusively that a suspected ten percent increase in cancer incidence has actually occurred. Moreover, the long delay between cause and effect common with radiation injuries complicates the matter even further, by making the detection of radiation damage possible only many years more into the future than is the case with chemical poisons.

For these reasons it is difficult to get a consensus among radiation-safety people as to whether a trend toward an increase in the cancer rate is real or simply a normal fluctuation in the yearly rate, to be balanced off by a corresponding decrease some years later. Accordingly, while one scientist might believe that a real increase in the cancer rate has already been proven, another might insist on waiting many years for more data before he is convinced of the same thing. Therefore, at any time there can be several schools of thought regarding the extent of the dangers associated with atomic radiation.

Unlike public-health and medical people, the AEC did not restrict itself to the most conservative interpretation of radiological health data; as an engineering organization unburdened by such traditions, the AEC *took its choice* from among the various opinions offered. Predictably, then, the AEC has always chosen that view which impeded its progress least. Accordingly, it was safe in making such self-serving interpretations of the scientific debate of the day as "Over a period of many years, a human being may safely receive a total amount of radiation which would cause a fatal illness if administered to his whole body within a period of a few minutes." Or: ". . . low levels of radiation produce no *detectible* somatic effect; that is, the body is able to repair the damage virtually as quickly as it occurs. Such low level exposure can be continued indefinitely without any detectible bodily change."[94]*

As late as 1957 the AEC assured the public, in connection with its atmospheric program in Nevada: "A Geiger counter can go completely off-scale in fallout which is far from hazardous . . ."[95]

Not only is all of this information known to be untrue today, but it was known to be untrue then. The only difference between then and now is that *at that time a minority of scientists held those views, whereas today none do.* But the crucial point is not simply that the AEC was wrong, but that it made the official decision, then as now, *to opt for whatever view among many impeded its technical progress least,* despite the fact that under the Atomic Energy Act it was responsible for public health as well as the promotion of nuclear energy.

At the outset of their testing program, AEC scientists naïvely believed that radioactive-fallout particles would disperse evenly throughout the world's atmosphere. They were totally unprepared for what actually did happen: the fallout particles partitioned themselves among the great rivers of air which circulate around our planet, thereby depositing much more fallout over the populous North Temperate Zone than near the equator. In this way, fallout became much more concentrated and therefore far more dangerous than they had originally estimated.

Another and far more important aspect of its blunder was that the AEC advertised for many years that the main danger from fallout was radiation external to the body. AEC scientists ignored or just didn't take the time to worry about the real threat from fallout, the internal radiation dose produced by radioisotopes which are taken into the body with foods. Although they were aware of the danger of strontium 90, which can produce bone and blood cancers, they overlooked the main pathway by which this component of radioactive fallout can enter man—through drinking milk. At the

* Emphasis added.

same time, they were totally unaware and thereby ignored the importance of iodine 131, which can produce thyroid cancer. It wasn't until secrecy concerning fallout was lifted in the middle 1950s that the truth became known, and then only through the efforts of non-AEC scientists and even, to a small extent, the Joint Committee, all to the great embarrassment of the AEC.

In those days of the middle 1950s, the Joint Committee was far less closely tied to the AEC than it is today. Representative Holifield branded the AEC "grossly tardy and negligent" in telling the nation the truth about fallout from atomic tests. He accused the AEC of intentionally playing down the effects and dangers of radiation.[96] Before the "turning point" in the early 1960s, the Chet Holifield of the 1950s sounded very much like the nuclear critics of today whom he so caustically condemns. He said then:

I believe from our hearings that the AEC approach to the hazards from bomb test fallout seems to add up to a party line—"play it down." As custodian of official information, the AEC has an urgent responsibility to communicate the facts to the public. Yet time after time there has been a long delay in issuance of the facts, and oftentimes the facts have to be dragged out of the agency by the Congress. Certainly it took our investigation to enable some of the Commission's own experts to break through the party line on fallout.[97]

4 · FALLOUT: HOW DANGEROUS IS IT?

BUT "PLAYING DOWN" the dangers of radiation from fallout was important for the AEC, because it foresaw (correctly) that radioactive fallout would spell the end of its atmospheric-nuclear-testing program. Accordingly, the findings of the Atomic Bomb Casualty Commission (ABCC) were unjustly minimized and still are. The ABCC is a research organization which since 1947 has been conducting epidemiological studies of the Japanese survivors of the atomic blasts at Hiroshima and Nagasaki. Financed by the AEC (to the extent of over $50 million so far) and directed by the National Academy of Sciences (with token funding by the Japanese National Institutes of Health), the ABCC has included perhaps 200,-000 individuals in its massive survey.

Small increases in general mortality, growth retardation and cataracts were observed,[98] but the main effect was that "the incidence of leukemia [a fatal blood cancer] was abnormally high among survivors, reaching a peak about 1951."[99] Leukemia, of all the cancers, is the first to appear after exposure to atomic radiation. Increases in other cancers among the survivors, as well as mutations in the yet unborn, would become obvious only decades later, due to the long delay between cause and effect known to exist with radiation effects other than leukemia.

Despite these facts, the AEC played down the increase in leukemia and concentrated its public announcements on those effects which were not expected to have appeared for decades anyway. At the very time that leukemia was still occurring at its highest rate among the survivors of the atomic blasts, the AEC focused attention elsewhere, announcing: "Data collected by the ABCC in Japan indicate an insignificant increase in the number of detectible *mutations* in children of persons subjected to radiation . . ."[94]* But this statement was made only eight years after the exposure; mutations take generations to appear.

Like mutations, cancers of the uterus, the bones and the thyroid don't show up for a very long time. For twenty-five years the rates of those cancers among the survivors had not been dramatically higher than other places in Japan, and the AEC quoted this fact yearly as an endorsement of its position that radiation from fallout was simply not as dangerous as AEC critics have said. However, in 1971 the ABCC announced what had been predicted by many, that other types of cancers were beginning to be seen and that "now, 25 years after exposure, the accumulated increase is striking, with

* Emphasis added.

no evidence yet that a peak has been reached." The ABCC felt that it was going to get worse as time went on, because "during the next ten years these persons will be entering upon ages when, ordinarily, cancer-rates begin to increase strikingly."[100]

Dr. Glenn T. Seaborg conceded to the Joint Committee that "after nearly twenty years of largely negative results—except for leukemia induction—positive findings are now beginning to emerge" from the ABCC in Japan. But, as chairman of the AEC, he still felt the need to minimize the importance of these results: "We are just beginning to establish a *barely discernible effect* from the statistical point of view . . . I want to indicate it is a *very small effect* . . . there is a *barely discernible effect* now . . . I don't want this to be misunderstood . . . It is *only an indication* at the present time. *It is not an established fact.*"[101]*

But it wasn't the wartime bombing of Japan which created the problem of radioactive fallout in the world, it was the atmospheric weapons-testing program that began in 1946 in the Pacific, in 1949 in Russia and in 1951 in Nevada. The widespread use of radiation-measuring instruments by the public caused the AEC some problems; as late as 1957 the AEC reassured nervous Southwesterners with misleading statements such as "Many persons in Nevada, Utah, Arizona and nearby California have Geiger counters these days. We can expect many reports that 'Geiger counters were going crazy here today.' Reports like this may worry people unnecessarily. Don't let them bother you."[84] The AEC exulted the next year that no claim for radiation damage "has ever been settled on the basis of alleged radiological injury to humans" and that a suit against the AEC for damages from facial cancer developed by Mrs. Daniel Sheahan as a result of assorted burns from radioactive fallout in the 1952 series was dismissed by the Court."[102]

Testing in the atmosphere was substantially ended by the Nuclear Test Ban Treaty of 1963,[6] and so were the massive injections of radioactive fallout into the open air. Accordingly many people believe that the hazards of radioactive fallout have vanished. But quite the opposite is the case: "Debris from atmospheric nuclear tests

* Emphasis added.

continued to be the most important man-made radioactive contaminant of the environment";[103] this is because it takes such a long time for all the fallout to come down to earth.

It is also widely assumed that most of the fallout still around remains on the ground, safely away from the public, at the AEC's Nevada test site. But "observations during the past decade indicate that less than ten percent of the total strontium produced from nuclear detonations at the Nevada Test Site has been deposited within 200 miles from the point of detonation";[104] the other ninety percent is somewhere else, of course.

Surprisingly, only one eighth of the total amount of strontium 90 produced by the nuclear tests had actually "fallen out" by the end of 1967, and only one tenth of the dose from the carbon 14 produced will have been delivered by the year 2000. So however harmful radioactive fallout is, it is almost as serious a problem today as it was ten years ago.

It is well known that atomic radiation can cause death from cancer, but it is less well known that at sustained low doses radiation affects general longevity, with individuals dying of "natural" causes but sooner.[105] Thus, the scientific debate revolves around only the rate of death for a given radiation dose—not whether it occurs at all.

To assess the harmful effects of nuclear fallout, we need only to know two things: how much radiation each person receives from worldwide fallout each year, and how much harm this radiation causes. Fortunately, there seems to be general agreement on the amount each person on earth receives from radioactive fallout: it is 5.7 millirem per year today[106] although it was ten times higher in the late 1950s and again in the early 1960s.

The best current estimates for the harm that atomic radiation causes indicate that "one statistical death" is caused by approximately 1,000 rem (radiation equivalent man).[107] By this scientists mean that this amount of radiation will reduce one person's lifetime by seventy years (death at birth), or two lifetimes by thirty-five years each (death at mid-life), or the lifetimes of 25,000 men by one day each (since 25,000 days are about equal to seventy years), or any combination of possibilities. For this reason the AEC never uses the word "death" but prefers to use the term "life shortening."

With the entire world, 2.7 billion people, affected, this gives 15 million man-rem per year. If 1,000 man-rem produce one "statistical death," then radioactive fallout produces 15,000 "statistical deaths" among the world's population each year. Repeating, this does not mean that 15,000 infants will die (one extreme) or that each man on earth will lose three hours of life (the other extreme), but rather a statistical distribution of all of the possibilities in between. But there are other effects besides "statistical death." Linus Pauling has estimated that a single year of testing produces "an estimated total of about 55,000 children with gross physical or mental defects."[108]

Fortunately, this high rate won't go on forever, since radioactive fallout eventually decays to nonradioactive products. But, using a United Nations estimate[103] of the total dose from all the fallout worldwide, 140 millirem, and assuming that 1,000 rem produce one "statistical death," a simple calculation predicts that about 400 thousand "statistical deaths" will occur before it is all over. Not surprisingly, this is about the same number arrived at in a formal study of the subject.[109]

Although these estimates are really educated guesses, they are nonetheless the best that science can offer currently. Furthermore, they are neither the highest nor the lowest, but those numbers that are in use by most people in the field today. If they are wrong, they are probably not far wrong, but, if the history of health standards for radioactivity is any judge, these estimates probably underestimate the hazard. They do not take into account mutations or "genetic deaths." Pauling estimates that 170,000 stillbirths and 425,000 embryonic and neonatal deaths are caused by a single year of testing.[108]

So fallout, it turns out, was and still is a very serious threat to health after all. It was a great and costly scientific blunder. No matter how you look at it, lives have been shortened or lost by at least tens of thousands yearly.

Hindsight, it is said, is a great gift, and if the AEC were merely wrong it would be one thing, but the AEC was more than simply wrong: as it is with bureaucracies, once the AEC committed itself to a position it rarely reversed itself, however obvious its error. Furthermore, many individuals within the AEC and the Joint Committee on Atomic Energy, in their zeal to promote nuclear energy, often confused that goal with the protection of the reputation of the AEC itself. Thus, when independent scientists began to point out AEC errors in connection with fallout, they were often ignored at first, then their statements were attacked, and in some cases an attempt was made to discredit the critic personally. This type of response to criticism began in the days of the fallout controversy and has abated only since 1970.

Not the least important result of their self-serving protectionism was that it served to delay for years a resolution of each problem. During that unnecessary lag, radioactivity was being poured into the environment from nuclear air blasts, miners were dying underground needlessly, and homes were being built on radioactive sand taken from the waste piles at AEC-licensed uranium mills.

5 · SECRECY

BUT in the early 1950s fallout data was still secret. Since no critical word was raised against the AEC's estimate of the dangers, it is not surprising that, in its zeal to protect its interests, grossly irresponsible statements were made. After all, public concern about radioactive fallout was the one thing that could put the AEC's atmospheric testing program out of business, and in the end it did. Quite naturally, therefore, the AEC devoted much effort publicly to minimize the hazards of radioactive fallout and no meaningful effort toward measuring the spread of fallout or investigating its dangers. This same effort to keep the public from becoming worried still pervades the Atomic Energy Commission.

Difficult decisions are more easily made when the hazards they include are not well known. So until the middle 1950s the AEC was content to dismiss publicly the dangers of radioactive fallout even though they had no idea what they were talking about. Dr. John C. Bugher, then director of the AEC's Division of Biology and Medicine, provides an example of this kind of lack of foresight. In a speech in 1954, he said of strontium 90, "I estimate that the amount of such material now present over the United States would have to be increased by the order of *one million times* before an increased frequency of bone [cancer] from this cause could be *recognized*."[110]* Remarkably, he said this after the massive Castle series of tests in the Pacific in the spring of 1954, which, according to Bugher himself, had deposited 100 millicuries of radioactive fallout per square mile (there is only about three or four times that amount on the ground today). Bugher's estimate of one million times that amount, or 100,000 curies per square mile, is regarded today as many times more radiation than is necessary to insure the destruction of the human race.

Not only was Bugher wrong in relation to current knowledge, but his statement of how much fallout man could tolerate was much greater than the then current highest estimates made by the AEC fallout study group at the Oak Ridge National Laboratory, the scientists who had the *only* data from which estimates could be made.[111] In the speeches made by AEC bureaucrats at the time, it was common to find AEC scientific data similarly exaggerated. Fortunately, our nation did not follow Dr. Bugher's guidelines.

In those days, even Holifield wondered at these extreme statements: "As a layman I was somewhat shocked to find out how much the experts admitted they did not know. In fact, when I thought over how little is known for sure, I wondered how some government officials could be so positive that bomb tests were so safe."[97]

Part of the AEC's lack of appreciation of the dangers of fallout

* Emphasis added.

followed from its ignorance of the precise dangers associated with the concentrating effect of the food chain. Scientists both in and outside the AEC have long known that the element strontium acts in the body like calcium, and that it is thereby built into the calcium-rich tissues, such as the bones, of any animal who eats strontium. Its radioactive isotope, strontium 90, is one of the most dangerous of all components of radioactive fallout because it is quickly built into living systems, its radioactivity lasts a long time, and it is concentrated by the food chain.

Here is how that effect works: A nuclear blast releases large quantities of strontium 90 into the air (about one hundred curies per kiloton of fission). Slowly, this radioactive dust comes to earth, brought down by rain or snow or simply by settling. It lands everywhere, on tobacco, tea leaves, leafy vegetables and, of course, pastures. Cows grazing on grass containing the fallout eat the radioactivity, with some of the strontium 90 concentrating in their bones and milk. Children who drink the cows' milk build their growing bones out of the calcium as well as the radioactive strontium 90 which the cow originally obtained by grazing over large areas of pasture. Thus the child concentrates in his bones the strontium 90 (and the calcium too) which was once spread over many acres. Once incorporated into his bones, the radioactive strontium remains there, irradiating bone marrow (where blood is formed) and bone as well, greatly increasing the child's chances for bone cancer, leukemia and other forms of malignant neoplasms.

But the AEC scientists differed from scientists outside the AEC on a crucial point. Astonishingly, the AEC believed that the main danger of strontium 90 came from *eating the bones* of grazing animals, and so they ignored the major route by which strontium 90 can enter man: cows' milk.

In response to the first stirrings of public criticism against the AEC (outside scientists pointed out that milk was the most important carrier of strontium 90, not bone), the AEC said, in its formal report to Congress that year,[112] that "*the only potential hazard to human beings would be the ingestion of bone splinters* which might be intermingled with muscle tissue in butchering and cutting of the meat. An insignificant amount would enter the body in this fashion."*

The report went on to say: "As to the taking in of radioactivity by animals eating plants growing in soil affected by the fallout from the tests, *experiments have indicated that there is no hazard to human health* from this source."* These "experiments" of course, were conducted in secret, if in fact they ever were conducted at all. Since the conclusions drawn were so wrong, the possibility that they will ever be released for public scrutiny is vanishingly small. But if these "experiments" had been released at the time, there is no question but that they would have stirred up a healthy debate and scientists outside the AEC would have been able to point out the error long before so much damage was done.

The hazard of radioactive iodine was utterly ignored until it was already too late, and former AEC Commissioner Willard Libby breezily dismissed the dangers of carbon 14 by stating, "Fortunately, this radioactivity is essentially safe because of its long life-time and the enormous amount of diluting carbon dioxide in the atmosphere."[113]

Thus from ignorance did the AEC guarantee the public that fallout was nothing to worry about. Surely those arrogant assurances would still be forthcoming if, without the help and interference of outsiders, the AEC were still allowed to run its own show today.

In the 1950s, before the turning point, Joint Committeemen still complained publicly about AEC practices. But since secrecy prevented them from finding out very much, they had little to complain about except the secrecy itself. It was not as if each man on the Joint Committee didn't have his AEC supersecret "Q Clearance"; there are other ways of handling congressional busybodies. Consider the words of Chet Holifield himself in 1957:

It has been my experience that a Congressional investigation is often the only way to make the Atomic Energy Commission come out into the

* Emphasis added.

open. We literally squeeze the information out of the agency. Except for the Congressional hearings, the AEC would withhold some important information that the public should have. Then, too, when the commission releases information on its own initiative it comes in forbidding technical form or in driblets through speeches of commission members or other high-ranking personnel. Even skillful newspaper reporters, not to mention the layman on the outside, have difficulty piecing together the information or understanding its significance.

Tardy release of information is bad enough in itself. But there is something worse. That is the selective use and release of information to favor a political position. The Atomic Energy Commission is supposed to be an independent agency. By direction of the Congress it commands vast resources and decides what the public shall know and what shall be withheld from the public. This is a great burden of responsibility. The chairman of the Atomic Energy Commission, by virtue of his dual role as Atomic Energy adviser to the President and head of an independent agency, has at times blurred and confused the situation. The prestige and resources of the Atomic Energy Commission have been lent to the fulfilment of partisan purposes in at least two instances.[97]

6 · SECRECY ENDS

ABOUT 1954, secrecy concerning fallout was relaxed and scientists outside the AEC got their first chance to examine data that until then was kept from independent review. In a very short time they discovered that the AEC was quite wrong in emphasizing external gamma radiation from fallout as the greatest danger, and that it was radioactivity taken into the body that was the greatest threat.

Commoner has observed that

the importance of iodine-131 as a hazard to the child's thyroid gland was first suggested by a geneticist, E. B. Lewis, from the California Institute of Technology. The noted chemist, Linus Pauling, first demonstrated that carbon-14, generated by nuclear explosions, is an important biological hazard. Evidence of high local concentrations of fallout in regions near the Nevada test site was first developed by Norman Bauer, a chemist, of Utah State University, and by E. W. Pfeiffer, a zoologist, of the University of Montana. The great value of large scale analysis of baby teeth as an index of strontium-90 absorption by children was first suggested by a biochemist, Herman Kalckar, of Harvard, and the first actual project to collect such teeth, the Baby Tooth Survey, was initiated by the St. Louis Committee for Nuclear Information. The Canadian botanist, Eville Gorham, first reported the extraordinary capacity of lichens to absorb fallout and indicated the significance of this effect in amplifying the fallout hazard in the Arctic.[114]

Some of these findings had already appeared in the press when, through the efforts of Dr. Ralph Lapp, the first and most effective nuclear critic,[115] something even more frightening was brought to the attention of the public. While AEC officials admitted that local fallout near the site of a nuclear test could be severe, they had always minimized the risk of a concentrated rain-out of radioactive particles causing a "hot spot" many hundreds and even thousands of miles away from an atomic blast. But a concentrated rain-out of nuclear debris is just what happened in Troy, New York, one rainy evening in 1953 just a few days after and two thousand miles away from an atmospheric nuclear blast at the AEC test site in Nevada.[116] From then on, the issue of radioactive fallout was no longer left exclusively to the "experts" at the AEC. The public began to take an interest, too, because it finally realized that you don't have to live near the Nevada test site to get irradiated; it can happen anywhere.

In response to the growing interest in fallout, the Joint Committee on Atomic Energy held hearings on the subject in the spring of 1957.[3] These hearings provide the first public record of the extremes to which some AEC officials went in order to protect a position officially held by their bureaucracy. Later on we will see examples of how self-righteous zeal turned into fanaticism as the AEC attempted to justify its mistakes and to avoid blame.

Testing was in high gear at the time; it was only three years after the "Bikini incident," wherein, through an AEC miscalculation of the explosive yield of a nuclear test called Bravo on March 1, 1954, and the incorrect estimation of the behavior of its fallout cloud, radioactive ashes reached well beyond the established "danger area" then prescribed. Heavy fallout contaminated all sixty-four inhabitants of Rongelap Atoll in the Marshall Islands, who were quickly evacuated, not to return for several years. But even at that they were lucky: fallout on the uninhabited northern end of their atoll was many times higher, almost certainly high enough to kill all human life there.[54, 117]

"Bikini ash," as the Japanese press called the fallout, also covered the decks, the catch and the twenty-three crewmen of the Japanese tuna trawler *Fukuryu Maru* (*The Lucky Dragon*) at sea eighty miles east of the explosion. The men suffered severe radiation sickness but all eventually recovered except the radio operator, who died seven months later. A million pounds of fish were seized and destroyed by the Japanese health authorities, resulting in heavy losses to Japan's fishing industry. At a mass meeting in Tokyo one month after the test, a banner of protest said "IT DOESN'T TAKE A BULLET TO KILL A FISH SELLER—A BIT OF BIKINI ASH WILL DO THE JOB."[54] The Japanese began to study radioactive fallout in the Pacific a year before the American studies began,[118] and it was a time when "in Washington you could swipe a Kleenex over a car top and cause a Geiger counter to respond readily."[3]

Dr. Ralph Lapp cut short a trip to Japan to testify before the 1957 Joint Committee hearings, calling the committee's attention to some "reckless and non-substantiated statements" made by AEC officials, perhaps the most arrogant and indelicate of which was made by Dr. Richard Doan in Japan on May 13 of that year. In a country where "some people . . . are so keenly aware of fallout they actually take showers after being out in the rain" and where public demonstrations against nuclear testing were still common, Dr. Doan stated that the bomb tests would not have "the slightest effect on humans."

But another matter exposed by Lapp was far more serious, because it had been presented publicly by an AEC official as an absolute fact when it wasn't any such thing. Lapp told of how Merril Eisenbud, the manager of the AEC's New York Operations Office, was quoted in a New York newspaper article[119] under the headline "Man Who Measures A-Fallout Belittles Dangers" as saying that "the total fallout to date from all tests would have to be multiplied by a million to produce visible deleterious effects except in areas close to the explosion itself"—a replay of John Bugher's statement, still used by AEC officials at that time, presented as fact and since proven very wrong. Eisenbud's assertion is all the more reckless since, just one year before he made that statement, the AEC had sent him to Yaizu, Japan, the home port of the *Fukuryu Maru,* where he could see for himself what can happen quite far from the blast.

Eisenbud's expansive assurance of public safety was considerably softened when he was subjected to close examination, by Senator Anderson in his case. Not denying the statement's accuracy, he said that he was "talking about the immediate gamma radiation from the fallout which occurs in the eastern United States within a matter of a day or so after a detonation in Nevada. This is not in the statement because the statement has been taken out of context."

In or out of context, it was just as wrong. Dr. Lapp, permitted a question from the audience, asked Eisenbud about the idea that present fallout could be multiplied by one million and still be safe. He asked for the radiation dosage of the rain-out of radioactivity in the Troy-Albany area in New York State after the April 1953 nuclear blast in Nevada. Eisenbud replied that the upper-limit estimate was "something under one hundred milliroentgen."

MR. EISENBUD: I would personally estimate it at about ten milliroentgen.

DR. LAPP: Is it proper for me to respond? I have done a little arithmetic. Let us take ten milliroentgens, as Mr. Eisenbud estimates, and we multiply [by a million] . . . that would be . . . ten thousand roentgens.

SENATOR ANDERSON: Ten thousand roentgens would kill everybody in sight.

MR. EISENBUD: Yes.

SENATOR ANDERSON: So that would mean there would not be any immediate danger if you kill everyone in sight?[3]

Because of the technical complexities involved, Eisenbud might have succeeded in duping the Joint Committee, as AEC functionaries do with such ease, but Lapp was in a position to rebut instantly, a fortunate and rare accident. Most of the time, of course, AEC officials are free to present distortions of a subtle technical nature to the Joint Committee and get away with it.

Though the Joint Committee members cannot be blamed for having less scientific training than their AEC witnesses, they certainly are to be faulted for their gullibility and lack of critical intelligence. There has never been anything to prevent them from obtaining their own independent scientific advisers, but as far as it is known they have never felt the need.

7 · THE CHANGING DEFINITION OF DANGER: STRONTIUM 90

FALLOUT and public interest in the subject increased rapidly in the next few years. Sixty-nine nuclear explosions were detonated in 1958, the highest rate in history. A two-and-a-half-year-long UN study by eighty-seven scientists from fifteen countries was finally released the same year, calling public attention to the dangers from fallout.[120] The strontium-90 content of tea leaves had already passed the maximum permissible concentration, according to the U.S. Food and Drug Administration; according to the AEC itself, strontium-90 levels in milk were rising dramatically all over the country,[121] and the strontium-90 content in wheat from Minnesota and the Dakotas was half again as much as the AEC's own safe limit for human consumption.[122]

About the same time, the National Committee on Radiation Protection (NCRP), a private organization having no government affiliation at all but, paradoxically, the only organization publishing applicable health standards, doubled its "maximum permissible body burden" of strontium 90 that may be tolerated by persons under occupational conditions. Suddenly someone was saying that the "safe level" of strontium 90 could be raised: man could take a bigger dose. Remarkably, this decision was handed down just at the time the strontium 90 released by nuclear tests was approaching the old "safe" limits. For many scientists outside the AEC it was a cause for alarm. The question naturally arose, "If fallout levels rise, should standards follow?"[123]

Also, "the question was quite properly raised" by the president of the NCRP himself, "How could the government find itself in the awkward position of being committed to using standards developed by a non-governmental organization over which they had no control?"[124] Representative Holifield and Senator John O. Pastore of the Joint Committee resolved part of the matter by simply sending a bill through Congress giving a federal charter to the newly renamed National Council on Radiation Protection and Measurements. This gave a certain amount of respect, if not the force of law, to its recommendations. But whether the NCRP ever was an organization independent of the wishes of the Joint Committee or the AEC is still a subject of contention.

Also, in direct response to public interest and confusion regarding radioactive fallout,[125] Dwight D. Eisenhower created the Federal Radiation Council (FRC) to "advise the President with respect to radiation matters directly or indirectly affecting health, including guidance for all federal agencies in the formation of radiation standards . . ."[126] Not to be upstaged by the President (in a field where it felt it was in exclusive control), the Joint Committee, in an act of complete redundancy, saw to it that a law was passed setting up the already established FRC.

But in bureaucracies, regulatory agencies are most often controlled by those very interests who are supposed to be regulated; accordingly, the regulating agencies tend to have built-in mechanisms designed to emasculate any attempt to change the status quo. Unfortunately, the Federal Radiation Council turned out to be a classic example of this, with two out of six of its members being the prime producers of radioactive pollution: the Secretary of Defense and the Chairman of the Atomic Energy Commission.[127] They became, of course, the Council's most active members.

Furthermore, the executive director who was picked for the FRC was Dr. Paul C. Tompkins. Just as Dr. Glenn T. Seaborg fairly typifies the weapons scientist, Dr. Tompkins represents a new kind of public-health official with all-purpose credentials, nominally able to serve the polluter and the polluted as well. Dr. Tompkins began his career at the Metallurgical Laboratory, the code name fore the plutonium and bomb-design laboratory at the University of Chicago during World War II. Serving at Oak Ridge and later as the director of the Navy's Radiological Defense Laboratories, he became the deputy director of the AEC's Office of Radiation Standards and even served for a year as the technical consultant to the Joint Committee on Atomic Energy. Replaying his role at the FRC, he is presently the acting director of the Division of Criteria and Standards of the Radiation Office of the newly formed Environmental Protection Agency (EPA), and the man who attempted to weaken EPA's position when two of its representatives voted against the AEC in a 1971 dispute over radiation standards in Colorado (see Chapter V). And so organizational nepotism, so characteristic of the atomic bureaucracy, became more complete as arm's-length dealing was lost even with the public-health "watchdogs."

In addition to resolving the confusion regarding the standards themselves, the FRC was supposed to be the one single agency to which the rest of government and the public could look for the last word on radiation standards. Now that there existed official guidelines, fallout levels could be more intelligently dealt with, or so it was thought at the time.

As if allowing the producers of fallout—the AEC and the Defense Department—to regulate it as well weren't enough to eliminate the FRC as a meaningful force, the FRC itself, in one of its first acts, finished the job. When President Eisenhower approved the first set of recommendations of the FRC, the following language was also contained in that document: ". . . the guides may be exceeded only after the *Federal agency having jurisdiction* over the matter has carefully considered the reason for doing so in light of the recommendations in this paper."[128]*

Thus, the FRC, at the beginning, achieved the very opposite of

* Emphasis added.

what the public was told to expect:[125] "Instead of placing responsibility in a single agency of the Federal Government, it opened the door wide for each Federal agency to establish its own standards."[129]

Radiation standards over the next few years made an interesting study of the corruptive influence of self-regulation. With increasing knowledge, radiation health standards had become increasingly conservative until that time. Since 1902, through many stages of re-evaluation, standards have gone down five hundred fold.[130] One of the *first acts* of the FRC was just the opposite. It was to liberalize the then accepted standard[131] for strontium 90 sixfold.[132] Thus the strontium-90 problem was "solved" by the FRC by the simple expedient of changing the definition of what is "safe."

Even President Eisenhower was misled on the dangers of strontium 90, as Joint Committee Chairman Holifield implies:

How can we be sure that the President is getting the best scientific evaluation of the problem? Mr. Eisenhower says that he bases his judgment upon the National Academy study. But this Academy report is complex and technical. Who interprets it for the President? As special Presidential advisor to the President on atomic energy matters, [AEC Chairman Lewis] Strauss is in a most favored and influential position. My question is simply this: Has the President been "fully informed"? Have the views of eminent scientists, who hold contrary views on strontium-90 to those of Mr. Strauss, been brought to the President's attention? This subject is of such great importance that the President should seek opposing viewpoints in order that he may exercise independence of judgment. Have any eminent scientists discussed the strontium-90 problem with the President?

I have no information to lead me to believe the President really understands this particular hazard.

Holifield went on to indict the AEC for keeping the Joint Committee in the dark as well: "The Atomic Energy Act of 1954 directs the chairman of the Atomic Energy Commission to keep the Joint Committee on Atomic Energy 'fully informed,' and Mr. Strauss has failed, in my opinion, to fulfill this legal mandate."[97]

8 · SLIDING STANDARDS: IODINE 131

BUT WITH INCREASED TESTING, fallout levels kept rising, and as deplorable a page in the history of the atomic bureaucracy as the strontium-90 blunder came to be, it was overshadowed by something even worse: it was discovered that the AEC had largely ignored even the *existence* of iodine 131 as a dangerous component of fallout. Again the AEC had been looking in the wrong place at the wrong time. Because of the short half-life of iodine 131 (eight days), radioactive iodine had long since decayed to nonradioactive products by the time AEC technicians got around to measuring for it. (Radioactive substances decay naturally to harmless products; some take less than a second to do so, and others require more time than the earth has been in existence. A measure of this rate for each particular radioisotope is called its half-life. It is that time required for half of the radioactivity originally present to disappear).

The fact that the AEC so neglected radioactive iodine was entirely the fault of top management of the AEC and its misplaced priorities. Throughout that period, the AEC had budgeted for only thirty to fifty technicians responsible for measuring fallout over the whole United States.

In the summer of 1962, the iodine 131 levels in milk in many areas in Utah reached into the highest range provided for by the Radiation Protection Guides of the FRC[133] and in some areas far exceeded the highest danger levels. In late 1962, the AEC admitted that the radiation dosage from iodine 131 may have reached 1.5 rem per year in some parts of the country;[134] this was three times the official FRC guidelines.

Fallout kept the Joint Committee busy with hearings in 1962[3] and in 1963[135] as well. It was during these hearings that the full importance of iodine 131 was revealed, first with the disclosure of a University of Utah study headed by Dr. Robert C. Pendleton.[136] A co-worker, Dr. Charles W. Mays, testified that this study, which began by the accidental discovery of iodine 131 in milk, revealed that "approximately a quarter of a million of the children in the State of Utah may have been exposed to average thyroid doses of 4.4 rads prior to age two."[135] This is over eight times the maximum safe limit established by the FRC, and, being an average number, it doesn't take into account the fact that "hot spots" were considerably higher than this level.

Dr. Mays also estimated that as the result of an AEC test in Nevada in 1953, seven hundred infants in St. George, Utah, received average radiation doses to the thyroid gland that were from 136 to 500 times higher than the existing permissible level. St. George is about one hundred miles from the atomic-test site in neighboring Nevada and is the seat of Washington County, Utah, the county with the highest reported level of fallout in the nation.[137]

That fall, a U.S. Public Health Service team arrived at St. George to investigate the reasons for the extraordinarily high incidence of thyroid nodules among the children there. Thyroid nodules are small wartlike bumps on the thyroid gland and are believed to be a precursor to cancer. They also appeared among the natives of Rongelap Island who were exposed during the Bikini tests[138] as well as the survivors of the Hiroshima and Nagasaki blasts.[139] But until 1957 the AEC was still making its usual reassuring statements, like ". . . Nevada test fallout has not caused illness or injured the health of anyone living near the test site."[84]

For the first time in the United States, official preventive action was taken and "Utah diverted contaminated milk from the market, an action for which, remarkably, the Federal Radiation Counsel 'spanked' Utah Health officials."[140] Utah also told the Joint Committee that it planned to bill the Atomic Energy Commission for the cost of such measures.[141] (It never did.)

With fallout levels approaching the Radiation Protection Guides of the FRC at places all over the nation (and of course far exceeding them in the isolated "hot spots"), the growing ranks of AEC critics naturally looked to the FRC for some action to lower the rising levels of radiation in the environment. As early as June of 1962, the FRC was asked even by the Joint Committee to resolve the many questions concerning standards for fallout.[4] After three months and at least one follow-up letter, Anthony J. Celebrezze, the chairman of the FRC, finally answered, suggesting that, contrary to what everybody thought, the Radiation Protection Guides *did not apply to fallout after all!*

In September of 1962 the FRC made it official, taking the position that the Radiation Protection Guides did not apply to nuclear fallout[142] and even going so far as to say that the protective measures taken by the states of Utah and Minnesota to protect consumers against large doses of iodine 131 in milk were unnecessary.

The original FRC Radiation Protection Guides (RPG) were defined by it as "a radiation dose which should not be exceeded without careful consideration of the reasons for doing so."[132] But scarcely a year later, as radioactive iodine approached its RPG all over the country, the FRC decided that fallout was exempt. But that wasn't the end of it. Because the FRC guides threatened to hinder the AEC, the Federal Radiation Council *proceeded to discredit its own guidelines,* established less than two years before, in the following language:

> Based on the advice of a special panel convened by the Council in the summer of 1962, it was concluded that radiation doses to the thyroid *many times higher than those provided in FRC Report No. 2 would not result in a detectible increase in diseases such as thyroid cancer. . . .* It is similarly concluded in this report that iodine-131 doses from weapons testing conducted through 1962 have not caused an undue risk to health.[143]*

Many scientists outside the AEC feared that these statements were merely trial balloons for a liberalizing of standards across the board. They were right. The next year, the FRC raised its health

* Emphasis added.

guidelines for radioactive iodine by twenty times[144] and even went so far as to suggest that in the special case of fallout from a foreign weapons test, a *higher* "acceptable dose" might be set.[145]

The remarkable attitude of the Federal Radiation Council was best illustrated by Dr. Paul C. Tompkins, its executive director, in testimony in 1969 reviewing those days:

> DR. TOMPKINS: You will remember that the annual intake [for radioactive iodine] was starting to approach the . . . Radiation Protection Guide for thyroid . . . and there was an important national question at that point, what, if anything, should the present government do? One of the things we considered was various ways of reducing it. Well, it turned out that practically anything we could think of . . . when you actually feed that back to the price of milk, turned out to be [an economic] risk. We had to take our choice between that much iodine or a predictable level of malnutrition from pricing the milk off the market. We made the choice . . .
>
> CHAIRMAN HOLIFIELD: . . . here you are faced with the situation of a *slight amount of iodine in the milk,* and if you prohibited the milk from being available to the children, you have a malnutrition problem that might be far greater than the potential danger that might occur from a *small amount of iodine in the thyroid gland.**
>
> DR. TOMPKINS: That is exactly the situation.[146]

Never mentioned is the simple fact that because of the very short half-life of iodine 131 (eight days) the problem could have been solved without cost, quickly, easily, and with no one the loser. The radioactive milk could have been diverted to drying plants; by the time it was dried, packaged, shipped and ready for use, the radioactive iodine would have reduced itself to well below safe levels. In the meantime the affected population could have used already available stocks of dried milk. All of this could have been done without increasing the price of milk in any way: the "malnutrition" threat seems just a hoax, invented to provide an excuse to continue to engage in atmospheric nuclear testing. It does, however, illustrate the extremes of rationalization to be expected from individuals in a situation where checks, balances and virtually all control, for that

* Emphasis added.

matter, have vanished. The same men are still around, and they have the same responsibilities as they did then.

It's no wonder that the FRC quickly became regarded as a kept organization, a creature of the producers of radioactive pollution. Every act of the FRC served only to provide administrative sanction for whatever the Department of Defense or the Atomic Energy Commission was going to do anyway. The FRC set rules; when the rules were broken, it broadened them and thereby put its scientific and political blessings on that sham.

9 · ATTACK-COUNTERATTACK

IN THEIR ZEAL to convince everyone that fallout was less dangerous than the public was being led to believe by scientist-critics outside the Atomic Energy Commission, certain individuals within the AEC threw honest science out the window. These men were not dismissed. They were even allowed many repeat performances. One example occurred in the summer of 1962. A group of children from St. Louis was sent to New York for thyroidal iodine 131 measurements. According to *The New York Times*,[147] the AEC's Merril Eisenbud, the man skewered by Ralph Lapp at the Joint Committee hearings described a few pages back, reported that "tests completed at the New York University Medical Center indicate that the amount of radioactive iodine entering the thyroid glands of children has not approached the danger level." Ignored was the fact that because of the short half-life of iodine 131, those tests were performed well after most of the radioactivity had disappeared.[148]

Another technique used to convince people that fallout is nothing to worry about involved public endorsements of that view by the only scientist left in the atomic establishment whose name is well known: Dr. Edward Teller, the "father of the H-bomb." In a book,[149] excerpts of which were given wide publicity in *The Saturday Evening Post* and *Reader's Digest,* he said that "radiation from test fallout might be harmful to humans. *It might be slightly beneficial or have no effect at all.*"* Having covered all possibilities with that observation, he disposed of the fallout controversy with such statements as "fallout from nuclear testing is not worth worrying about," and "fallout from such testing is dangerous only in the imagination." These opinions, presented as facts from a scientist, were not accompanied by any supporting evidence and depended entirely upon the reputation of Dr. Teller for their credibility. In the same book he advocated preparation for limited nuclear war and, as a civil-defense precaution, putting schools permanently underground.

As AEC mistakes became more obvious, critics began appearing, even inside the AEC itself. In 1962, Dr. Harold A. Knapp, a scientist at the Fallout Studies Branch of the AEC's Division of Biology and Medicine, completed a study relating iodine 131 found in milk to its deposition in human thyroids.[150] Knapp estimated that during the 1950s the dose to the thyroid from the iodine 131 in cow's milk approached ten times those levels considered safe by the FRC. He pointed out that this hazard was ignored at the time because the AEC was measuring for radioactivity long after the short-lived iodine 131 had decayed to nonradioactive products. Dr. Charles L. Dunham, the director of the AEC's Division of Biology and Medicine in 1962, conceded the point at the time, explaining that "we were too busy chasing strontium 90."[151]

Predictably, the AEC was reluctant to make public the Knapp report and did so only on the condition that the report be reviewed by a special AEC committee constituted for this purpose and composed of "qualified scientists with specialized backgrounds." Furthermore, the report of that review committee had to accompany the Knapp report once it was presented to the Joint Committee, so as "to provide additional perspective." It was a technique used later in the Pitzer Panel case, a time-honored bit of deception.

However, protectionists inside the AEC were surprised, and dis-

---

* Emphasis added.

appointed, because the report of the Langham Committee, as the review committee became known, ranged "all the way from favorable to completely negative." But a close examination shows that of the five members of the Langham Committee only four were actually "qualified scientists with specialized backgrounds" as the AEC required; they regarded the Knapp report favorably, and at least one AEC scientist-reviewer felt that it was even too conservative.[28] But the single nonscientist on the committee, Oliver R. Placak, was the chief of the Off-Site Radiological Safety Organization of the Nevada test site! Knapp himself commented:

[Since] the committee member who was "completely negative" with regard to the nature and the utility of the report *happens to be the person in charge of the Commission's Off-Site Radiological Safety Organization, and thereby responsible* both for an accurate appraisal of gamma levels and the levels of iodine-131 in milk, I would say that to a considerable extent the burden of proof is on him to either produce a better estimate or to admit that he has no knowledge of and no way of estimating the levels of iodine-131 which may have resulted from past tests.[152]*

It is an underhanded technique, the practice of constituting committees of inquiry with the guilty party sitting in judgment of himself. It is a procedure which would be regarded as highly irregular elsewhere, but it is standard operating procedure for the AEC. The AEC made a great point of the fact that the Langham Committee was "not unanimous." But it didn't say what the lone dissenter, Placak, did for a living. Thus weakened, the report was used to mislead the public and, like President Eisenhower before him, even President Kennedy himself,[153] the public was lulled into believing that not enough is known about fallout to make an intelligent decision until more research is done.

Participation on the Langham Committee must have been a shock to the four scientist members, exposed as they were to the not so subtle although unsuccessful attempts of the AEC bureaucrats to repress technical data in order to protect the agency from public embarrassment. Interestingly, it was this experience that caused one member, Dr. John Gofman, to reevaluate his opinion of the objec-

* Emphasis added.

tivity of the AEC methods and motives, and that eventually made of him, somewhat late in the game,[154] one of the AEC's most potent critics.

As far as Harold Knapp is concerned, it was over a year after its completion that he finally saw the release of his final report. His first version was suppressed by the general manager of the AEC on the recommendation of the head of the AEC's Division of Biology and Medicine, Dr. Charles Dunham. His second report was classified secret, and his third version, the one finally published, was handed over to the director of the Division of Biology and Medicine on the day Knapp resigned from the AEC (for a new job at the Pentagon).

Other criticism came from the defense establishment. It was widely asserted by the AEC that radioactive iodine was entirely due to atmospheric tests. Dr. Edward A. Martell, a West Pointer, army man, and then at the Air Force Cambridge Research Laboratories, published information indicating that much of the iodine 131 detected within the United States had actually come from our own underground nuclear tests in Nevada, which, through error, vented radioactive iodine to the atmosphere.

Mr. James T. Ramey, then the executive director of the Joint Committee (later to cross over and become the single most powerful commissioner of the Atomic Energy Commission), delayed the printing of Martell's five-page testimony until the AEC could give it the Pitzer-Knapp treatment. The AEC put together over fifty pages of rebuttal, blaming the Russians for the radioactive iodine observed by Martell; when Martell's testimony was finally printed, the long rebuttal was also there.[155] This is roughly the equivalent of injecting the cross-examination of a witness into a legal transcript at some later time without the witness's knowledge or presence, a procedure surely in violation of fair play if not due process of law. But again, what could cause outrage elsewhere is standard operating procedure at the Atomic Energy Commission.

Dr. Martell's articles on the subject in *Science* magazine[156] invoked some malicious innuendo in the record, as AEC Commissioner Gerald F. Tape *incorrectly* suggested that Martell had had some trouble in the past in getting his scientific material accepted by that journal. (In the scientific world, this amounts to saying that your work is not acceptable by your peers.) Senator George D. Aiken, in a remarkable display of ignorance, actually suggested that Martell was paid $10,000 for writing the piece, and even Holifield was surprised when Commissioner Tape had to tell them both that scientific articles are contributed to journals "with no remuneration whatever."[157]

What the AEC would not admit and what the Joint Committee would not accept then is now public knowledge: many millions of curies of radioactivity have left the Nevada test site, leaked from at least eighteen accidental ventings of underground blasts.[158]

The controversy concerning radioactive iodine raged for several years,[159] but in the end even the AEC accepted Knapp's results. But then as now AEC strategy was mindless and straightforward: when attacked, counterattack.

10 · THE DEBATE CONCLUDED, THE AEC NEVER RECOVERS

BUT AEC intransigence could not stand forever against the hard technical data brought against its position from outside scientists. Consider how our official attitude toward fallout has changed since the AEC allowed independent scientists to inspect fallout data.

In 1956 President Eisenhower said, "The continuance of the present rate of H-bomb testing, by the most sober and responsible scientific judgment . . . does not imperil the health of humanity."[160] Compare that view with President Johnson's remarks in 1964, only eight years later:

This Treaty [the Nuclear Test Ban Treaty] has halted the steady, menacing increase of radioactive fallout. The deadly products of atomic explosions were poisoning our soil and food and the milk our children drank and the air we all breathe. Radioactive deposits were being formed in increasing quantity in the teeth and bones of young Americans. Radioactive poisons were beginning to threaten the safety of people throughout the world. They were a growing menace to the health of every unborn child.[161]

The AEC's fallout blunder was, of course, a serious embarrassment not only to the Joint Committee but to the President as well. But as of today, the only discernible reprimand ever received by the AEC for its mishandling of radioactive fallout was that the chairman of the AEC, once number four on the State Department's Protocol List, has slipped down to number sixteen; the real price for the AEC's mistake was paid by everyone else.

After all, to have mistakenly assumed that fallout would distribute evenly throughout the world's atmosphere instead of concentrating in the temperate zones, as it finally did, was an understandable error in view of the knowledge of global meteorology at that time. But for the AEC to have been concerned only with the external radiation dose from fallout, thereby ignoring the effects of the food chain, was clearly an incompetent and unwarranted conclusion. To compound this by advertising that its "experiments have indicated that there is no hazard to human health" from fallout[112] was unquestionably irresponsible, and to maintain this position, by implication and by innuendo, ten and twenty years after it was known to be false became truly scandalous.

The reaction to the criticism inside the AEC was a disaster, too, for it destroyed much of the spirit, if not eventually the flesh, of that agency. AEC personnel were *actually directed* that no such mistakes are to be made in the future to cause such embarrassment again, and the AEC even had an unsuccessful witch-hunt for the guilty party. Instead of admitting their error publicly and profiting by it, a reaction not unknown in federal circles,[162] AEC bureaucrats no longer addressed themselves primarily to the job title of their particular task, but, from that time on, generated mechanisms within the bureaucracy so as to make responsibility impossible to follow and to invent and use language whose sole purpose appears to be an attempt to obscure fault and blame.

The course was thus set which served to reduce the AEC to what it is today: an agency which divides its best efforts between, on the one hand, justifying its past mistakes (see Chapters III, IV and V) and, on the other, promoting atomic energy beyond all reasonable limits and into wildly inappropriate adventures (see Chapter VI).

But all that could not have happened without the assistance of the Joint Committee on Atomic Energy. For it was the committee's reaction to the fallout blunder which permitted even worse abuses to take place later. Duped since the beginning by the AEC, the committee was the unwilling partner in the AEC's embarrassment and blame. At that point it would have been appropriate for the Joint Committee to have held hearings into the competency of the AEC. But for the committee to have done so would have amounted to an admission of its own negligence and gullibility. Courage of that sort is almost unknown in Congress, and so the committee took another course. If the AEC's errors were to reflect upon the adequacy of the Joint Committee, then the committee from that time forward would protect the AEC from such charges, just as if it were protecting itself. Accordingly, the last vestige of checks and balances disappeared and the Joint Committee and the AEC were in bed together for good.

Many abuses and excesses in the use of political power by the stewards of the Atomic Energy Commission and the Joint Committee on Atomic Energy took place since then. The unfortunate result has been the erosion of public trust, to the detriment of those real benefits which could come from the orderly development of nuclear energy (see Chapter VII).

IV
RADIATION
ON THE JOB: THE
URANIUM MINERS

I would just like to ask some of these men here, particularly the ones from the Atomic Energy Commission, if they ever saw anyone they love die because their bones were rotting away. My father went very slowly. My uncle went quite fast. He only had two months.

> —PAT ELLISON, daughter of a uranium
> miner, testifying at a U. S. Department
> of Labor Hearing, November 21, 1964,
> Washington, D.C.[163]

1 · INDUSTRIAL SAFETY

EXPANSIVE CLAIMS of atomic industrial safety have been made for years by the Joint Committee on Atomic Energy and by the AEC itself. They say in public that their weapons factories and nuclear plants have had a safety record that is second to none, and that at no installation has there been either an accidental atomic explosion or an unintentional release of massive quantities of radioactivity to the outside. But AEC technical reports tell another story.

AEC public statements, only partially true, ignore the several criticality accidents, the worst of which was the explosion of the SL-1 reactor on January 3, 1961, at the National Reactor Testing Station, forty miles west of Idaho Falls, Idaho. It will never be known exactly what caused that accident, since the three men who were there died shortly afterward. The Oil, Chemical and Atomic Workers local union there petitioned the Joint Committee for relief from "laxness on the part of the AEC." They accused the AEC of "whitewashing" the whole incident, and complained that "highly radioactive parts of the [victims'] bodies were removed; heads, arms and what have you were removed and unceremoniously buried at the hot waste dump at the site. The remainder was put in small lead boxes and placed in the caskets for burial." They asked to have "lead caskets" of the proper size available at the reactor sites so that the next of kin may give a husband or son a proper burial, "in one piece . . ."[164] Other atomic fatalities are not so rare as is generally believed, either. Leo Goodman, an atomic consultant for the United Automobile Workers as well as the AFL-CIO, presented a partial list of atomic-reactor accidents to the Joint Committee.[165] Six years later he completed a list of 139 "atomic science fatalities" which occurred between 1944 and 1967.[166] The AEC disagrees violently with Goodman's conclusions, but that is to be expected. It is very difficult to get any federal agency to admit that atomic radiation has caused any particular cancer. Of fifty-four cancer cases and other conditions alleged to have been caused by radiation on the job, the AEC says only seven were "allowed or settled."[167] An AEC Division of Operational Safety report lists the three men killed in the SL-1 accident above as having died of "skeletal and internal injuries,"[168] perhaps accounting for the union's "whitewash" charge.

Thus, the AEC's industrial safety record is not entirely without blemish, but, more importantly, the claims of atomic industrial safety that its record is supposed to support are frequently not true. For, while the AEC seldom lies, it often tells only that part of the truth necessary to create a favorable impression—which is, after all, in the nature of a promoter.

The *only* reason the AEC can give its record of industrial safety good marks is because it uses a grading system designed to ignore its most obvious industrial accident: long-term injury due to atomic radiation. The claim of a good record is based solely on a low number of lost-time accidents. Significantly, accidents at AEC plants are counted only if they result in time lost from the job. Thus, when a worker at the Dow-AEC atomic-bomb plant near Denver, Colorado, for example, accidentally cuts himself while machining plutonium, the accident is counted only in proportion to the time lost because of the cut (even small cuts involving plutonium sometimes require surgery to remove all traces of the metal, because, in addition to its chemical toxicity, even tiny amounts left in the body can cause cancer). So when an accident involving radiation is recorded as costing only a few hours or even days of lost time, it can and does produce death from cancer many years later—a death that will never be included in the lost-time accident statistics. Because the victim is often retired by then, many job-connected cancers are never even recorded at all.[169]

The AEC's method of grading itself thus permits it to ignore completely what many have come to suspect, that the cancers which occur among workers in atomic plants are caused in large measure by radiation exposures on the job. The commission's disregard of this obvious possibility is, of course, disputed, but the truth probably will not be known for several years (if then), until a new AEC study is completed.[170] Until then, the much talked-about safety record of atomic plants will be irrelevant to the problem of radiation, even though radiation is what people worry about most in connection with atomic plants. Nevertheless, the atomic industry's safety record is used by the AEC in its relentless efforts to convince its critics and the public that fear of radioactivity is unfounded.

2 · DEATH UNDERGROUND

THERE IS one area of atomic safety, however, where exhaustive health studies have already been made and where the dangers are accurately known, because men have already begun to die in large numbers—and that is the matter ot the highly lethal health hazards to which uranium miners have been subjected. This problem came about because of the AEC's crash program to obtain a domestic supply of uranium, and it is beyond a doubt the most shameful page in the history of the atomic establishment. It is a story of the needless deaths by cancer of many hundreds of uranium miners on the Colorado Plateau—deaths predicted in advance[171] and caused by airborne radioactivity in the mines.

In addition to uranium, ore veins contain radium. By radioactive decay, uranium slowly changes to radium which in turn slowly changes into a radioactive gas called radon which slowly seeps out of the rocks and into the mine atmosphere. Radon gas rapidly changes into a series of highly radioactive solid particles called "radon daughters," and it is these that were breathed by the miners and caused so much lung cancer. It is important to realize at the outset that this problem has an easy solution, ventilation of the mines, and that this solution was known long before the AEC's crash program to obtain a domestic source of uranium ever began.

For an idea of the magnitude of the problem, consider the words of Charles C. Johnson, Jr., the administrator of the Consumer Protection and Environmental Health Service of the U. S. Public Health Service, who said in 1969 that "of the six thousand men who have been uranium miners, an estimated six hundred to eleven hundred will die of lung cancer within the next twenty years because of radiation exposure on the job."[172] This is a very large number considering that at its peak year the American uranium-mining industry employed only twelve hundred miners.[173] In a study done for the state of Colorado, Woodward and Fondiller, an actuarial firm, estimated that the workmen's-compensation bill for this particular AEC blunder will cost the state over $20 million.[174]

Miners complained that if someone "who works in the mines has lung cancer, he is not told about it." The threat of breathing the radioactive air was minimized as the workers were told, "If you take an hour after being out on the surface, all the radiation of radon gas which you inhaled that day would have left your system."[175]

This particular assurance was made not uncommonly in the early days. Its viciousness lies in the fact that it's true: the radon gas does leave the system rapidly, but *radon is not the problem*. It is those solid particles which are produced by the radon, the "radon daughters," which cause lung cancer. After formation, they remain suspended in the air, and, being electrically charged, they adhere tenaciously whenever they strike a surface. A pair of human lungs, breathing air down in the mines, serves as an excellent trap for these highly radioactive particles.

In seeking the reason for this tragedy it is hard even today to understand how such a monstrous mistake could ever have been allowed. In the several hearings before the Joint Committee on Atomic Energy and the U. S. Department of Labor, State Workmen's Compensation Commission officials, other state representatives, and even mine owners all testified that the special dangers of uranium mining were never even mentioned, much less explained to them, by the AEC. Feay Smith, an attorney for the State Workmen's Compensation Insurance Fund of Colorado, put it this way: "Nobody told us that we had radiation in the mines—and nobody told us that we didn't; the AEC just led us down the primrose path."[176]

3 · THEY KNEW . . .

IN THE CASE of atomic fallout, the AEC officials were unaware of the problem until outsiders pointed it out to them. In that they were incompetent, their moral culpability began only when they refused to accept legitimate criticism and attempted to silence the dissent. In this respect, the death of the uranium miners was no different. But there is something more: *The reason why this tragedy is the AEC's most shameful blunder is that the AEC knew all about the problem well before the miners ever went underground.*

One hundred years ago, the Europeans had noticed that their uranium miners were dying from lung cancer at an extraordinary rate,[177] later determined to be between fifty and seventy-five percent.[178, 179] The Germans investigated the problem carefully[180] and by 1930 had determined that airborne radioactivity in the mines had caused the cancers.[181] By the early 1930s the problem of airborne radioactivity in the Czechoslovak mines was solved by simple ventilation.[182] The French had found the costs of ventilation to be only *one percent* of the operating cost of the mines.[183] All of this information was published in Europe and America, and an extensive review article was published in this country in 1944.[179] Indeed, as early as 1947 the AEC had *itself* measured the airborne radioactivity in American mines[184] and found it to be even higher than the mines of Europe, mines which *had already claimed a thousand lives!*

So when the AEC began buying huge amounts of American-mined uranium, creating the uranium boom of the 1950s, it was well aware of the hazards of this newly rejuvenated occupation; but American miners were permitted to go down into the unventilated mines anyway, just as if nothing were wrong. Predictably, the miners began dying and have continued to die of cancer to this day, although some of them have not set foot in the mines for years.

It is now a decade or more since the miners were receiving their maximum radiation exposures underground. Accordingly, enough time has passed to view the problem with some detachment. Even so, the most restrained view is still frightening in its implication of guilt. Dr. Brian MacMahon is professor of epidemiology at Harvard and chairman of the advisory committee on this subject to the National Academy of Sciences. In 1971 he said: "The epidemic of lung cancer now in progress among American uranium miners could readily have been—and indeed was—predicted on the basis of experience in other parts of the world.[171]

4 · WHY THE AEC DID IT

IF THE AEC concealed the dangers, what could possibly have been its motive? The answer is in the printed record of the period, in the official history of the AEC. When John Gustafson became the AEC's first director of raw materials in 1947, "it shocked him to discover that the nation's huge investment in atomic energy . . . rested on the production of uranium ore from one mine deep in the Belgian Congo . . ."[185] Moreover, "Gustafson estimated that the low uranium content and the high development costs for domestic ores would force the price of [uranium] from American sources up to $20 per pound or higher, compared to $3.40 for the [Belgian Congo] material delivered in the United States."[186] But the AEC couldn't pay twenty dollars to the American miners and expect the Belgians to take $3.40 for very long. When the AEC contract with the Belgians expired in three years, the Division of Raw Materials could look forward to paying the same higher price for its Congolese uranium. This was no small matter, since in 1949 about eighty-five percent of the AEC's total uranium procurement came from the Congo. The cash differences are impressive: at the low price, the 1949 bill for uranium ore was about $16 million; at the higher price it would have been over $90 million. It just isn't that easy to come up with an extra $75 million, even for the AEC.

Incredibly, the AEC solved the problem in 1948 by "guaranteeing" the *same minimum price* to the American miners that it was paying to the Belgians, despite the fact that by its own estimates American ore should cost the AEC six times more. According to the AEC history, "the guaranteed minimum price was *far below expected costs,* but it could not be higher *without jeopardizing the* *price the Commission was paying for Belgian Congo material.*"[186]* It is difficult to determine today whether the subsequent development of the domestic mines is a tribute to excessive cost-cutting on the part of the mine owners or an indictment of an incompetent government economic projection, but at any rate, within a few years a thousand men were engaged in digging uranium ore out of the Colorado Plateau. As late as 1966, the AEC admitted that when a much higher price for uranium was established ($8 per pound), it was still "substantially below the going price of uranium from all sources."[187]

As the Europeans found out a generation before, the only way to reduce the airborne radioactivity in the mines was to use ventilation equipment; mine safety, of course, costs money. Since the AEC had committed itself early in the game to pay a price for uranium which by its own estimates was one sixth of the true value, and was still getting a bargain eighteen years later, it could not very well ask the mine owners to provide those services, such as safety, that are part of the true cost. Nor could it very well warn the states of the dangers, without at the same time laying itself open to demands for uranium price increases.

In the words of the official AEC history, "cost, not quantity, was the issue." We got what the AEC paid for—a cancer epidemic.

5 · THE AEC'S OFFICIAL POSITION

THE AEC DID not make its first public statement on the matter until 1959, a decade after it started the problem in the first place, and just past the peak year of uranium mining in the West.[173] In the face of the European experience, the AEC's own measurements of

* Emphasis added.

hazardous levels of airborne radioactivity in the mines, and, by this time, the predicted appearance of lung cancer deaths among the miners, the commission finally admitted that the problem *may* exist after all.

Jesse Johnson, the director of the Division of Raw Materials of the AEC, responded to the challenge with what has become an AEC trademark by now (see Chapter V): by suggesting that perhaps the "lung damage" (they never use the word "cancer") had *some other cause* than radiation, and by asserting that a long study was needed in order to find the answer. At a speech before the American Mining Congress in Denver he said, ". . . mines having concentrations of radon products in excess of permissible limits *may* present a definite health hazard. However, an *extensive medical examination program extending over a considerable period* would be required to determine whether uranium miners have a higher incidence of *lung damage* than those employed in other mines or in other occupations.[188]*

This is a favorite tactic of bureaucracies in general and the AEC in particular in dealing with health matters: when put to the wall by state and federal public-health agencies, it will admit that "extensive research" is needed. In other words, before the AEC would accept the fact that a health hazard existed, it wanted more data; that is, the effect had to become "noticeable." The "data" demanded by that "body-in-the-morgue approach"[92] were simply more cases of lung cancer, enough additional cases so that there would be no doubt in anyone's mind that the costly procedure of ventilating the mines was an absolute necessity.

Most of the radiation exposure of the miners was taking place just at the time Johnson's statement was made. What was needed was not research (it had already been done in Europe), but immediate control procedures in the mines (procedures already developed in Europe). But for the Atomic Energy Commission and the Joint Committee to admit to this would be to admit to error, and to date this has never been done.

Checks and balances gone and "built-in objectivity" a failure, the

* Emphasis added.

AEC's Division of Raw Materials won out over the AEC's Division of Biology and Medicine; eight years passed while miners were dying and the problem was studied.

6 · "BUILT-IN OBJECTIVITY" FAILS AGAIN

THE AEC POSITION was that although all the uranium was being mined exclusively for its own use (it even owned over a dozen mines itself), it still had no authority to regulate worker safety until the ore had left the mine. The AEC neglected to mention that the Walsh-Healy Act of 1936 provides for federally supervised worker safety in such situations involving federal contracts. Why AEC attorneys did not point this out to the states and the U.S. Secretary of Labor is another question that can best be answered again by the fact that this would increase the price of uranium ore, to more than the commission cared to pay.

So AEC lawyers came up with a self-serving opinion (never adjudicated, by the way) to get the commission off the hook. Their interpretation of the Atomic Energy Act, as presented by Commissioner Ramey, contends that "since AEC's authority to regulate source material is limited to material after removal from its place of deposit, mining of uranium is not covered."[189] That opinion invariably appears *without* a complete definition of the terms as they are defined in the Atomic Energy Act itself.[6] There uranium ore is defined as "source material," but "its place of deposit" is spelled out much more clearly than the AEC lawyers reveal. The phrase in the act is "its place of deposit *in nature,*" and although it is not further defined the phrase is used there several times. Clearly, the AEC lawyers suggest that the mine is the "place of deposit in nature" despite the fact that the phrase is widely used in mining law to mean the ore vein itself.

Now, any law must be read using everyday logic and the common definition of words. Therefore it's doubtful that this obviously self-serving interpretation would ever be upheld by a court. Remarkably, it's this flimsy argument upon which the AEC bases its entire position of nonresponsibility. The act regulates uranium ore in all circumstances, even requiring a license for possession. It covers the entire field of atomic energy, regulating uranium ore, uranium itself and its byproducts, but nowhere in the entire act is there to be found, even by implication, any effort to exclude the licensing of mines. The commission's weak argument, never challenged, is the sole basis for its claim that the cancer epidemic among the uranium miners of the Colorado Plateau is someone else's responsibility and not the responsibility of the Atomic Energy Commission.

7 · THE STATES INHERIT THE AEC'S PROBLEMS

THIS MEANT that the various state departments of health in the mining states were faced with the job of enacting regulations which would inevitably be restrictive to a booming uranium industry. Furthermore, it meant that this had to be done not only in the face of a tacit approval of the existing mine conditions by the AEC (Johnson's speech was made after the boom was on for ten years) but also against the very powerful and active opposition of the various mine owners' associations. Norman Blake, deputy inspector of mines for Colorado, says, "It was often hard to get anything done about radioactivity in the mines in those days. Anybody that said a thing against uranium mining was suspected of being a Communist."[190] The uranium boom and the Cold War shared the 1950s.

So effective was this opposition that only in Colorado of all the nine uranium-mining states did the State Health Department succeed in being heard, and then only after the miners began dying. So, except for Colorado, what leaving it up to the states meant was to have no control at all. It's inconceivable that the AEC was not aware of this at the time.

The man most responsible for calling attention to the dangers was P. W. Jacoe, the former director of occupational and radiological health for the state of Colorado. Reminiscing, he said, "Many people at that time accused state health officers of inventing the whole problem. They tried to get people to believe that what we were really interested in was to expand our departments and our power."[191] This accusation, common in Grand Junction, Colorado, at that time, was again made there twenty years later, when health officials discovered new problems involving radioactivity, this time much closer to home than the mines. As we will see later, it turned out to be the radon daughters again, right inside five thousand private homes in that town. But it was not the AEC that made the first public statements describing the dangers of uranium mining; it was the Colorado State Department of Health, in 1949.

The department received for its trouble intense criticism from Grand Junction, the center of the uranium-mining industry. There was even "scientific" opposition: there is in the files of the Colorado State Department of Health a copy of a letter from a Grand Junction physician to the Vanadium Corporation of America, assuring the mine owners that the "principal radiation from uranium 238 is alpha radiation which is harmless"—an excellent example of the irresponsibility and monumental ignorance passing for expertise in those days. The physician goes on to say that he has examined ten employees of the Vanadium Corporation of America who work in "so-called radioactive occupations," and they showed no ill effects from radiation.[192]

The press was hardly objective in Grand Junction, a town which has the same atomic decoration on its city seal that appears on the emblem of the AEC itself. The Grand Junction *Sentinel,* long a blind supporter of the area's largest industry, has always reserved its short supply of skepticism for news unfavorable to the atom. Even the

Denver Post, the largest newspaper in Colorado, though discretion the better part of valor and (according to the reporter himself) yanked its 1955 story "Cancer Safeguards Needed in Mines" out of the paper before Denver metropolitan readers could see it.[193]

The miners continued to die of cancer in increasing numbers, but the AEC was so successful in causing people to doubt that radiation was the cause of the cancer epidemic, that state workmens'-compensation funds were slow to acknowledge that lung cancer was job-related. The misery was none the less real, however, and increasing every day as miners died and families were left destitute.

One woman wrote the Colorado State Department of Public Health:

My husband . . . worked in the uranium mines in 1954. Last January he became sick and when he had X-rays and examinations taken he was practically alive with cancer. He passed away April from cancer of the lungs and from what my doctors said, all over. This has left me with enormous bills from X-ray treatments, hospital bills, etc. I myself make around $36 per week if I get in a full week so you see I am pretty well up against it. I wonder if there is anything that could be done to help me.[194]

Multiply this by a thousand and you will get a feeling for what uranium means to the families of the miners on the Colorado Plateau who have already died or whose excess exposure has already doomed them to an early death.

As the problem became publicized through the next year, many company representatives simply refused to believe in its existence. In Wyoming there was a brief scandal when mine owners tried to get the governor to fire Robert Sundin, the chief of radiological health for the state. It developed that Mr. Sundin had discovered falsified information in a report to his department by a Wyoming mine owner.[195] These were just some of the pressures that state radiological health officers faced as they tried to make public-health sense out of a situation dumped into their laps by the Atomic Energy Commission.

Another problem faced by state health officers was the AEC's secrecy. In 1949 Colorado's Department of Health requested some technical information about the hazards of uranium mining. The AEC's Los Alamos Scientific Laboratory replied, but the word "RESTRICTED," stamped in red, appeared twice on every page of their answer.[196] It was only four years after World War II; health officers didn't know whether they could freely use that information or not. That same year P. W. Jacoe, of Colorado's Health Department, visited the uranium mills at Naturita and Durango. His visit was reported in the newspapers, and shortly after the articles appeared the AEC denied him access to the mills until he could get his supersecret Q clearance from the AEC many months later.

Time went by while the miners continued to work in unventilated mines and to die from cancer. The studies went on, too, useless studies that could be likened to the reinvention of the wheel, because all they could show was what was already known from the European cancer studies: *if you sent men underground and let them breathe airborne radioactivity at levels known to exist in our mines, you will have a cancer epidemic.*

In time the Colorado Workmen's Compensation Board was besieged with death claims. A contract with Woodward and Fondiller, the New York actuarial company (and sometime contractor to the AEC itself), confirmed the fiscal fears of the state[174]: the evidence indicated that the miners were dying at such a rate that if the claims were allowed, it would bankrupt the Workmen's Compensation Insurance Fund and possibly the entire state. The total bill would be well over $20 million, with no relief in sight from the Joint Committee, the AEC or the mine owners. In short, the situation attained scandalous proportions.

8 · FEDERAL INACTION

BY THE MIDDLE 1950s the U.S. Surgeon General described privately the dangers of uranium mining to the AEC and later to the Joint Committee on Atomic Energy. In 1957, the U. S. Public Health Service reported that "early environmental studies in American uranium mines reveal concentrations of radioactive gases and dust considerably *in excess* of those reported in the literature for the European mines,"[197]* an observation that has stood the test of time.[178] The Public Health Service published a bulletin about that time describing the ventilation methods already proven successful in reducing airborne radioactivity in the mines to a safe level.[198] But it wasn't until 1959, over a decade after the AEC's massive ore-procurement program began, that the Joint Committee finally held the first public hearings into the matter.[199]

Still, states weren't notified of the acute nature of the problem. That finally happened in December of 1960 at a "Governors' Conference," convened for the purpose at the request of Secretary Flemming of the Department of Health, Education and Welfare.[200]

Subsequently, only Colorado appropriated any money for additional mine inspectors. New Mexico provided funds for one additional engineer; Utah and Wyoming provided no one at all, and Arizona would not even provide its existing mine inspectors with the necessary additional authority,[184] thereby providing further evidence of the futility of expecting the states to handle so large and complex a problem.

The Joint Committee on Atomic Energy was not yet defending the AEC by reflex action; the "turning point" had not yet been

* Emphasis added.

reached. At hearings on "Employee Radiation Hazards and Work-men's Compensation" in 1959,[199] committee members agreed that uranium mining did indeed need regulation and enforcement. They even pointed out that all AEC contractors "fall under the Walsh-Healy Public Contracts Act [and accordingly] the AEC had direct control over their procedures and methods of operation." The Joint Committee even suggested that *"in these cases a simple directive to the contractor results in the necessary changes being made, with the cost of the changes being borne by the AEC."** But still nothing was done.

The handwriting was on the wall: we were already years into a replay of the European tragedy. It took ten years for the Joint Committee to get the message, a message that the AEC had known all along: something was very wrong down in the mines.

9 · CHECKS AND BALANCES FAIL AGAIN: THE DEPARTMENT OF LABOR ACTS

BUT THE YEARS continued to roll by and nothing was done. By this time the fallout controversy was over, the "turning point" was passed, and the Joint Committee and the AEC were pals forever.

Accordingly, corrective forces to change the policies of the Atomic Energy Commission had to come from the outside—unfortunately, though, only after a situation became intolerable. In this case the first meaningful step toward a correction of the uranium miners' problem came in 1967, two decades after the AEC first contracted for the purchase of domestic uranium.

Secretary of Labor Willard Wirtz took the initiative and issued the first standards which made any public-health sense for the control

* Emphasis added.

of airborne radioactivity in the uranium mines. In a statement before
the Joint Committee on Atomic Energy,[201] he said:

> After seventeen years of debate and discussion regarding the responsi-
> bilities for conditions in the uranium mines, there are today . . . no ade-
> quate and effective health and safety standards . . . for uranium mining.
> There is unmistakable evidence of a high incidence of lung cancer
> among uranium miners; ninety-eight have died from it, and another 250
> to one thousand—the estimates vary—are already incurably afflicted
> with it. The best available evidence is that over two thirds of the ap-
> proximately 2,500 underground uranium miners are working under con-
> ditions which at least triple their prospects for dying from lung cancer
> if they continue this work and these conditions remain unchanged. . . .
> There is no more critical imperative today than this society's assertion
> of the absolute priority of individual over institutional interests and of
> human over economic values.

As the hearings went on it became clear that the Joint Committee
on Atomic Energy was not in agreement with Wirtz's last sentiment.
But the Joint Committee is nonetheless very sensitive when people
find this out. Representative Craig Hosmer (R., Calif.) complained,
"People were going away from here yesterday and saying that the
Joint Committee was for love, motherhood, apple pie and lung
cancer."

And small wonder, too, because the Joint Committee fought hard
and long against every point which would support controls in the
mines. Thus it joined the AEC in its moral guilt of frustrating any
solution to control of the hazards in the mines.

10 · THE JOINT COMMITTEE
COUNTERATTACKS

IT'S IMPOSSIBLE to know why they took such a brutal position. Perhaps they can see things only from the mine owners' point of view,
as some union men testified, or perhaps they were simply piqued by

the fact that someone else had to do their job, a job they were supposed to do all those years. (Only four years before, Senator Edmund S. Muskie had to hold hearings on water pollution produced by uranium mills,[187] a situation widely regarded as a slap at the Joint Committee.) In any case, they were certainly chagrined, and Secretary Wirtz did not get a warm reception. Representative Wayne N. Aspinall (D., Colo.), one of Holifield's parrots on the Joint Committee, told him, "If you had given us a chance to act and we had not acted, then some of us would have been a little bit more sympathetic to your position, but you did not do that; you haven't given us that chance."

But Secretary Wirtz believed that the Joint Committee had had its chance and blew it. He replied, "I felt that this was far and away the best way to bring this thing to a head after seventeen years."

Joint Committee members, when cornered, are fond of using the Russian threat to national security to buttress their cause, even when it's wildly inappropriate; this time was no exception. Shortage of uranium was hardly an issue; a half-billion dollars' worth of the stuff was stored then, as now, in barrels at the AEC's Grand Junction operations office in Colorado; the AEC hasn't signed a new contract to buy uranium ore since 1962, and uranium purchases ceased entirely at the end of 1969 after a "stretch-out" program was completed. There was such a surplus of uranium concentrates that four years later even the AEC decided to sell off *the whole stockpile*.[202] But that didn't stop Senator John Pastore from suggesting that Secretary Wirtz might just be compromising our national security: ". . . I am going to point out the fact that this is a momentous decision that you have made. No question at all about it. As a matter of fact, it was resisted by the chairman of the commission, the Atomic Energy Commission, who under the law is responsible for all the fissionable material that is necessary for us to keep up our defense, that's how serious it is."

But, as usual, it was Chet Holifield who carried the ball; he felt that the Joint Committee had been singled out, and asked, "Why didn't the Secretary place this [standard] on copper mines, on coal mines, on zinc mines, tin mines and all the other mines where [there is radioactivity]? . . . But he has not and he has the same power to put it on the other mines as he has to put it on the uranium mines. Why didn't he?" It's hard to conceive how Holifield, the most powerful single person in Congress where atomic matters are involved, could not know that it's simply a matter of degree—that airborne radioactivity is a problem of uranium mines and that it's simply not a problem in most other mines. But although Holifield was mixed up in his facts, he was almost certainly right about the Joint Committee being singled out; however, it shouldn't have been a question in his mind. Secretary Wirtz made it clear that men were dying and "seventeen years of debate and discussion" had produced nothing: when he said "produced nothing," he was talking about the Joint Committee.

Although it is not a fundamental law, as a practical matter nothing gets through the Joint Committee on Atomic Energy unless Representative Holifield approves. If the issue involves any restriction on the AEC, he is virtually impossible to convince. In that connection, the uranium miners' hearings are his finest hours.

11 · THE JOINT COMMITTEE ATTACKS THE SCIENTIFIC EVIDENCE

WHEN THE scientific testimony to support Secretary Wirtz's new health standard began, Holifield even rejected laboratory experiments on mice as invalid, wisely pointing out that mice are not men and thereby betraying a fundamental lack of understanding of the nature of experimental science. He said, ". . . as far as I know you haven't had any mice down in the mine, either, but the point I am making is that he took an assumption that . . . mice to man was in direct ratio and he built upon it a theory which in my opinion was unsupportable."

Holifield then attacked Secretary Wirtz's new standard as too idealistic: "Mr. Secretary, of course all of us subscribe to the high and noble sentiments which you have expressed . . . however, the point of obtaining one hundred percent perfection has never been attained by man." He also contended that the standard would be unworkable, because it would be too hard to measure: "You have gotten into such a fine area of measurement . . . it is an impossibility for it to be practical and workable . . ." This criticism, of course, holds true for almost any instrument—the widely used electronic speed trap, for example. But even an AEC report[203] discussing the accuracy and reproducibility of monitoring techniques in uranium mines implied that the safest standards suggested by Wirtz could be monitored reliably.

When Colorado introduced the Woodward and Fondiller report predicting one thousand deaths due to airborne radioactivity in the mines, Holifield nearly lost control, suggesting that the cause "could be practically all smoking, because there is ample evidence that heavy smokers have a greater incidence of cancer than a nonsmoker in the general population."

But Holifield's skepticism suddenly evaporated when Dr. Robley Evans, the Joint Committee's star scientific witness, took the stand. Dr. Evans is the proponent of the "threshold theory," which holds that there is a threshold level of radioactivity below which there is no harm to man. But by 1967 the sole criterion by which theories were accepted by the Joint Committee was not whether the theory reflected the truth or not, but rather whether a theory supported the position of the Joint Committee. The "threshold theory" was a minority view among scientists at the time, and it has since been repudiated entirely.[204] It is this "threshold theory" which supports such frankly wrong statements made by the AEC in 1953 as ". . . the body may safely receive a small dose of radiation because the effects are repaired virtually as rapidly as they are produced. A large number of small doses may be given over a period of time, as the body is able to repair itself between doses."[94]

Evans expressed his "conviction that there does exist an absolute threshold for inhaled radon daughters below which these nuclides are innocuous." But Dr. Victor Archer of the U. S. Public Health Service testified at those hearings that on the basis of actual recorded deaths the levels thought to be innocuous by Evans (on the basis of the threshold theory) were actually producing lung cancers at twice the expected rate. About the same time Robley Evans was giving this testimony, other scientists[205, 206] found that abnormal chromosomes (implying cancer and genetic damage) turned up under conditions of radioactivity one tenth as severe as Evans' cut-off point for "no harm." By then it was clear that the safety factor built into Evans' recommendations weren't nearly as large as he believed. Still later studies confirmed chromosomal breaks in blood cells taken from the miners themselves.[207]

Dr. Karl Z. Morgan, head of the Health Physics Division of the AEC's Oak Ridge National Laboratory, also disagreed with Dr. Evans' theory, registering "strong opposition to setting [standards] on the basis that there is or may be a threshold dose . . . below which there is no damage."[208]

In addition to Dr. Morgan, no fewer than five scientific groups have provided "detailed rejections of the Evans claim,"[209] and in 1970 the Bureau of Radiological Health reviewed the Evans studies and others upon which he based his theory and found that ". . . human experience to date is not sufficient . . . therefore, in the low dose regions expected to be experienced by the general public, the assumption of a linear, non-threshold model continues to be a prudent public health philosophy for standards setting."[204]

But even as late as 1970 Evans was still testifying on behalf of the AEC in favor of his "threshold theory."[210] This time in federal court, Dr. Evans not only emphasized his theory's continued validity but said that this view "is a majority theory" in the scientific community. This was flatly contradicted by Dr. Morgan, who stated that "the majority of scientists feel that there is no true threshold,"[211] which may explain why the Joint Committee hasn't been able to bring in other scientists to support Dr. Evans.

The record of the 1967 hearings also indicates that Dr. Evans has, during his career, received several million dollars from the AEC in support of his research, and that Evans himself admitted that he consults on the side for a uranium-mining company whose spokesman, *at the same hearings,* testified that compliance with the new standard would present insurmountable difficulties to his company. Mindful of this, Holifield asked Evans, "The statements you are going to make . . . are based on your best professional judgment? . . . without any regard to the retainers which you may have?"

Dr. Evans replied, "Intellectual honesty is the only thing I know, sir."[212]

12 · ECONOMIC COUNTERATTACK

UNABLE to shake the scientific testimony supporting the new standards, the Joint Committee retreated to the real issue: economic expediency. Representative Hosmer introduced the new line of testimony by saying, "What I am seeking to do . . . having heard Secretary Wirtz and his crew expound on the regulation, is to get a feeling on our record of what the recipients of these regulations do when they run up against [this] kind of problem . . ."

Ben F. Bolton, the vice-president of Kerr-McGee Corporation, a large uranium-mining company (and part-time employer of the Joint Committee's star scientific witness, Dr. Robley Evans) said his firm wished to show "the virtual insurmountable problems which an underground uranium miner will encounter in endeavoring to comply with the recent directive issued by the Secretary of Labor," adding that "that directive would unnecessarily greatly increase the hazards to uranium miners employed by Kerr-McGee." How a safer standard could *increase the hazards to miners* is certainly a new argument, and, not surprisingly, Mr. Bolton did not explain.

Until this time, only the French had studied the economics involved in achieving lower levels of radiation in the mines; they had concluded that the necessary improvements would add one percent to the cost of uranium.[183] Later an American study by the A. D. Little Corporation,[213] commissioned by the AEC in 1970 (under FRC auspices), concluded that somewhat better improvements than the French had in mind would add only three percent to the cost of mining uranium. This conclusion was adopted also by the National Academy of Sciences and the National Research Council in their 1971 report on the problem.[214]

Secretary Wirtz testified to this point when he said that "the AEC estimate is that about ninety-five percent of the industry's production capability is in the mines that should ultimately be able to meet a one-working-level exposure standard." Wirtz added later that mine operator reaction to compliance with his directive showed "eighty-one responses to these letters are encouraging; only one letter replies that compliance is not possible." It appeared that even the mine owners themselves weren't nearly as much against the new standard as the Joint Committee would have everyone believe.

Chet Holifield's anger was especially reserved for the union representatives who came to the Joint Committee to ask for help after waiting the seventeen years. Anthony Mazzocchi, the legislative director of the Oil, Chemical and Atomic Workers' Union, was asked by Holifield, "Why do you make a statement like that: 'There has been much talk but no action on any of the various issues?' There has been a great deal of action . . . I think if you will reconsider that sentence that you will withdraw it from the record because it is absolutely false." Mr. Mazzocchi, attempting his answer, said, "I would consider withdrawing it only if my own experience had demonstrated otherwise. I was a president of a local union that represented—" Holifield cut him off with "I don't care what your experience is."

Not surprisingly, union men complained that they have been denied a voice before the Joint Committee, to which Holifield replied, "There has never been a time when . . . a representative of a labor

union to this committee asking to be heard [has] been turned down."
Leo Goodman, atomic consultant for several unions, called out from
the audience, "You yourself turned me down several times, sir." He
was silenced by an abrupt "Sit down or leave the room!" from
Holifield.

Union men angrily asked that the burden of proof should be on
those who would call for a higher exposure level in the mines rather
than a lower exposure level, and expressed their hope that the Joint
Committee "would commend the Secretary of Labor rather than
harass him." Holifield didn't help matters much with remarks like
"Let us not get off into the emotion of miners dying. . . . We are
aware that people are dying on the highways as a result of automobile
accidents, but we are not closing down the automobile plants."

Small wonder, then, that Chet Holifield is despised in union circles. Leo Goodman has even proposed that a new unit of measurement of underground exposure to radiation, sufficient to double one's
chances of lung cancer, be established and called a "holifield."[215]

13 · FURTHER DELAYING TACTICS

STILL, after the dust cleared, a new, safer standard, on a graduated
scale at least, did go into effect immediately, and this standard was to
be made three times safer on January 1, 1971, four years later, or
so it was thought.

But, remarkably, the Joint Committee held new hearings in 1969,
only two years afterward, and opened the question again.[216] Richard M. Nixon had become President in the meantime, and Willard
Wirtz had been replaced as Secretary of Labor as had Wilbur Cohen,
the Secretary of Health, Education and Welfare. Both men were
advocates of the tightened health standards for uranium miners.
By presenting all the old evidence to a "new team" in Washington,

the Joint Committee hoped to regain some of the prestige it lost in the 1967 hearings, but most of all the Joint Committee sought a reversal of Secretary Wirtz's guidelines. Representative Price set the tone accurately by stating, "I would like to point out that several of the government witnesses at this hearing are members of a new team; as such we are not holding them responsible for what went on before they came to office."

Chairman Holifield brought the issue up by saying, ". . . our questions are not intended to harass the present Secretary. We felt that [the tightening of standards for the uranium miners] was done in haste, that there was a certain amount of, let us say, pressure or coercion involved on the part of at least two members of the council, Secretary Cohen and Secretary Wirtz, to obtain a conforming to their viewpoint. As I said, they were laymen, not scientists . . ."

Robert E. Finch, the new Secretary of Health, Education and Welfare, told the Joint Committee that since there was a sharp disagreement among his staff regarding the new standard, he would have his expert explain. Commenting on the expert's credentials, and even before the testimony began, Holifield added a new wrinkle in intimidation and prior restraint; he said, "That is a very fine background. I will just warn you *in advance* that we can put on some scientists on the witness stand with equal background who will probably take a different position from what you will take."[217]

There was even a replay of the mouse-to-man problem. Holifield asked a scientist, "You would also say that even though the experiments have been made on mice, that the transfer to man is another extrapolation on which you have no real evidence?" It seems that in the two years since the last hearings, Chairman Holifield hadn't yet learned that when experiments involve damage, there is a long tradition in science (hardly ever broken) of using animals instead of men.

Perhaps because his testimony received so little support from the other scientific witnesses at the 1967 hearings, Dr. Robley Evans didn't appear at the 1969 hearing. The Joint Committee relied upon the testimony of Dr. Geno Saccomanno, a pathologist at St. Mary's Hospital in Grand Junction, Colorado. Dr. Saccomanno testified at a

November 1968 Labor Department hearing that his records show a recent decrease in lung cancer cases, suggesting that perhaps the original projection of total deaths was wrong. He also suggested that cigarette smoking may be more to blame for lung cancer among miners than radiation.

As with Robley Evans two years before, Saccomanno's new data were received uncritically by the Joint Committee, and much was made over his testimony. Predictably, he was uncritically believed by the mine owners; one mine operator representative said, "Dr. Saccomanno says the majority of evidence indicates that tobacco, not mine exposure, only is the culprit."

It's only fair to point out that it wasn't Dr. Saccomanno but rather the Joint Committee members who inflated his suggestion out of all proportion to his supportive data. Dr. Saccomanno himself says that his data "naturally [are] incomplete because if some of these cases die outside of our immediate area, we will not have a record of them."[218] Just how incomplete the data might be is indicated by a 1961 study showing the migratory character of uranium miners: only twenty-six percent of a group of over one thousand miners were found working in uranium mines seven years later.[219]

Secretary of Health Finch disposed of Dr. Saccomanno's theory with clarity and dispatch: "Dr. Saccomanno's statement is not persuasive. Dr. Saccomanno is reporting a personal experience which is not interpretable in any true statistical sense. . . . Dr. Saccomanno admits he does no more than give a personal guess as to whether the observed deaths are significant. . . . Because his experience is anecdotal rather than statistical, it is entitled to little weight when compared with the highly statistically significant observed excesses of lung cancer mortality . . . of the Public Health Epidemiological Study. Dr. Saccomanno's recommendation of reliance on a ban on smoking in the mines to reduce the risk of lung cancer . . . has little scientific foundation." Undersecretary of Labor James D. Hodgson added that "European pitchblende miners were dying of lung cancer before the introduction of tobacco to Europe."

The result of the 1969 hearings was simply that the safer standard originally proposed by Secretary Wirtz stayed in force and, on a graduated basis, the new three-times-safer standard would take effect on January 1, 1971. But the Joint Committee persisted; it had not given up yet. Representative Melvin Price wrote letters to HEW Secretary Finch and Labor Secretary Schultz, as well as the White House, pushing for the abandonment of the new safer standard scheduled to go into effect in 1971. The committee was "extremely interested in safeguarding the health of miners," he said. "It is also interested in protecting the miners' means of livelihood as well as the stability of the uranium mining industry."[220]

As a result, just three weeks before the new three-times-safer standard was to go into effect, the Joint Committee won a six-month postponement[221] so that "all pertinent information, including epidemiological data, miner exposure records, health considerations, mining practices and costs thereof," could be—you guessed it— studied some more.

But the Joint Committee's delaying tactics are no longer as effective as they have been in the past. The postponement won by the Joint Committee served only to weaken its position. The National Academy of Sciences–National Research Council report, the justification for the six-month postponement, not only supported Secretary Wirtz's original recommendations (made *four years earlier* by now), but, because of new data available, found that danger existed at a lower level than heretofore believed.[214] Finally a safer standard went into effect in the mines on July 1, 1971.[222]

14 · WHY?

BECAUSE OF THE WAY they have mishandled the uranium miners' tragedy, the credibility and even the motives of the Joint Committee are suspect in official Washington. The nagging questions remain: Why did the Joint Committee on Atomic Energy stand in the way of the establishment of a safer standard for uranium miners, a standard that in no meaningful way could harm the uranium industry or the AEC? In particular, why did it permit seventeen years to pass before something was done and why didn't the Joint Committee do it finally, rather than Labor Secretary Wirtz? Why did it greet Secretary Wirtz's standard with such obvious and unprofessional antagonism? Why did it schedule new hearings only two years later, just after the "new team" (the Nixon Administration) took over in Washington? Why does the record of those hearings reflect an obvious and barely controlled hostility for those standards, their authors and their supporters? Having failed finally to discredit the new standards, why did the Joint Committee members continue tenaciously to attack them in letters to the White House, an effort which achieved a six-month delay before the standards became law in 1971? Every delay was a deadly serious matter for the miners who had to work in air more radioactive than it had to be. Every delay meant that many more cases of lung cancer; it's that simple.

After so many hearings on the matter, it was clear that on a technical basis there could be no possible justification for the intransigent stance of the members of the Joint Committee. Surely at one time the Joint Committee had good reason to go along with its experts, but as the mortality statistics began to come in, as the miners died, its position became indefensible. At such a juncture, organizations typically do one of two things: they admit to error, get some new experts and try again, or they refuse to acknowledge their error and become defensive, harden their original attitudes and seek still more experts to justify their original position. Unfortunately members of the Joint Committee on Atomic Energy took the latter course.

Another nagging question is, how could the Atomic Energy Commission have ignored the European tragedy, causing it to be replayed again here, and, once it saw it happening here, how could the AEC have allowed it to go on as long as it did? As mentioned earlier, the inordinately high death rates (due to lung cancer) of the uranium miners of Europe was well known and widely published in English medical and scientific journals long before there ever was an AEC.

Likewise, it was also known that it was the airborne radioactivity in the mines that was the cause of death, a known problem which had a known solution. Indeed, even the precise levels of radioactivity in the European mines were published. That the AEC itself had measured the same radioactivity in our mines before its massive procurement program began, and found the levels at least as high or higher than in Europe, and did not act to lower these levels simply cannot be justified for any reason. The commission says that it alerted the states to the dangers, but it can provide no evidence for this until 1959, more than *ten years* after the first large domestic uranium buying by the AEC began, and when uranium mining in the West had *already begun to decline.* That the AEC made no attempt to lower radioactivity levels in the more than a dozen mines it owned outright surely cannot be blamed upon the states.

The real irresponsibility on the part of the AEC is not that it didn't warn the states soon enough or strongly enough, but that it ever gave the full responsibility to the states in the first place. In so doing, the AEC dropped a new and totally strange problem onto the various state health departments and into the laps of people who could not be expected to have the competence, in that age of atomic innocence, to know even what to regulate. This left the state health officials with the problem of having to deal unassisted with the powerful mining interests in those mining states, because to safeguard the health of miners requires enactment of regulations that would inevitably be restrictive of a booming new industry; it's no wonder that the states failed and Secretary Wirtz had to act "after seventeen years of inaction." It is inconceivable that the AEC was so politically naïve that it could not have anticipated that result.

The efforts of public-health people were further diluted because they were required to convince their respective state legislatures of the urgency of the situation, and because they had to do it in the face of the tacit approval of the existing conditions by AEC field employees. Under such circumstances, it is easy to see why state health officials were criticized locally as "empire builders" and derided for "inventing problems that didn't exist."

The AEC ducked the job because to regulate mining would mean to accept responsibility for reducing airborne radioactivity in the mines and that would inevitably raise the price of uranium. Although the recent AEC-sponsored research indicates that this would result in an increase of only three percent in the cost of uranium, an AEC study done in 1948—about the time the AEC decided that mining was not its responsibility—suggests that domestic ore would have cost six times more than what it was then paying.

Thus, it would appear that an error made twenty-four years ago, the 1948 decision to peg the domestic price of uranium at one seventh of its predicted value, hardened any future position of the AEC. With no money for mine safety in its uranium price, it couldn't very well require mine safety unless it raised the price drastically. Thus the AEC and ultimately the Joint Committee were caught in a dilemma: the miners were already dying, and to raise the price of the uranium to pay for mine-safety measures would in effect fix the blame for those miners already dead squarely upon the AEC. So the AEC and the Joint Committee solved the problem by ignoring it until—as is always the case—forces from outside the atomic bureaucracy exposed the problem and finally solved it.

V
RADIOACTIVE
WASTE: THE MOUSE
THAT ROARED

Our decision to go to salt for permanent high-level disposal is one of the most far-reaching decisions we, or for that matter, any technologists have ever made. These wastes can be hazardous for up to a million years. We must therefore be as certain as one can possibly be of anything that the wastes, once sequestered in the salt, can under no conceivable circumstances come in contact with the biosphere.
— ALVIN M. WEINBERG, Director,
Oak Ridge National Laboratory[223]

1 · THE PROBLEM

PERHAPS the most vexing and far-reaching decision our society must make in the next few years is what to do with our growing pile of radioactive wastes.

According to Dr. Glenn T. Seaborg, plutonium will be the mainstay of our energy economy within thirty years, and in only twenty years our annual production of this metal will exceed sixty tons.[224]

But plutonium is toxic almost beyond human experience. It is nearly as hazardous as botulism toxin:[225] quantities of less than a thirty-millionth of an ounce will produce cancer.[226] Plutonium's co-discoverer, Dr. Seaborg, regards the description "fiendishly toxic" as an understatement,[227] and no wonder: if ten pounds of the stuff were administered with absolute efficiency, it could produce cancer in every human being on earth. About the same amount would be enough to produce an atomic bomb. But such unimaginable toxicity does not impress some people whose job it is to handle the stuff. Perhaps the most blatantly incorrect statement ever made in connection with radiological dangers is found in a handbook discussing plutonium safety, where the statement is made that "in order for plutonium to be hazardous to an individual who swallows it, one must swallow enough to go critical"[228] (enough to make an atom bomb).

Byproducts of the weapons-building program and the nuclear-fuel-reprocessing plants, radioactive wastes are made up of many elements, but the most troublesome have been strontium 90, cesium 137, iodine 131, radium and plutonium. Although some wastes decay to nonradioactive products in a few hundred years, radium remains unsafe for more than ten thousand years and plutonium for more than two hundred thousand years.[229]

Because of their obvious danger, it is vital that radioactive wastes be completely isolated from the environment. But consider how difficult that is to do: *If radium wastes had been interred in the Great Pyramid at Giza, in Egypt, at the time it was built, almost 5000 years ago, more than ten percent of that waste would still be radioactive. If the waste had been plutonium instead, decay would have reduced the radioactivity hardly at all: ninety percent of the amount originally present would remain there today.* And if those ancient Egyptian technologists had not been infallible in their judgment of the hazards, we would be living with the consequences of their mistakes today.

Yet as inconceivable as it may seem, radioactive waste disposal problems of the nuclear age present that staggering responsibility to our civilization—our technologists must be no less than infallible. Accordingly, everything must be done to increase our chances of being right when we finally decide what to do.

The analogy of the pyramid brings grave robbers to mind. The pharaohs didn't survive them, and it's possible the plutonium won't, either. Terribly expensive (about \$5,000 per pound), its prolif- eration worries even the AEC. Commissioner Clarence E. Larsen regards a rapidly growing nuclear black market as "likely" in the future, leading not only "to serious economic burdens to the indus- try" but to "a threat to national security" as well.[230] "Such a black market could put the five kilograms it takes to make an atomic bomb into the hands of anyone willing to pay."[231] This would make an ideal companion piece for the laser-ignited do-it-yourself "basement" hydrogen bomb already suggested.[232]

And so what our society produces in the way of waste, how much we produce and what we are going to do with it all are very serious questions; they are decisions far too serious to be left to the experts alone. For despite Dr. Seaborg's opinion that it is irresponsible to point out past failures of the AEC,[89] its past record is our only gauge of its competence to handle problems of the future. They were wrong before; could they be wrong again? As we shall see in this chapter, the record of the AEC's competence in handling radioactive wastes in the past is poor, far too poor to justify relying on it alone to do the very much bigger job our society faces in that connection in the future.

2 · THE FIRE

IRONICALLY, the public became involved in this far-reaching decision only recently. For that matter, the AEC wasn't very involved until recently, either: Senator Frank Church of Idaho calculated that in its entire history the AEC has spent less than one tenth of one percent of its entire budget on waste-disposal research.[233] But that's all changed now. Neglected for years, radioactive-waste disposal has suddenly emerged as one of the more serious technical problems ever faced by the AEC; and it all started with the fire.

On May 11, 1969, the most expensive single industrial accident in American history took place. Even though it was more costly than the great General Motors fire at Livonia, Michigan, fifteen years before,[234] the remarkable fact that the damage caused by the fire could hardly be noticed outside the two buildings in which it occurred attests to its special nature. It was a plutonium fire, and the problem was not so much destruction as it was radioactive contamination.

Dow Chemical's Rocky Flats atomic plant, located just eight miles upwind of the densely populated areas of suburban Denver, Colorado, is the Atomic Energy Commission's only facility for the mass production of plutonium parts for atom bombs, now the trigger for the modern thermonuclear weapon. The importance of this plant, and the two buildings in which the fire took place, can be appreciated by the fact that a serious impact on weapons delivery schedules and stockpiles would have occurred had the fire taken place a year later. According to Major General Edward B. Giller, the director of the AEC's Division of Military Applications (and one of the most able scientific military officers in the country), "The fire occurred at a particular period in which our requirements for deliveries of new devices was at a minimum. . . . If we are unable to get back into production in April, in the spring [of 1970], then we will not be able to meet our commitments to the Department of Defense and our production will indeed slip."[235]

The day after the fire, Robert Hollingsworth, the general manager of the AEC, appointed a special board to investigate. Its report received little publicity, because, *by a remarkable coincidence,* it was released on November 18, only hours before the Apollo-12 astronauts landed on the moon. But what it said was worth noting.[236]

The fire began in a "glovebox" area where plutonium is machined. Plutonium, like phosphorous, can *ignite spontaneously* and produce the intense heat characteristic of burning metals. The report suggests that the source was some loose scrap plutonium which was improperly stored in uncovered cans under the glovebox. The glovebox liner itself was made out of six hundred tons of *combustible* material. The first indication of the fire was an alarm finally sounded by the heat-sensing system installed throughout the buildings. However, by this time the fire was well out of control, because the astonishing facts are, as the report states, that "since the heat detectors were located outside and under [the glovebox] and *were insulated* by the floor of the storage cabinet, *they were incapable* of sensing the fire."*

Similar industrial installations, subject as they are to state, local and insurance-company fire regulations, typically have fireblocks along production lines. Not so for this top-secret installation; the report went on to say: "The long interconnected conveyor system without physical barriers provided a path for the fire to spread. The closed metal door in the North Line demonstrated the effectiveness of even a simple firebreak in the line."

On May 20, an AEC delegation, in closed-door testimony before a Senate commission, requested and received the funds needed to restore Rocky Flats to full operation. In retrospect, it is tempting to speculate how many of these contributing causes would ever have been allowed had a private insurance company instead of the general public carried the fire risk.

At hearings for extra funds "to eliminate fire and safety hazards at various AEC installations," Representative Glenn R. David of Wisconsin observed, "Are we fairly subject to the charge of negligence in failing to have some of these basic things at these installations? Nobody would permit operations to go on without firewalls and automatic sprinklers and things of this kind unless they were under the jurisdiction of the federal government where they can do nothing about it, I suppose."[72]

It was at these same hearings (over a year after the fire) that the AEC finally admitted to the real danger that the fire had presented to the public. Describing it as "a near catastrophe," General Giller testified that if the fire had burned through the roof (it didn't), "then hundreds of square miles could be involved in radiation exposure and involve cleanup at an astronomical cost as well as creating a

* Emphasis added.

very intense reaction by the general public* exposed to this. . . . If
the fire had been a little bigger, it is questionable whether it could
have been contained."

Clearly, then, this fire was not simply an accident that could happen anywhere, as Dr. Lloyd M. Joshel, then Dow's general manager
at Rocky Flats, implied at a meeting in Denver.[237] It was caused by
the everyday incompetence and negligence inevitably found in any
system which polices itself. Joshel, fifty-seven, retired at the end of
1971.[385]

3 · THE TROUT FARMER

OF COURSE, newspapers all over the country carried the story.
Robert A. Erkins, president of the Snake River Trout Company, the
world's largest trout farm, received a *New York Times* clipping in
the mail from one of his customers back East.[238] The story said that
for "several months, hundreds of railroad cars will be carrying from
Rocky Flats to the Snake River plain of eastern Idaho an estimated
330,000 cubic feet of contaminated waste to be buried below ground
by the Commission's National Reactor Test Station."[239] The customer was worried that his trout might become contaminated with
plutonium. So was Mr. Erkins.

He wrote a letter to Idaho's Governor Don W. Samuelson, ex-
pressing worry that the Snake River aquifer (an underground river
and the largest in the country), which feeds the springs that support
the state's trout farming industry, might become polluted with radioactivity.[240] He had reason to worry: it turned out that the open
trench which was used for plutonium disposal was separated from
the underground aquifer by a layer of basalt rock only six hundred

* Emphasis added.

feet thick, and according to the chief of the Water Pollution Section of the Idaho State Health Department it was "crevassed and fissured all the way down to the aquifer."[241] Not only that, but deep disposal wells are used in Idaho to inject liquid radioactive wastes directly into the aquifer.[242]

As usual, AEC assurances were extravagant. "We have substantial technical experience. There's no real or potential basis for alarm—*ever*," said William F. Ginkel, manager of the AEC's Idaho Operations Office. He went on to say that his operation was "reviewed continually by the Department of Health, the AEC and people like the National Academy of Science."[241] Ginkel thereby implied something not true, that the National Academy of Sciences (NAS) had examined his Idaho operation and found it safe. Ginkel never mentioned the fact that the NAS had reviewed AEC radioactive-waste-disposal practices for years and roundly condemned not only the Idaho operation but AEC atom dumps everywhere they existed!

4 · THE "SUPPRESSED" 1966 REPORT OF THE NATIONAL ACADEMY OF SCIENCES

THE EXISTENCE of the NAS reports became known, but nobody outside the AEC could obtain copies (at least one author couldn't even get a copy for himself).

Idaho's Senator Frank Church became involved and asked for an independent federal review of the AEC's waste-handling practices in his state. He also asked AEC Chairman Seaborg, "I would appreciate a report from the AEC explaining why this report has not been made public."[243] The unpublicized report Senator Church was asking about was the National Academy of Sciences Report of 1966 (the same one referred to by the AEC's Mr. Ginkel, above).

The AEC's official reasons for hiding this information are contained in Seaborg's response[244] and in two unsigned AEC "staff critiques"—one of the NAS report itself (the Pitzer-Knapp-Martell treatment)[245] and the other of a newspaper article on the subject.[246] The reason is simply that "the May 1966 (NAS) report went *beyond its purpose* of appraising the AEC's research and development program on waste disposal, and *commented at length on operational activities.*"* The comments, of course, were very unfavorable. It's tempting to speculate how the AEC would have handled the situation if, having gone "beyond its purpose," the report were laudatory.

But *five months later* Senator Church was still without the "suppressed" report. He said, "I am increasingly troubled over the trend towards secrecy in our government. If security reasons are involved, or the Commission does not feel the report is factual, it should say so. But to simply indicate that the Committee did more than the AEC felt it should, and use that as a basis for not releasing the report is a dubious procedure. The AEC, like all government agencies, is created for the benefit and protection of the people, and should make public as much information as possible."[244]

The very next day, "The AEC, denying that it had suppressed the report, made a copy of it available to *The New York Times.* Asked why Senator Church could not get his own copy, the AEC said that Senator Church had *not requested a copy* of the report."[247]* It would seem that Seaborg had denied Senator Church a copy of the NAS 1966 report, but AEC-watchers will recognize immediately the little game Seaborg was playing. Senator Church may have thought he was asking for the report five months before, but he was actually asking Seaborg for a report explaining "why this [NAS] report has not been made public," and that's what Seaborg gave him: a report on a report. (Thus Seaborg could always point out the fact that Senator Church did not actually *ask* for the report.)

But the NAS report was finally released, even if it was *The New York Times* that had made the first direct request for it. And it confirmed the fears of a worried Idaho public. The National Academy of Sciences—National Research Council report,[242] calling at-

---

* Emphasis added.

tention to the fact that the AEC's waste-disposal operations in Idaho "are conducted over one of the largest of the country's remaining reserves of pure fresh water," found cause for worry in 1965 "over the prevailing belief" that the basalt surface layers of only "several hundred feet provide a reservoir for safe storage of tremendous quantities of wastes of all levels of radioactivity and that no hazardous amounts of radioactivity will percolate down to the water table."

Furthermore, the report calculated that with water movement in basalt "as high as 15 million gallons per day per foot," the radioactive waste would take only fifty to sixty years to reach the springs in the Snake River Canyon that the trout farmers were so worried about. Recalling the fact that, on human time scales at least, plutonium lasts forever, Mr. Ginkel's assurances that there was no basis for alarm "ever" suddenly looked rather reckless.

The NAS committee went on to say that it left the AEC's Idaho disposal site in 1965 "with two unrelieved major anxieties: (1) that *consideration of long-range safety are in some instances subordinated to regard for economy of operation,* and (2) that some disposal practices are conditioned on *over-confidence* in the capacity of the local environment to contain vast quantities of radionuclides for indefinite periods without danger to the biosphere."*

As early as 1955 the committee concluded that "continuing disposal of low-level waste . . . above the water table, probably involves *unacceptable* long term risks."*

Consider the judgments which we can presume afforded the AEC its basis for suppressing the entire report; the so-called comments on "operational activities" are no such thing. They were technical judgments concerning geology, judgments squarely within the mission of the NAS committee.

As early as 1960 the NAS committee said: *"No existing AEC installation is in a geologically acceptable location for disposal of highly radioactive liquid waste . . ."* In 1965, it went even further: *". . . none of the major sites* at which radioactive wastes are being

---

* Emphasis added.

stored or disposed of is geologically suited for safe disposal of *any manner of radioactive wastes* other than very dilute, very low-level liquids."*

But the trout farmer had done his work. About a year after the NAS report was released to the public, the AEC announced that the buried waste in Idaho would be removed from his state.[248] But just as Colorado's waste started Idaho's problems, Idaho's waste was to go elsewhere as the problem became national in scope.

5 · QUICK ACTION IN KANSAS—TOO QUICK

NEWSPAPER reports and magazine articles began calling attention to the fact that the AEC's waste-disposal practices are indeed sloppy. Many millions of gallons of boiling liquid wastes are stored in large tanks in the states of Washington and Georgia in addition to those solid wastes buried in shallow trenches in Idaho that called attention to the problem in the first place. There are exposed liquid wastes as well. A week after the NAS report was released, the AEC admitted that ducks feeding on algae in waste-water trenches at the Hanford, Washington, works were so radioactive that they "would have given a person five times the maximum permissible dosage of radiation if eaten."[249]

The public was surprised to learn that although the liquid wastes will continue to be dangerous for thousands of years, the tanks have a life expectancy of only twenty-five years or so. Many leaks have already occurred, one releasing seven hundred gallons of an intensely radioactive liquid.[233] An unsigned AEC "staff analysis" of the incident exults: "In each of these cases . . . the radioactivity was absorbed in the soil . . . and in the worst case . . . did not reach within 100 feet of the ground waters."[246]

* Emphasis added.

In Idaho the situation was even more haphazard. A worker at the AEC's installation there says:

The way that they dispose of their radioactive waste is, they take heavy equipment and they go out and they dig a big trench. They put the smaller particles in a pasteboard box and the rest of the stuff is dumped directly into the ground. This includes the material from the Colorado atomic plant. As you know, the Idaho Falls disposal burial ground is right over the nation's largest underground water supply, which handles water for the vast Northwest. We know that we have tanks of radioactive material, a liquid, that is leaking into the ground. Hanford has the same problem, and the same problem exists in other places.[250]

Pictures of this process were made public only in January 1971, a year after these methods were discontinued.[251]

The AEC was on the spot, and it went into action fast. In January of 1971 it announced the establishment of a $25-million National Radioactive Waste Repository in an abandoned salt mine near Lyons, Kansas,[252] breathing life into its Salt Vault Project, a study which four years before had provided data indicating the feasibility of storing high-level radioactive wastes in underground salt beds.[253]

Unnoticed in the flurry of activity was the fact that the AEC had been urged to establish such a waste depository sixteen years before by the National Academy of Sciences,[242] by its own Salt Vault Project in 1967,[253] by the General Accounting Office in 1968 and 1971,[254] by the National Academy of Sciences again in 1970[255] and by the Comptroller General in 1971,[251] and had still not acted.

It's highly unlikely that the AEC would *ever* have acted if it weren't for the trout farmer. After all, one tenth of one percent of its total budget over the years spent on waste is an expression of waste's priority among the other AEC programs: waste management, as important as it is, and as central as it is to the AEC's responsibilities under the Atomic Energy Act, just had to take a back seat to the more glamorous and far more frivolous AEC efforts described in Chapter VI. Again, it took public embarrassment to impress upon the stewards of the AEC that action was required.

Before the AEC announced its commitment to create the National Radioactive Waste Repository at Lyons, Kansas, it had already spent well over $100 million, during a fifteen-year period, studying salt-bed disposal of radioactive wastes. Most of that time and money was spent in the salt mine at Lyons. The AEC was so sure that Lyons was the place that in March 1971 Milton Shaw, the director of the AEC's Division of Reactor Development, told the Joint Committee, in a very unusual declaration, that "another year's work of research and development in this area on top of fifteen years of work *will not be particularly productive.*[256] We need the project and are ready to proceed with it. Moreover, we are convinced that the Lyons site is equal or superior to the others. The valuable data gathered there during [our study is] *unique to the Lyons mine.*"[257]*

Seldom in the history of the error-prone AEC has a technical commitment been stated so positively. The momentous decision, the decision men will have to live with for a million years, had been made: Lyons was the place.

Accordingly, the AEC made an unorthodox request. Normally, it asks first for an appropriation sufficient to complete the initial stages of a project ($3.5 million in this case), and if all goes well it returns to the Joint Committee later on to request sufficient funds to complete the job. In this case the AEC not only asked for the entire cost of the project at once ($25 million) but wanted the funding to begin in only three months' time instead of a year later as is the usual practice.

But even Joint Committeemen could see why the request was made that way; Senator Pastore told Milton Shaw, ". . . if you get authorization of 25 million, it would be a fait accompli; whereas if you get the 3.5 million, you would have to come in and ask for a new authorization next year. . . . [The critics'] argument is that once you have grabbed this thing, you are not going to let go. And they would rather have you prove it before you grabbed it."[258] The AEC had received some criticism of its project by then and Milton Shaw simply wanted all of his money right away, to avoid a new

* Emphasis added.

appropriation hearing the next year and the new criticism such a hearing would evoke.

But it was 1971; the AEC didn't have the free hand it had in the fallout controversy of the late 1950s and the uranium miners' tragedy of the early sixties. Today people just aren't ready to accept an AEC plan without some scrutiny.[259] For one of the first times, the public could read about an AEC proposal before it took place,[260] and some of them just weren't buying.[261] Governor Robert B. Docking was aroused, Representative Joe Skubitz, a Kansas Republican, raised hell in Congress,[262] and the Kansas Geological Survey was sharply critical of the AEC's plan on technical grounds.[263] Outside scientific scrutiny, as usual, proved to be the undoing of the AEC this time as well.

6 · OH, WELL, BACK TO THE DRAWING BOARD!

ONE OF THE MAIN REASONS for choosing a salt mine for the disposal of atomic wastes instead of some other subsurface deposit is that salt layers are among the least likely place for water to exist underground. For the most serious hazard to the AEC's waste plan would be if somehow quantities of water entered the salt vaults. The wastes, red-hot and well over one thousand degrees Fahrenheit, would vaporize the water instantly and violently expel steam, water, salt and waste particles throughout the mine and up through and out of the main shaft to the outside. Thus the ultimate disaster would be a "radioactive volcano." Depending how much water entered the mine, an accident of this sort could easily contaminate a large part of the state of Kansas for thousands of years, rendering it uninhabitable and seriously endangering downwind areas for many hundreds of miles.

The Kansas Geological Survey had been very critical of the AEC's haste, pointing out that not enough is known about the underground water there. Dr. Ernest Angino, associate director of the Survey, said, "Water is probably the ultimate disaster for the whole project." A few months after the appropriation hearings, the American Salt Company wrote a letter to the AEC. A company spokesman told the *Denver Post* that the letter "expressed concern about the presence of water" and that his company "had been injecting water into the formation for fifty years; as we remove salt, the water replaces the salt."[264]

Another month or two later, an AEC staff report, examining "certain additional information," revealed that tunnels of the American Salt Company's mine come as close as five hundred yards to the AEC's proposed atom dump. Also, the report said: "In the course of drilling small holes . . . water started leaking into the mine" because one of the many gas or oil bore holes in the area had been intercepted.[265] "Water and mud came spurting out" but there was no record of a well nearby.[264] Dr. William W. Hambleton, the director of the Kansas Geological Survey, remarked, "We felt the Lyons site increasingly looked like a leaky sieve. I think they [the AEC] are realizing that, too."[266]

And so after fifteen years and a hundred million dollars' worth of studies and experiments, the AEC had arrived at a point in March of 1971 where Milton Shaw could tell the Joint Committee that no further research was needed. The AEC had made what Oak Ridge Director Alvin Weinberg has called "one of the most far-reaching decisions . . . any technologists have ever made,"[223] and Lyons was it. But in September 1971, only six months after Shaw spoke with such certitude, AEC Assistant General Manager John A. Erlewine conceded that because of "certain additional information" the AEC would have to consider "possible alternative sites" to Lyons, Kansas, for its atom dump.[265]

Technical blunders are almost always blamed on having ignored facts which if considered at the outset would have resulted in a better course of action. Justifiable ignorance of those facts is the usual excuse for the blunderer, as new information is constantly being discovered. But seldom, if ever, has a technical organization so positively stated that its plan is fixed, further research is useless, and full and immediate funding is required, and then been proven so wrong so soon. It's not as if some complex new scientific fact were discovered in the meantime. It is simply that despite all that time and money, the AEC completely missed what the Kansas Geological Survey, Representative Joe Skubitz and everybody else in the area knew and had been trying to tell the AEC all along—that there was a lot of water moving around down there only five hundred yards away from the AEC's mine, and nobody knew quite where it was.

Thus, unable to admit to the limits of its competence, and blinded to outside criticism by its arrogance, the AEC very nearly committed this nation to a blunder of colossal proportions. If the AEC were allowed to go ahead with its plan to store the hot wastes at Lyons and if the millions of gallons of water that are known to be hidden somewhere in that salt deposit should flood into the waste vaults, there is a real chance that we could write off substantial areas of Kansas to another AEC bungle.

But, fortunately for Kansas (and the rest of the country), the AEC's incipient disaster was arrested. Representative Joe Skubitz commented in October of 1971 that the Lyons site is "dead as a dodo for atom waste burial."[267]

But suppose the AEC had been competent enough to pick a dry salt mine. The $25 million would have been appropriated and the project could have proceeded according to plan. Let's examine only one aspect of that plan. At the Joint Committee hearings in March 1971 Senator Howard H. Baker, Jr., asked the AEC witnesses, ". . . if these computations are wrong, what do you do about it? . . . Just briefly, ever so briefly if you will, tell me what you would do on retrievability or to provide a 'back door.' "[268] We are, after all, dealing with an irreversible situation. Containers which will hold the hot radioactive wastes are acknowledged to be temporary—they will last for no more than a few years; the container is just to "get it there." Soon the radioactive waste becomes a red-hot blob with internal temperatures as high as 1,650 degrees Fahrenheit. (The salt melts at 1,470 degrees.) Suppose it is discovered someday that the wastes are in danger of entering the biosphere and it is necessary to remove them—what then?

The AEC's Milton Shaw answered that "in nine out of ten cases the cans will be retrievable . . . but in the gross sense, we do not feel retrievability . . . will be worth the investment in the waste repository."

Floyd Culler, deputy director of the Oak Ridge National Laboratories, testifying at the same hearings, said that the blob could be drilled out and removed with a machine, but he went on to say, ". . . have we yet conceived of the machine to do this removal? The answer is No. . . . Let me assure you that at some point during the preliminary design we will conceive of a machine . . . that will make retrieval possible."[268]

But to "conceive of a machine" and to build one are two different things. Consider the conditions under which such a machine must operate: the canisters gone, each blob of radioactive waste will be at temperatures well over one thousand degrees Fahrenheit and release more than a billion rads of radiation.[269] Radiation doses that great are almost beyond imagination: there will be more than enough radiation in each blob to give every person on earth double the present recommended maximum permissible radiation exposure (170 mr), and there is not just one blob to contend with, there are many. Assuming a machine can be built, how long will it take, considering that it has yet to be conceived? Will it be ready for an unforeseen emergency *or will that be the signal to begin the design work?*

Culler went on to make an observation crucial to all the disputes that have ever taken place between the AEC and the public: "For what I think are sound reasons, *there is no conceivable sudden emergency* that will demand that we remove these wastes from the mine in a hurry."* He said that just as if it hadn't been said before about

* Emphasis added.

other AEC waste problems, by other AEC spokesmen, who later turned out to have been dead wrong. In almost the same words, an official AEC summary once said about the uranium-mill-tailings (waste) problem: "We find it *difficult to conceive* of any mechanisms whereby the radioactive material, which is now so widely dispersed, could become so concentrated so as to exceed current acceptable standards for protection against radiation."*[270]

But just because the AEC can't conceive of something doesn't mean it can't happen. The statement is remarkable because *at the very moment it was made a mechanism was operating which was doing just that.* Doing what the AEC could not conceive of: concentrating the radioactivity so as to "exceed current applicable standards for protection against radiation."

And so, before our society entrusts the AEC solely to handle the vital problem of permanent and irreversible storage of radioactive wastes, it is imperative to examine the way in which they solved the previous waste problem that they had. Dr. Seaborg's opinions notwithstanding, those who have not learned the mistakes of history are doomed to repeat them.[271]

7 · TAILINGS: HOW THE AEC HANDLED ITS PREVIOUS WASTE PROBLEM

DURING the uranium boom of the fifties, all uranium ore was transported from the mines either to AEC-owned mills or to mills owned by corporations which were licensed and controlled by the AEC; it could not be otherwise under the Atomic Energy Act.

Now, when uranium is extracted from its ore, other radioactive impurities, notably radium, are left behind in piles of gray sandlike mill wastes called tailings. Because the rock has been pulverized, from the point of view of radium and its decay products (radon gas

* Emphasis added.

and radon daughters), tailings are even more dangerous than the ore itself, the same ore which, inside the mines, was responsible for more than a thousand lung cancers in Europe and America and an unknown number in the Belgian Congo.

Despite their obvious danger, uranium mill tailings were piled just next to the rivers while the liquid wastes were dumped directly into the water.[272] Today these tailings piles amount to over 100 million tons,[273] scattered mostly throughout the Colorado River Basin at six active mills and eleven abandoned mill sites.[274] They contain about fifty-eight times more radium than the entire U.S. supply of sealed radium sources combined, the kind which periodically makes the front pages when one is lost in transit.[275]

Regulations in the AEC licenses were widely assumed to be highly restrictive of how the company mills handled the radioactive ores, since the regulations contained broadly phrased health and safety provisions. It was not surprising, then, that the mills were able to operate for about ten years without a complaint. Everyone assumed them to be safe, and, of course, they were so represented by the AEC.

But in the late 1950s, at the request of the states, a biologist from the Federal Water Pollution Control Agency of the U. S. Public Health Service was asked to collect fish samples from the Animas River downstream from the AEC-licensed uranium mill at Durango, Colorado. He not only found no fish there but no life at all; what he found was described as a "biological desert."[276]

8 · RADIUM IN THE DRINKING WATER

SINCE the sandy tailings were in intimate contact with the rivers, dissolved radium in the river water was immediately suspected as being the cause of the "biological desert" on the Animas. The Federal Water Pollution Control Agency quickly established that the radioactivity downstream from the Durango mill was almost five hundred times normal levels, and that this radioactivity was eight times more than the maximum amount permitted in drinking water. It was even higher downstream of uranium mills elsewhere in Colorado, but this finding was particularly alarming because thirty thousand people lived down the Animas, primarily in Aztec and Farmington, New Mexico, and because river water exclusively is used for drinking and irrigation there.

The U. S. Public Health Service then measured the radium in the drinking water of these towns and found that although the radioactivity there was less than upstream, the concentrations there were nevertheless "considerably in excess" of the established limits for radiological health.[277, 272] Furthermore, they found that the dissolved radium in the river was concentrated by the stream plants as much as nine hundred times and that food crops irrigated by Animas River water showed a similar increase.[278, 279]

As with the strontium 90 and iodine 131 from fallout, the worry here is that whenever radioactive elements concentrate, man at the end of the food chain will concentrate the radium into his bones still further.

For example, hay and alfalfa irrigated with water containing radium accumulates radium in concentrations one hundred times higher than normally. Cows eating this forage concentrate the radium still further, in their bones and in their milk. Milk from cows exposed to uranium-mill pollution was shown to contain as high as thirty-two times more radium than milk from other areas.[278] When men (and children in the bone-building ages especially) drink that milk, the radium concentrates still further in their bones and greatly increases their chances for bone and blood cancer. But it's difficult to measure the results of radium consumption, for two reasons. The affected population doesn't stay in one place long enough, for one thing, and, for another, effects such as bone cancer are observed only decades after the original exposure.

The vast spread of the problem became obvious when it was dis-

covered that the bottom sediments of Lake Mead had three times the
radium contained in similar sediments taken upstream of the ura-
nium-milling operations.[280] Although this concentration was far less
than those found closer to the mills, the fact that Lake Mead supplies the drinking water for Los Angeles illustrates the potential
dangers in permitting, as the AEC did for ten years, the *direct discharge* of uranium tailings into the waters of the Colorado River
Basin.[281]

9 · THE AEC'S RESPONSE

ONCE THE PROBLEM was discovered, the response of the AEC was
hardly in the interests of public health. Just as with virtually every
other problem it has faced before or since, the AEC directed its efforts not toward solving the problem, but toward economic expediency
and the protection of its own reputation. Despite the fact that through
its license the AEC had direct control over the mills, it relied on per-
suasion to solve the problem. It had little choice, because, as with
the uranium-mining tragedy, the AEC had not built into the uranium-
milling pricing schedules any money for public safety. As a consequence, no attention was paid to health hazards at all. The Grand
Junction plant, formerly a sugar mill, was still being used for the
storage of sugar fifteen years after the uranium milling began there.
A state inspector discovered uranium-oxide dust so thick on the
sugar sacks that "you could write your name on them with your
finger."[282] A Farmington, New Mexico, physician, worried about
radium in the drinking water of his town, visited the Durango mill
upstream and found the radioactive dust so thick in the company's
offices there that he was "afraid to breathe." He also saw "the fur-
rows through the tailings which carried the material directly into
the river."[283]

But as the Joint Committee observed in 1959, the AEC could solve any problem with its contractors (mines and mills) at a moment's notice, since "a simple directive to the contractor results in the necessary changes being made, with the cost of the changes being borne by the AEC."[199] The AEC, however, was not interested in making such directives, especially if it had to bear the cost. At a conference on the pollution of the Animas River in 1958, the AEC was asked, "Does the licensing division of the AEC really expect industry to police itself . . . ?" And Mr. Barker of the AEC's Division of Licensing and Regulation said, "Yes, that is about it." He followed this later on with the remarkable admission ". . . we will not, in a sense, move in with the idea of trying to put them out of business, *because that in turn would put us out of business.*"[279]*

By 1959, public clamor downstream forced the AEC, after ten years of inaction, finally to issue regulations to its licensed mills to "assure that concentrations of radioactive material in mill areas and in waste discharged into streams are brought within permissible limits." But at the same time the AEC press release said: "The Commission believes that no *immediate* health hazard exists as a result of the discharge of the mills' effluent into the Animas."[284]*

This is another example of AEC semantic duplicity: nobody else was worried about the "immediate" health hazards, either; the danger was acknowledged all along to be a long-term hazard. But by thus diverting attention from the real problem, these statements convinced many of the affected people that there was no hazard of any kind.

As with the uranium miners, the AEC met its criticism by refusing to acknowledge the seriousness of the problem. In a speech later that year, for example, Jesse Johnson, the director of the AEC's Division of Raw Materials, said, "There are some natural water supplies both in this country and in Europe that have a similarly high radium content. These have been used for years as a source of domestic water."[285] There is a fallacy and a tragedy in this kind of irresponsible remark—fallacy in that, contrary to his implication, neither Jesse

* Emphasis added.

Johnson nor anyone else *knew* whether those other water supplies he spoke of had been causing an increase in cancer all those years. The natural rate of cancer is about one in 340 persons each year.[93] Most of the areas of which he spoke are remote and don't even have as many as 340 persons to begin with. If they did, and if their cancer rate were doubled, only one extra case would appear, hardly an obvious phenomenon (except to the extra victim). The tragedy in this remark is that it uses the prestige of the Atomic Energy Commission to lure people into the false security that nothing really is wrong, thus serving to delay the necessary corrective measures.

AEC attempts to explain away the high concentrations of radium in the food crops displayed a remarkable ignorance in high places within the AEC. The director of the AEC's Division of Operational Safety, Dr. Peter A. Morris, said during Senate hearings on the matter, "On the agricultural problem, it is my understanding that the study shows that the radium came from the topsoil and not from the irrigation water. I would like to be corrected on that. This was my understanding."[286] Senator Edmund Muskie had to point out the obvious to Dr. Morris: that when you irrigate with radioactive water, any radioactivity found in the food crops is likely to have come from the water and not from the topsoil. The subject was quietly dropped.

Naturally the question of responsibility came up. As with the uranium miners' tragedy, the AEC tried to fix the blame elsewhere, first on a nonradioactive cause for the "biological desert" downstream of the Durango mill. They blamed the chemical toxicity of an "organic raffinate" discharge from the mill rather than the radium itself.[287] However, state officials have pointed out that although the organic-raffinate compound itself is not radioactive, the waste fraction called "organic raffinate" which was dumped directly into the river contained more radium than any other waste leaving the mills.[282]

10 · POLLUTION AS A WEAPON?

AT LEAST one person realized the potent pollution power that Durango, Colorado, had over its downstream neighbors in New Mexico: In those days there was a water dispute between Colorado and New Mexico. Arthur Ballantine, Jr., the publisher of the Durango *Herald News,* suggested (in a signed editorial) that unless New Mexico's senators came around to his way of thinking in the dispute, a resumption of the release of all radioactive effluents from the Durango mill should commence forthwith so as to pollute the water supply of Farmington, New Mexico, again. He went on to say that "this may not seem nice, but the most effective way to fight fire is with fire."[288] But pollution can go both ways: Although Farmington is *downstream* from Durango, Durango is *downwind* from Farmington. Ten years later the massive Four Corners Power Plant near Farmington, a single plant which produces more air pollution than New York and Los Angeles combined, was described in the Durango paper as an "unqualified disaster," as smog drifted from Farmington up to Durango, the other way this time.[289]

11 · AIR POLLUTION BY URANIUM TAILINGS

WATER POLLUTION by radium isn't the only hazard to be expected from 100 million tons of uranium tailings. As polluters, tailings are versatile. The radioactive dust itself blows for many miles, but more dangerous than that is the radon gas which percolates up through the tailings, changing to its daughter products on the way, causing high concentrations of airborne radioactivity above and around the piles. State and federal health authorities measured this radioactive air and found high levels outdoors. They had cause for concern, because many of the piles are very close to centers of population; the huge pile at Durango, for example, towers two hundred feet just above the town.

Even the AEC made measurements on and around the piles. Although some administrators there were clearly interested in covering up the problem, there were others in the AEC who simply went about their business measuring things without ideological bias. In 1958 the AEC's Health and Safety Laboratories made their own measurements around the mills and found that in all cases even the air above these vast piles contained high levels of radioactivity.[290] They even went so far as to recommend that such areas be restricted and that *the public be excluded*. Two years later another AEC study called attention to the possible hazards from the tailings piles themselves[291] and recommended additional studies.[292]

But again the built-in mechanism designed to separate the AEC's promotional interests from the regulation functions within the same organization failed, because it was *nine years later that the public was finally excluded from the piles*.[293] It was during these nine years, as we shall see, that the worst abuses took place.

Although these studies clearly didn't worry the AEC, they certainly worried the Colorado State Department of Health, because although the most dangerous concentrations measured were directly over the piles, the potential for unknown hazard was certainly real and the record of the AEC by now was hardly reassuring. Even today the air in downtown Grand Junction, Colorado, is three to four times more radioactive than the air in similar towns without uranium mills.[294] So the Colorado State Department of Health asked for an explanation of the dangers suggested by these AEC studies. The AEC's acting chairman at that time, Gerald Tape, replied that the AEC studies were not valid to prove dangers, since *they were designed only to develop analytical techniques and not to prove danger.*[295] The AEC has subjected state and federal public-health officers to that sort of evasiveness and arrogance for twenty years. Much of the AEC's problems today stem from its tactical error in presenting that same face to the public, in connection with the AEC's massive promotion of nuclear electric-generating stations across the country.

12 · WHAT TO DO WITH 100,000 TONS OF RADIOACTIVE SAND

WHAT WORRIED the states most was what was going to happen to the piles in the future. By 1966 most of the piles were pulled back from the rivers, and the tailings were in direct contact with the water only during the spring floods. The only pile actually owned by the AEC itself was flattened, covered with topsoil and grassed over at a cost of over $300,000,[296, 297] and even this ambitious project was described by the Federal Water Pollution Control Agency as only "adequate for a period of twenty years or so."[281] Considering the cost, the states did not expect that all the other piles would be similarly covered voluntarily by the owners, a job that the AEC estimated would cost about $10 million[275] but would probably cost five times that today. Moreover, since the best treatment was good for only "twenty years or so," it became clear that perpetual maintenance would be required, because the fact is that the piles will continue to be dangerously radioactive for an incredible ten thousand years. Aware that unless responsibility for these tailings was assigned quickly it would be only a matter of time until, through bankruptcy or other corporate changes, the states or, in one case, the Navajo Indians[298] would inherit the entire lot by default. The abandoned coal mines throughout the East and the placer mining operations in the West testify that it had happened before.

But the AEC didn't want the albatross around its neck, either. Through its mill-licensing program, it still had control over all the piles and could under law require the stabilization and covering over of them all at any time. Despite promises to the states that no mill license (and, hence, responsibility) would be permitted to terminate without a complete review of the tailings problem,[299] the AEC, no stranger to ducking responsibility, arbitrarily decided in 1966 that when a mill owner's license terminated, further control of tailings was not required.[300] The AEC's arguments about the responsibility of the states notwithstanding, the effect of this action was to remove the uranium-mill tailings from any control at all.

The state of Colorado protested this action, with the support of the U.S. Public Health Service,[301] but it did no good. The AEC, without outside consultation and without publishing any supportive data, and in the face of the opposition of every single state and federal agency that had anything at all to do with the problem, arbitrarily concluded that the uranium tailings piles presented no hazard to the environment, *either short-term or long-term.*[302]

And so the millions of tons of radioactive sand were suddenly no longer the responsibility of the AEC. With the exception of Colorado, where state control took over immediately, the tailings piles would just have to wait until they caused some real trouble before anyone else would step in with control measures. And by that time, of course, it would be too late.

In its summary, the AEC made the same sanctimonious assurance found in its pitch for the Lyons, Kansas, atom dump and for virtually every nuclear promotion before or since: *"We find it difficult to conceive of any mechanism whereby the radioactive material, which is now so widely dispersed, could become so concentrated as to exceed current applicable standards for protection against radiation."*[303]*

As I pointed out earlier, at the same time this was said a mechanism was operating which was doing the inconceivable. The radioactive material did become concentrated, but this was not the first

* Emphasis added.

time that everyone else was right and the AEC turned out to be wrong, despite its arrogant certitude; by now it was getting to be a habit.

13 · INDOOR RADON

HERE'S HOW it happened: Early in 1966, federal and state radiological health officials were in Grand Junction, Colorado, evaluating a new means of detection for radioactive atmospheres in the mines. The device, called a radon film badge, never did amount to much,[304] but what the two men learned on that trip amounted to a great deal.

Robert D. Siek, the director of the Radiological Health Section of the Colorado State Department of Public Health, and Robert N. Snelling of the U.S. Public Health Service's Southwestern Radiological Health Laboratory, were walking past some new construction when they noticed some trucks unloading fill into an excavation. What caught their eye was that the fill material was not the ordinary sand usually used; it was a gray, finer sand, characteristic of uranium tailings. (Fill is used to level an area before a concrete floor is poured, to fill in behind newly poured cellar walls and generally to round out an excavation after the concrete foundation is completed.)

Starting with the truck drivers, they questioned many people and quickly determined that for over ten years most of the sandy fill material used for new construction in the area was uranium tailings, taken from the big AEC-licensed Climax Uranium Company mill in downtown Grand Junction.

The health officers were alarmed because they knew that to put tons of uranium tailings beneath a home is to duplicate very nearly the situation in a uranium mine. There the radium contained in the ore slowly changes into radioactive radon gas, which seeps out of the rocks and into the mine, continuously changing into radon-daughter particles on the way. As already mentioned, radium is not removed from the uranium ore during the milling process. Therefore, tailings are at least as dangerous as the ore itself and probably more so, since the radium in tailings is far more concentrated, being undiluted by the waste rock surrounding the ore in the mine.

When tailings are used under homes, the same radon gas seeps up through the cement slabs upon which these buildings are built and accumulates inside the home. Just as in the mines, the radon gas changes to radon daughters, and people who stay home are thereby exposed to the same dangers as the miners underground. But this is not the only hazard. Radon daughters failing to make it through the cellar slab are entrapped in the concrete and still emit gamma rays, which can penetrate the concrete and are particularly strong near the floors, where children spend much of their time. The amount of the radioactivity in the air inside those homes, as in the mines, is variable, depending greatly on ventilation. Consequently, the situation is far more dangerous in the winter, when windows are closed, than in the summer, when breezes sweep the radioactive particles outdoors.

The threat of radon gas in thousands of homes in Grand Junction was truly alarming to the Colorado State Department of Health. It appeared even worse than the problem with the miners, because there were many more people involved and they were of all age groups, but the special worry was for those most sensitive to atomic radiation: small children and the unborn. It was the babies who would suffer most. Not only are they more sensitive to atomic radiation than adults generally, but they would receive the highest dose of radiation of the whole family; they spend more time at home than adults, breathing the radioactive air, and they would get most of the gamma-ray dose, being closer to the floors. It would develop later, as the problem became larger with each investigation by the Colorado Department of Health, that their older brothers and sisters were going to radioactive schools all those years.

The Colorado Department of Public Health projected that by

1971 there would be five thousand homes in that state which had used tailings for construction purposes. In order to make comprehensible the doses that were involved, the department calculated that the lungs of the occupants in ten percent of those homes are ex posed to radiation equivalent to 553 chest X rays per year for *each occupant*.[305] Furthermore, that report describes the radiation dose to the lungs alone, due to inhaled radon-daughter particles; it does not account for the exposure that might be the most serious of all, the gamma rays that emanate through the cement floors themselves.

On November 17, 1971, Colorado's Board of Health voted to begin notifying Grand Junction homeowners of the dangers beneath their feet.[306] The letter reads in part:

DEAR SIR:

An official report on our survey of your property for the presence of uranium mill tailings is enclosed. The study, as you will note, confirms the presence of uranium tailings on your property.

There is little precise scientific information about the long-term health effects of low-level radiation such as exists in your home. However, all scientific authorities agree that all exposure to man-made radiation should be removed or reduced to the lowest possible level, and we consider any use of uranium tailings for building construction purposes potentially hazardous from a health viewpoint.

A gamma map of your property, showing where the tailings are located, is enclosed for your guidance. The shaded areas are those in which the radiation readings are the highest. . . .

As if the threat to public health wasn't enough, owners of the radon homes found that the value of their houses decreased markedly in value. The first among many, a candy company promising six hundred new jobs for Grand Junction, changed its plans. But Grand Junction's problems didn't stop there: Rex Johnson, a Veterans Administration loan guarantee officer, indicated that the VA was considering blocking loan approval for purchases of homes where the radiation indoors exceeded safe levels.[307]

An engineering study prepared for the AEC concluded that the cost of removing the tailings from beneath the homes in Grand Junction would be very high.[308] In the case of one home valued at

$32,000, the AEC determined that more than $15,000 worth of work would be required to remove all the tailings. AEC Commissioner Larson estimated that the entire bill could run as high as $15 million,[309] which is about fifteen percent of the assessed valuation of the entire county.[310] But Larson's estimate was biased, of course; it did not include the ten school buildings or the many business establishments involved, nor did he take into account the structures in over a dozen other communities in Colorado alone or the several areas in other states believed to be similarly affected.

How this problem came to be, and who is responsible, is still being bitterly argued. Because, as the history of the problem demonstrates, all the tailings were removed from mills which were under the strict authority and control of the AEC. (The state assumed control only in 1968, when Colorado became an "AEC agreement state.") Furthermore, the tailings were used for construction purposes with the full knowledge of the AEC. Not only was the big mill within a mile of the AEC's Grand Junction Operations Office, but the piles there were inspected by the AEC on a monthly basis. Between 1952 and 1966, some 200,000 tons of tailings were removed from those piles by the public, and at no time did an AEC inspector issue a "noncompliance citation" to the mills for permitting this practice.[311] Much of the dispute centers around whether it was true, as most people assumed with good reason, that tailings were used with the approval of the AEC as well.

14 · THE AEC ATTEMPTS TO COVER UP

IN ANY CASE it was clear that the AEC made it difficult for health officials to get any cooperation in the early days, even to define the extent of the hazard. Small wonder, too, since it was clear (as AEC personnel conceded privately) that the indoor radon problem is potentially as great an embarrassment to the AEC as was its radioactive-fallout blunders of the 1950s and early sixties.

Even before the discovery of the indoor radon problem in Colorado, the AEC was aware that tailings were being used for construction purposes there and not only did nothing to stop the practice, but was unresponsive to inquiries into the questions of safety involved.

For example, in 1963, eight years before it was discovered that hundreds of homes in Durango, Colorado, were built on uranium tailings, Dr. Arthur L. Warner, the county medical director there, wrote to Dr. Donald I. Walker, then the regional director of the AEC's Division of Compliance.[312] The Vanadium Corporation of America's tailings pile caused "serious concern within this community," Dr. Warner said. He asked the AEC for information concerning the use of these tailings in the construction of "small buildings."

I asked Dr. Walker if he had ever answered Dr. Warner's inquiry. Dr. Walker, now director of the Health Services Laboratory at the AEC's Idaho Operations Office, acknowledged that he did not make a written reply[313] but that Dr. Warner did receive the AEC's "1961 letter" (referred to later), a warning letter that the AEC alleges it sent to nine different state health departments but that cannot be found by any one of those departments.

The next year, Page Edwards, manager of the Vanadium Corporation's Durango mill, also asked the AEC for advice concerning the use of tailings for construction purposes. The AEC did not answer that question but simply replied that "tailings . . . are not subject to the AEC licensing requirements."[314]

By then (still before the discovery of the indoor radon problem), even official channels record that there had been "widespread use of tailings in construction materials, for sand traps on golf courses and for *children's sandboxes*,"* according to one official's report of a Public Health Service meeting held in Cincinnati in 1964, a meeting attended by Dr. Walker and another AEC representative.[315] The AEC assurance that tailings were so harmless that they could be used

* Emphasis added

in children's sandboxes became so popular that even Senator Muskie had to settle that question during the Senate hearings on the subject.[316]

After discovery of the indoor radon problem by the Colorado State Department of Public Health, the AEC, both on an unofficial level and on an official level, sought to impede investigations into the nature of the problem.

The earliest example of this occurred in 1966, just after the discovery of the problem. Since children are the most sensitive to radiation, it was important to measure radioactivity in the schools. Robert D. Siek of the Colorado Department of Public Health and Robert N. Snelling of the U.S. Public Health Service, the men who discovered the problem in the first place, along with Dr. Cecil Reinstein, the Mesa County health officer, met with the superintendent of schools in Grand Junction in 1966 to explain the problem and secure permission to make measurements in the schools. Siek remembers that the superintendent said he would have to consult with his "scientific adviser" in such matters, James Westbrook, who was a member of the school board and also an assistant manager of the AEC's Grand Junction Operations Office. Remarkably, the health officer's request was turned down.[317]

Today, in his defense, Westbrook claims that the measurement technique proposed at that time (the radon film badge) was imprecise.[318] Siek acknowledges that the technique is only a fair one,[319] but even so it could hardly have failed to give an idea of the extent of the problem. Grand Junction is the county seat of Mesa County. In July 1970 the Colorado State Department of Public Health informed the Mesa County school board that fifteen of its schools had been built on tailings and that in at least one schoolroom (in Pomona Elementary School) the airborne radioactivity exceeded the federal limits permitted in uranium mines.[320]

On an official level as well, the AEC tried to hinder all meaningful efforts to arrive at a solution to the problem. Its tactics remained unchanged from the days of the uranium miners' problem. Using every means to convince people that the problem didn't exist at all, the AEC went so far as to sabotage the funding requests of the only other agency that was investigating the problem. In 1967 the Colorado State Department of Public Health (and the Southwestern Radiological Health Laboratories) requested funds from the National Center for Radiological Health of the U. S. Public Health Service. It needed support to carry out the surveys necessary to define the extent and seriousness of the indoor radon problem. The AEC, officially this time, managed to review the grant request and *on the AEC's recommendation* the U. S. Public Health Service turned down the state's request for funds. The AEC review,[321] a scientific smokescreen, actually suggests that the high levels of radon which were found in the homes by the health department could have come from *natural causes*. "Therefore," it said, "a further sampling program . . . does not seem warranted." Incredibly, the AEC blamed the problem on natural causes until early 1971.

About that time, the University of Colorado Medical Center in Denver applied to the AEC for funds to study chromosomal breakage, an early barometer of radiation damage, among children in the radon homes. In March of 1971, at a meeting between Governor Love, Colorado medical and health people, and six AEC representatives, AEC technicians, minimizing the hazard of indoor radon, indicated that a chromosomal study in Grand Junction "had no validity" and suggested that the Surgeon General's guidelines (discussed later) were invalid as well. AEC Chairman Glenn Seaborg turned down the grant himself in a letter to Governor Love. The governor managed to obtain other funds, and in a matter of months investigators uncovered some rather frightening findings (the Kempe-Ross testimony, to be discussed later).

Not only did the AEC seek to impede research efforts to identify the problem, but it refused to accept the existence of the problem and, on an unofficial level, and an official level as well, sought to convince the public and the Joint Committee on Atomic Energy that the problem either didn't exist at all or was due to natural causes and should therefore be ignored.

For example, Robert Catlin, the assistant director of operational safety for the AEC, came to Colorado to explain the indoor radon problem. He appeared on Denver television in February of 1970,[322] along with General Edward Giller, the AEC's director of military applications, and Dr. Edward A. Martell and myself, representing the Colorado Committee for Environmental Information, a group of scientist-critics.

Referring to the indoor radon problem, the moderator asked Catlin, "Is there an element of lack of responsibility in allowing such tailings to be used in this fashion?"

I have excerpted fairly three quotes from Catlin's complete answer which explain his main points: 1. "Well, I think in general that the use of mine tailings for construction purposes probably, from what I've heard, predates the Atomic Energy Program." 2. "Whether these constitute a risk is a moot point." 3. "I think it behooves us, however, to recognize at the same time that radiation in the home isn't just there because of tailings. There are materials of construction; if one uses bricks in a house or certain concretes, it's possible to increase the background radiation level."

While Catlin's statements were true, they are only the smallest part of what is true, and this must have been known to him at the time. The use of tailings for construction purposes he referred to in quote 1 above was the 1969 discovery of Colorado's Health Department that ten old homes in Uravan, Colorado, were built on radium diggings of the 1920s.[323] Radon levels in seven of those homes actually exceeded the level allowed in uranium mines. But twelve days before Catlin made those statements, an "Interagency Steering Committee" (referred to by Catlin on the TV show) had met, and those present learned that some hundreds of homes were already identified, and more than three thousand homes were suspected, as being built on uranium-mill tailings at that time, thereby contradicting his quote 1 above; and tentative U. S. Public Health Service guidelines, already known to be exceeded, were given out to those attending the meeting, thereby contradicting his quote 2 above. Three AEC representatives attended that meeting, which took place twelve days before Catlin made his statements, and one was Harvey F. Soule, an engineer in Catlin's own division. In his trip report[324] distributed to Catlin, Soule calculated that natural background radon could not account for the indoor radon levels being observed in Grand Junction and even said, "My own conclusions are that in some Grand Junction buildings over tailings, radon can be found in concentrations comparable to those in mines," thereby contradicting Catlin's quote 3 above.

On an official level as well, the AEC sought to convince its watchdog in Congress that the problem was of dubious existence. In February 1970 an AEC document was prepared to provide background information on the problem for use by members of the Joint Committee on Atomic Energy.[325] Presented in a question-and-answer format, the document asks: "What about radon in people's houses from tailings underneath them?" The answer contains these kinds of qualifications: "It was a *reported* practice to use uranium mill tailings"; "*in theory,* radon from this fill could diffuse into buildings"; "technical evaluation of this situation is *difficult* since traces of radium exist in virtually all soils"; "radon emanation is detectible in air almost *everywhere*"; "it is particularly detectible . . . in *masonry* structures."*

This answer strongly implies things which were known to be untrue at the time. "Reported practice" implies that it may never have taken place at all, yet the AEC was aware in February 1970 that the Colorado Department of Public Health had made hundreds of measurements proving that the problem was real and had already estimated that at least three thousand homes would be involved. To say "in theory . . . radon could diffuse into buildings" implies that it was not known whether it could take place or not; again the AEC was aware at the time of the results of the tests made by Colorado's Health Department, that the problem was not a theoretical possibility but an established fact. To suggest that radium and radon are "everywhere" is to suggest that the indoor radon problem is actually due to natural causes, a theory inconsistent with the high measurements being made by Colorado at that time and known to the AEC.

* Emphasis added.

Confronted with such skillful double-talk, it's not surprising that the Joint Committee on Atomic Energy was duped for so many years by the AEC. The Joint Committee joined the AEC in its culpability only when Jcint Committeemen refused to accept contrary testimony when it was finally presented to them (discussed later).

The AEC was so anxious to avoid having someone blame its tailings for the problem that even AEC employees assured townspeople in Grand Junction that the radon being measured by the state health people was due to natural causes.[282] Their statements, and the same allegations in the AEC review above, were made despite the fact that there was no evidence whatever to support this view.

So in order to lend believability to its claim that the whole problem was due to natural causes, the AEC began a research project entitled "Indoor Radon Daughters and Radiation Measurements in East Tennessee and Central Florida."[326] It was known that naturally high levels of radium exist in the surface soils in central Florida, and the AEC expected to find there a duplication of the indoor radon measurements made by the Colorado State Department of Health in Grand Junction. In this way the AEC sought to diminish the seriousness of the problem in Colorado by putting it in "proper perspective." As it turned out, the highest level (in Florida) reported by the AEC was only one percent of the highest equivalent measurements (five-minute grab samples) made by the Colorado Department of Health in Grand Junction,[327, 317] so the AEC report was put quietly to sleep. As a matter of fact, it has stamped on it: "NOTICE, THIS REPORT IS FOR INTERNAL USE ONLY. IT MAY NOT BE PUBLISHED." Interestingly, the AEC felt that it was all right to spend money for "research" to cover its tracks, but support of research to investigate the real problem in Grand Junction "does not seem warranted."[321]

Thus, the record of the AEC's handling of the indoor radon problem has at every point reflected a refusal to acknowledge the seriousness of the problem and a substantial effort to prevent others from doing so. The result has been that the solution has been impeded and the population at risk (the state's current estimate is fifteen thousand) has had its exposure unnecessarily prolonged, and that exposure, the equivalent of 553 chest X-rays each year per person, is nothing to ignore.

15 · THE AEC REWRITES HISTORY

IN THE UNSIGNED, undated "Staff Report" explaining "AEC Responsibilities Regarding the Mining and Milling of Uranium,"[328] major emphasis was placed on a claim that the AEC timely notified all the "applicable state health departments in early 1961 discussing the AEC's licensing authority over uranium mills and the health and safety considerations relative to the [selling or giving away] of sand tailings."[329] As indicated in the letter itself, ". . . *the radium content of these tailings may be such as to warrant control by appropriate state authorities . . .*"* A copy of the "1961 letter" was made a part of this document and given wide circulation. The AEC even used it before the Office of Management and Budget as late as 1971, as part of a request for supplementary money to conduct additional studies of the indoor radon problem. Heading each copy of the "1961 letter" is the legend "This letter was sent to the State Health Department of the following states on March 7, 1961: Colorado, Utah, Wyoming, New Mexico, Arizona, Oregon, Washington, South Dakota, and Texas."

If this letter had in fact been sent, it might vindicate, to some extent at least, the AEC's complete silence on the dangers it had left behind in the aftermath of its quest for raw materials. But nobody could remember the letter.

I asked the Colorado State Department of Public Health to search its files for the "1961 letter"; it could not be found. At my request, that department polled the other eight states named by the AEC

* Emphasis added

as having been sent that letter, and all of the appropriate radiation health officers of all of the state health departments named in the AEC's letter responded. Wyoming's Robert E. Sundin said: "We have searched our files and have failed to locate the March 7, 1961, USAEC Staff Report . . . The materials contained in the report are *interesting* and I believe *we would have no reason for not retaining it* . . ."[330]* Marshall W. Parrott of Oregon said: "I found the letter supposedly sent to Oregon in 1961 most interesting. Unfortunately, I have been unable to locate a copy of this letter in our files."[331] Arizona "could not find this letter in our files either."[332] South Dakota was "not able to locate the particular letter."[333] And neither was Texas.[334] Utah[335] and New Mexico, asked whether they had the letter,[336] responded in the negative as well, as did Washington[337] with a simple "We do not." Thus, not one of the states named has a record of this correspondence.[338]

I raised the question of the "1961 letter" before the Joint Committee at its first hearings into the indoor radon problem in late 1971.[339] It is interesting to observe that the 1961 letter was signed and dated. That's the way the AEC used to do things before the turning point came in 1962 after the fallout embarrassment. Since then AEC staff reports not only are unsigned and undated but also carry no identifying marks whatever, even to indicate that they have originated at the AEC. The author of that letter was Harold L. Price, the AEC's director of regulation and the man who first held that position after it was created in 1961 as a consequence of the internal reorganization of the AEC, designed to provide "built-in objectivity" (discussed in Chapter I). Although Price had resigned from the AEC only two weeks before,[340] he presented his position to the Joint Committee: he had sent the letter and could offer no explanation as to why it had not been found by the intended recipients. Remembering Seaborg's response to Senator Church (a "report on a report"—see Section 4, this chapter), all the AEC said was that the letter had been sent. It did not guarantee that it was received.

But as Robert D. Siek of the Colorado Public Health Department

* Emphasis added.

said, "It would seem that if such a letter was indeed sent to the indicated states, that at least one of the states would have some knowledge or record of the correspondence."[341] Thus, it seems inconceivable that nine such important letters could all get lost in the mail. But there is another possibility: the indoor radon problem is certain to become the AEC's greatest embarrassment since the days of radioactive fallout. Accordingly, many people in the AEC are very anxious to avoid blame for their agency, and rewriting history is one way of doing that.

16 · THE GRAND JUNCTION REACTION: *ENEMY OF THE PEOPLE* REVISITED

THE AEC WASN'T the only obstacle in the way of solving this problem. Grand Junction, Colorado, the town with the atomic motif on the city seal, was equally unfriendly to the efforts of the State Health Department, and it still is. But the hostility of town fathers in general toward health officers who discover a local problem is a very old story.[342] The problem is usually seen not as it is, a real danger to health, but only as a threat to property.

The business community, the first to express open hostility, still actively works against what it has said is an "imaginary problem." Howard H. McMullin, a local banker, actually requested the governor of the state to bring charges against the "empire builders" and "self-seekers" in the State Public Health Department for working "against the public good." He closed his letter to the governor with a sentence that says it all: "If matters like this continue, real estate values can be destroyed by loose talk and this would affect our business."[343]

There was opposition from the local doctors, too, despite their nominal commitment to public health. Dr. Geno Saccomanno, the same man who testified before the Joint Committee on Atomic Energy in 1967 that it was cigarettes and not radon that were causing lung cancer among the miners, had an even more remarkable observation about the indoor radon problem. A news report quotes him as saying at a public hearing, "We doubt that cancer is caused by radiation, even at high levels."[344] Dr. Bruce A. Ward, a radiologist from St. Mary's Hospital, is quoted in the local paper as saying, "It's inconceivable in any normally ventilated home, that a significant amount of radon daughters could be trapped in the lungs."[345] Apparently Ward could not "conceive" of what was public knowledge at the time, that countless measurements by instruments had established beyond doubt that airborne radiation was dangerously high in thousands of homes in his town.

The local press, the *Daily Sentinel,* has always reserved its limited supply of skepticism for critics of the AEC, but when it finally editorialized against the AEC it did so not for its concern for public health, but for its concern for property. Advocating immediate removal of the tailings by the AEC, it said: "If the question is taken into court it will be a lengthy procedure. It will cause extensive damage in *unfavorable publicity* for both AEC and Grand Junction."[346]*

The position of the politicians is particularly reprehensible. Mayor Stanley Anderson told *Cervi's Journal* that he believes the structures to be safe and that his opinion is shared by the majority of the citizens of Grand Junction, who are "snickering at" or simply "ignoring" reports of danger from mill tailings.[347] Congressman Wayne Aspinall said, "I have friends who wouldn't even let researchers into their homes for the simple reason it's so much trouble-making."[348] Aspinall is a member of the Joint Committee on Atomic Energy.

None of these attitudes could stand long if the public were in disagreement with them. Like the people in Lyons, Kansas,[349] Grand Junction folks ignored the evil to befall their pleasant little town. After all, for a booming decade Grand Junction owed a lot to the AEC. But with the AEC's Grand Junction Operations Office not

* Emphasis added.

worried, their doctors not worried, their mayor and their Congressman not worried, and their press and their business community worried only about property values, the people of that abused little town can hardly be blamed for feeling that the whole problem is just make-believe.

17 · DEFINING THE DANGER

ALTHOUGH the indoor radon levels in Grand Junction were high and known to be dangerous, there were no applicable public-health guidelines at the time to establish *legally* the danger or safety of the exposed population. Early in 1970 the Colorado State Department of Public Health requested the U. S. Public Health Service to provide some numbers so that the state could better determine how many of those homes built on tailings were dangerous to live in.

Fortunately scientists didn't have to start from scratch. Since the health hazard was identical to that with the uranium miners, all of the work already done on that problem[350] was applied to the new problem of determining a health standard for occupants of the radon homes. Of course, an adjustment had to be made for the fact that instead of a forty-hour work week, longer periods, typically, are spent at home. Also, consideration was given to the fact that the home population, containing infants, children and pregnant women, is more sensitive to radiation than a population of miners.

Six months later, Dr. Jesse L. Steinfeld, the U. S. Surgeon General, produced what has since become known as the "Surgeon General's Guidelines."[351] They provide three categories of exposure to radon daughters indoors, ranging from low (where no corrective action is indicated) through an intermediate level to a high level where "remedial action is indicated." That is bureaucratese for "Do something about it now "

Down but not out, the AEC prepared another of its unsigned "staff critiques," this time of the Surgeon General's Guidelines themselves.[352] Regarding the guidelines rather negatively, the AEC stated that the Surgeon General's "recommendations in their present form are difficult to implement" and it complained that they "do not identify the remedial actions contemplated." But this "staff critique" didn't have the steam and conviction of earlier ones, perhaps because the AEC position was becoming steadily harder to justify.

Well, now that they had some guidelines, the Colorado health people were finally in a position to make some judgments from all the measurements they had made for four years. In the summer of 1970 the State Public Health Department informed the Mesa County School District that radiation was a serious problem in the public schools (see Section 14, this chapter). In May 1971, letters went out to the Grand Junction city manager[353] and the Chamber of Commerce[354] recommending that real-estate sales be restricted until it can be determined that the property is free of tailings. On July 12 the Board of County Commissioners decreed that building permits would be granted only "with the provision that if tailings are present, they be removed prior to the erection of buildings."[355]

18 · WHICH HOMES ARE HOT?

WELL, what was the "remedial action" to be? The problem in the mines was solved by ventilation with big fans; could that even be considered for a home? Paul Smith, formerly of the Public Health Service and now the Denver representative of the Radiation Office of the Environmental Protection Agency, said early on, "The only way to avoid the problem is to remove the source." And that was what was finally agreed upon: the homes would have to be dug out and the tailings removed from beneath them.

The "Interagency Steering Committee on Indoor Radon," composed of representatives of the state of Colorado, the Environmental Protection Agency, the U. S. Public Health Service and the AEC, was formed in late 1970. It met in Grand Junction in August 1971,[356] and in Denver in September.[357] The unanimous recommendation of its own medical advisory group was reported by Dr. Robert Ross, then president of the Mesa County Medical Society: "In instances where tailings have been found under and adjacent to buildings in the Grand Junction area, it was agreed that the tailings should be removed and the AEC is the responsible agency for removal of the tailings."[358]

The Denver meeting, which, according to the press, was "punctuated by sharp dialog," was by no means unanimous in the view that the AEC pay for the damage. The final opinion of the Interagency Steering Committee was "to recommend complete removal of all tailings within ten feet of a habitable structure." The State Department of Health and the two representatives of the Environmental Protection Agency voted in support of this opinion; the AEC members, voting against the motion,[359] were "visibly shaken and angry" at the outcome.[360]

The state was encouraged by the vote, because it had been widely expected that the EPA would support the AEC's position. This was because most of the members and all of the bosses of the Division of Criteria and Standards of the Office of Radiation Programs of the newly formed Environmental Protection Agency (EPA) were formerly AEC people. The AEC men were moved over to EPA from the AEC as part of President Nixon's abortive effort to dilute the self-regulation aspect of the AEC.[361] The rest of the staff of that division, outnumbered two to one by ex-AEC personnel, were moved over from the U. S. Public Health Service. That shuffle accomplished far more mischief than it was designed to cure and illustrates some of the behind-the-scenes maneuvers which take place in Washington among the regulated agency, the regulator agency, and their watchdogs in Congress.

In the past, the AEC and Public Health Service people had their fights in the open record. Now in the same office, they hammer out their positions behind closed doors. There is an inevitable clash of philosophies between public-health officers and representatives of a promotional-minded engineering agency like the AEC; moving desks around within the federal bureaucracy doesn't change that fact. Judging from the composition of EPA's Division of Criteria and Standards, it might be expected that whenever a public-health judgment clashed with maintaining the good name of the AEC and their good friends back there, that judgment would always be made in favor of the AEC.

EPA's final resolution of this issue confirmed the state's worst suspicions. Dr. Stuart Black and Jay Silhanek, the EPA men who voted in Denver against the AEC position, were formerly with the U. S. Public Health Service. But the director of the Division of Criteria and Standards was there, too, and he was Dr. Paul Tompkins, the man who was the executive director of the Federal Radiation Council and who presented the FRC's justification for raising the standards for iodine 131 and strontium 90 when the fallout levels rose so dramatically in the early 1960s.[146]

Ex-AEC men within EPA opposed the vote of the EPA representatives at the Denver meeting and actually tried to get their men to change their votes. The next few days were spent in meetings between the EPA, the AEC and the Joint Committee, later described by Glenn E. Keller, Jr., the president of Colorado's Board of Health, as "midnight skulduggery."[362, 379] Black and Silhanek were subjected to close questioning by an EPA attorney (described by someone present as "an inquisition"), but it was too late; the Interagency Steering Committee meeting was over, the vote couldn't be changed. There was only one thing left to do. Paul Tompkins publicly disavowed the vote of the EPA representatives. Dr. Tompkins said, "We're not advocating tailings come out no matter how small the level or how expensive the cost."[360]

But twelve years had passed between the first hearings on the uranium miners' problem and the final establishment of the present standards. Colorado was not prepared to wait that long again; i had waited too long already. The AEC was first put on notice in the middle 1950s, that tailings were dangerous. The state of Colorado discovered the indoor radon problem in 1966 and first asked for federal guidelines in early 1970. While bureaucrats bickered, many thousands of Coloradoans had to spend that much more time living under conditions approaching the radioactivity of a uranium mine (or an average equivalent of several hundred X rays per year for each person). It became apparent that repeated assurance of "no immediate danger" was no longer appropriate. The exposure had already become chronic.

Furthermore, the national reputation of Grand Junction was suffering considerably. If that town's name was to become synonymous with radioactivity, then the pressure to relocate for manufacturing companies already there would increase, while new companies contemplating a move to Grand Junction would change their plans (and have already done so). Some community leaders perceived that if the problem wasn't resolved quickly the town would "wither away."

19 · WHO'S RESPONSIBLE THIS TIME?

REPRESENTATIVE WAYNE N. ASPINALL (D., Colo.), who not only represents the area but is also a member of the Joint Committee on Atomic Energy, said just before his election to his twelfth term in Congress in 1970 that "Uncle Sam had control of the ultimate product, uranium," and that "it may be necessary for Uncle Sam to take the lead" in solving the tailing problem. Regarding the AEC's position, that it didn't have legal jurisdiction over the piles (see below), Aspinall went on to say, "I have always believed that the Commission should not hide behind this technicality." He even put a price tag on the whole cleanup operation; it was somewhat low: $10 million.[363] Joint Committee watchers were surprised at his comments, even though it was a pre-election speech. Aspinall, like his mentor Holifield, has always been one of the most outspoken hawks on the Joint Committee.

But after his reelection to office, he resumed his normal position. Just one year later, in a complete about-face, the Grand Junction newspaper quoted the Congressman as saying, "The [U. S.] Public Health Service and the Colorado Health Department are trying to force the Federal Government to accept responsibility for removing the tailings." The paper went on to quote Aspinall: "The costs of removal are too great and government treasuries are too limited. The sooner we get this into our heads, the better off and the more logical we will be."[364]

Aspinall's post-election reversal drew criticism but, significantly, not a lot from his own district. In Denver, Glenn E. Keller, Jr., the president of the State Board of Health, said, "I should think Mr. Aspinall's first responsibility shouldn't be to the AEC . . . but to the homeowners in Grand Junction. . . . I submit that the Federal Government has exercised extreme irresponsibility in this situation and Mr. Aspinall is sticking his head in the sand when he disclaims that."[365]

But the Congressman found himself having to choose between two mutually incompatible positions. On the one hand, Aspinall could continue to "represent the AEC" and his long-time supporters, the mining and milling companies, who themselves are already preparing their legal defense should they be enjoined, with the AEC, in a damage suit.[366] If he did this, he would alienate his constituency and lose the next election. On the other hand, if he reversed his position and demanded federal reparations for the damage caused by the AEC in his district, he would thereby tacitly admit to his own negligence, because the chain of responsibility for the whole mess doesn't stop at the AEC; the worst than can be said about that agency is that it was incompetent. Ultimate responsibility lies somewhere in the AEC's watchdog committee in Congress. It turns out that the chairman of the Subcommittee on Raw Materials of the Joint Committee on Atomic Energy is where the buck stops—and that man is Wayne N. Aspinall. So to push for the federal millions needed to dig out the tailings would be to admit to his own incompetence in permitting the problem to have occurred in the first place. Or at least that is one popular explanation of the paradox of a Congressman representing the "federal view"[348] against his own constituents.

When he was AEC chairman, even Glenn Seaborg said that the AEC "is concerned now" and "we'll be there with our shovels to dig out the sand and replace it with clean dirt if it comes to that."[367] But perhaps he spoke impulsively (he was in Hawaii speechmaking at the time), because on an official level the AEC does not agree; an AEC "Staff Report" prepared especially for this problem states: "It is AEC's view that it has no legal responsibility for the disposition of the tailings in its role of purchaser."[328]

Although the AEC admits that its responsibility over source material begins "at the door of the mine," Joseph F. Hennessey, then chief legal counsel for the AEC, explains its basis for this self-serving legalism: "We do have the basic legal authority to license and regulate *all* uses of uranium [but] there is a limitation in [the Atomic Energy Act] that exempts . . . any quantities of uranium that are in such concentrations as to be considered *unimportant by the Commission* . . . so our present posture is that the concentration of uranium in these waste piles is so substantially lower than our minimum concentration standard for exercise of regulatory authority that we are not in a position to impose any restrictions . . . on the mill tailings that are left over from abandoned operations."[368]* But nobody was aware of this decision. As far as Colorado's Governor John A. Love is concerned, the AEC's loss of jurisdiction was kept a *secret* outside the AEC.[369] A check in early 1972 confirms that Hennessey's opinion is still AEC policy.

Mr. Hennessey, having decided that the AEC has no legal responsibility under the Atomic Energy Act for the indoor radon problem, even went further and addressed himself to the water pollution of the Colorado River Basin. In answer to a Presidential executive order which states that "pollution caused by all other operations of the federal government such as . . . contracts, shall be reduced to

* Emphasis added.

the lowest level practicable,"[370] he said that the order "was promulgated by the President in furtherance of the purpose and policy of the Federal Water Pollution Control Act. [This] Act, in my view, did not authorize any enlargement upon the regulatory authority conferred upon the AEC."[178] Mr. Hennessey gave no other reasons to support his view, now AEC policy.

Unnoticed in the legalisms is the 1957 license application to the AEC from the Climax Uranium Company, the owners of the mill from which most of the tailings under the homes had come. Under the heading "Inventory" (of those things to be regulated) appears "Mill Tailings," and elsewhere in that document the following restriction turns up: "Residues and tailings are to be stockpiled and are not discarded into the river."[371] So it would seem that the AEC really was supposed to regulate those tailings after all.

Furthermore, in response to a 1959 request by the Vitro Corporation of America to *sell* a substantial amount of tailings for use as fill,[372] an AEC interoffice memorandum *recommended approval* of the sale of tailings for use "around a proposed sewage disposal plant at Salt Lake City, Utah," as well as "for sanding streets and sidewalks."[373]

Curiously, Hennessey himself said in 1966 that if the AEC felt that the piles "represented a health hazard, I think we could within our licensing authority, impose a requirement that the piles be stabilized."[368] Clearly, then, the AEC accepts or refuses responsibility as it pleases, using its own interpretations of law, without regard for the *intent* of the law, to support its position of self-interest.

20 · THE HOTHOUSES OF AMERICA: WHERE ARE THEY?

BUT THE INDOOR RADON PROBLEM in Grand Junction, Colorado, was discovered and finally evaluated despite the opposition from community leaders and the delaying tactics of the AEC. It was suddenly a lot easier for the Colorado Department of Health to obtain support to evaluate the problem elsewhere in that state. Using a truck-mounted mobile scanning laboratory, the department quickly identified hundreds of homes in Durango, to the total surprise of everyone there. By the summer of 1971 over thirty thousand structures were checked in fourteen Colorado communities, and over five thousand indicated the presence of tailings.[356]

Salt Lake City has a large pile of uranium tailings at the abandoned Vitro mill right in the middle of town. Not so fortunate as Coloradoans, the people there had to rely on the Utah State Department of Health, which assured everyone that no tailings were used for construction purposes anywhere in their state. But a newsman easily found many homes and other buildings which were built on tailings,[374] in addition to the sewage-treatment plant, where the approval of the use of tailings for construction was recommended by an AEC official.[373]

Wyoming, with many homes built just near the tailings piles, is another candidate for the list of affected areas. Well in advance of any findings whatever, the AEC's C. L. Van Alstine issued assurances to the contrary. "There is no danger here. A lot of this is scare stuff," he explained, adding that even in Colorado "they have yet to find proof of physical hazards."[375] Several months after he spoke, the truck-mounted screening unit of the Environmental Protection Agency moved into Wyoming and found eighty-seven "anomalies" in Riverton "which need to be followed up," according to Robert E. Sundin, Wyoming's director of industrial hygiene.[376] (Anomalies are abnormal readings indicating the "possibility of tailings under structures.")

It seems that if there's a big pile of fine clean sand free for the taking, people will use it even though it's radioactive, before going out to buy ordinary sand. And if the AEC isn't worried about it, why should the people be?

With that possibility in mind, the Environmental Protection Agency has just begun a massive survey to measure the radiation in the homes near the uranium mills in nine Western states. Those who have been close to the problem predict that at least three thousand more homes will be identified as unsafe before it's all over, bringing the total to almost seven thousand.

21 · THE JOINT COMMITTEE'S ROLE

As WE HAVE already seen from its hearings on radioactive fallout in the early sixties through the uranium miners' hearings in the late sixties, the Joint Committee on Atomic Energy has functioned less as a watchdog over the AEC and more as an indulgent parent, stepping in only to rescue its naughty child when the AEC got itself into some trouble it couldn't handle on its own. The indoor radon problem was no exception.

Hearings were finally held before the Subcommittee on Raw Materials of the Joint Committee on Atomic Energy in October of 1971.[309] Because the chairman was Representative Aspinall, there was apprehension that the two-day hearing was to be a "whitewash" of the federal involvement in the problem. According to the press, "despite disclaimers . . . that the session wouldn't be weighted in favor of the AEC . . . it approached that condition repeatedly." AEC and other federal witnesses were heard the first day and received friendly and courteous receptions. At the end of that day Chairman Aspinall "was moved to point out that he had already read statements [that the Colorado Department of Public Health] would offer the next day: 'I can't conceive of what they contend, being the facts,' said Aspinall."[366]

Predictably, then, the state health officers were "keel-hauled" by Aspinall and Holifield. The next day no attempt was made to conceal the collusion between the Joint Committee and the AEC, as runners scurried back and forth between Joint Committee staff aides on the podium and AEC personnel in the audience, carrying messages. Then staff aides of the Joint Committee members "circled behind them, serving up prepared and pointed questions for the Coloradoans, some of them so edged that the hearing took on the spirit of a criminal courtroom with witnesses about to be impeached for lying."[366]

Colorado's press was aroused at the behavior of the Joint Committee and commented editorially on the "hostile" and "abusive" tactics of Aspinall, branding him as "rude and wrong."[377] But, historically, mean and petty behavior on the part of Joint Committeemen is standard operating procedure there. For example, it's not uncommon for members of the Joint Committee deliberately to mispronounce the names of witnesses appearing before them who don't share their views.[378] That's the way it always has been, but it has never been news until today. The public's concern for the environment and newly found hostility for government bureaucracy in general, and the AEC in particular, makes it an issue now. But as usual the antiquated Joint Committee will be the last to perceive that not so subtle change of the country's mood.

The week of the hearings was the week of "midnight skulduggery," as Glenn E. Keller, Jr., Colorado State Board of Health president, described it.[362, 379] Almost an object lesson in what is bound to happen when checks and balances disappear, the AEC, the Environmental Protection Agency and the Joint Committee on Atomic Energy, all supposed to be operating at arm's length from each other and representing the public, held secret joint meetings, planning just how to handle Colorado's testimony. Keller summed up the situation by stating:

We have observed the efforts of the AEC first to deny the possibility of a problem, then to admit possibility but pooh-pooh probability, then to recognize a problem and deny responsibility, and finally, in the last few weeks, to engage frantically in behind-the-scenes efforts to avoid recommendations of the Interagency Steering Committee and the Medical Advisory Committee that the tailings be removed. . . . It casts serious doubt upon any testimony from the AEC before this committee, as it indicates a clear bias. We suggest, most respectfully, that this committee should carefully examine any testimony before it which represents special interests or attempts at bureaucratic justification.[380]

Well, what testimony was it that the Joint Committee wanted so badly to keep from the public? History was repeating itself. Five years before, the Woodward and Fondiller report, which predicted the extra lung cancers among the uranium miners, was presented before the Joint Committee. Then members of the committee attacked that report (see Chapter IV), and for the same reasons they tried to discredit the medical testimony in the 1971 hearings on the indoor radon problem: they refused to believe that the problem was real and they did not want to be bothered with any facts except those already in their possession, facts carefully assembled for them by individuals inside the AEC with long experience in the handling of congressional watchdog committees.

What the Joint Committee was most particularly interested in keeping out of the record was the Kempe-Ross testimony. Several times during his own testimony, the director of Colorado's Health Department, Dr. Roy Cleere, asked that the Kempe-Ross testimony be included, but each time Aspinall refused. If it was included at all, Aspinall explained, it would appear accompanied by an extensive rebuttal. Belittling the Kempe-Ross testimony, Aspinall remarked that even if it was accepted by the committee, it "wouldn't be worth too much."[366]

But the Kempe-Ross testimony had a lot to say. Dr. C. Henry Kempe is a professor and chairman of pediatrics at the University of Colorado School of Medicine in Denver, and Dr. Robert M. Ross, Jr., now past president of the Mesa County Medical Association, is a practicing pediatrician in Grand Junction.[381] In 1969, Dr. Ross began to take notice of what appeared to him to be too many cases of cancer among his young patients: he saw blood, muscle and nerve cancers in what seemed excessive numbers. He also saw birth defects: mongolism and premature fusion of the skull bones of infants, also too many, it seemed. He discussed his concern with Dr. Kempe in Denver, and it was agreed that the matter was important enough to investigate in a more rigorous manner.

Funds were requested of the AEC in order to conduct a study. It was this request which was disparaged by the AEC at the March 1971 meeting with Governor Love and ultimately denied in a letter to the governor by AEC Chairman Seaborg himself (see Section 14 of this chapter). The study went ahead anyway, and the Kempe-Ross testimony is only the first result.[382]

While the death rate due to birth defects was decreasing in the rest of Colorado, it was rising in Mesa County and was already fifty percent higher than the rest of the state, the study found. Similarly, the death rate due to cancer, stable in the rest of Colorado, was "significantly higher in Mesa County" and "steadily increasing." Cleft lip and palate were twice as high as in the rest of the state, and, according to Dr. Herbert Lubs, one of the researchers, the incidence of mongolism among the newborn was "almost three times what you'd expect."[383] Even the birth rate there was "significantly lower" than the rest of Colorado. This was the testimony the Joint Committee didn't want to hear.

But it is only the beginning. According to health officials, no further results will be published for some time, but "when they do publish their findings on cancer and leukemia, mongolism and other birth defects, that's when we're going to get the real fright," observed Board of Health President Keller. "And if the study comes up with house-to-house correlations, then we're going to have a panic situation."[384]

22 · RADIOACTIVE WASTE DISPOSAL IS TOO IMPORTANT TO BE LEFT IN THE HANDS OF THE AEC

THUS, not only did the AEC and the Joint Committee on Atomic Energy make the mistakes to start with, but the terrible irony is that they placed almost insurmountable obstacles in the path of everyone who has tried to solve each of their major blunders before it became a tragedy. The AEC was dead wrong about radioactive fallout, the Joint Committee desperately tried to stop the efforts of Secretary Wirtz to help the uranium miners, the AEC was hostile to the efforts of the Federal Water Pollution Control Agency to cure the radium pollution of waters on the Colorado Plateau (while the Joint Committee ignored the problem entirely), and the AEC did all it could to suppress its latest embarrassment, the indoor radon problem in Grand Junction, Colorado.

The paradox is that despite these failures, our nation must still rely on the *same team* to solve the far more difficult question of high-level radioactive-waste disposal. Just as the AEC was convinced that fallout wasn't dangerous, that uranium miners faced no unusual hazards underground, and that Grand Junction's radon homes could be blamed on natural causes, so it is firmly convinced today that salt-bed disposal is the only permanent solution to the radioactive-waste problems of tomorrow. But the AEC has had fifteen years and several hundred million dollars to make that decision, and its choice was another potential disaster: it picked one of the few wet salt mines in the world.

No better example than its history is needed to demonstrate the incompetence of the AEC to handle future problems of radioactive waste. Today as in the past, technical competence has always been available to the AEC through its contractor laboratories; that has never been the problem. The AEC's incompetence lies in its inability to use available capabilities because of consistent bad judgment stemming almost entirely from a desire to serve itself instead of the nation. When the best talent of an agency is wasted on justifying its past mistakes and avoiding responsibility for new ones, there is not much left over for anything else.

VI
ATOMIC GADGETS

*The requirements problem . . . is the tendency to
hold back the development of new hardware until
a . . . requirement is formally established by the
agency that would use the hardware. . . . I believe
that without the requirements problem, the progress
to date could have been accomplished sooner and at
lower cost.*

—JAMES T. RAMEY,
AEC Commissioner[411]

1 · MIRACLES FOR SALE

PREDICTABLY, the breakdown of checks and balances allowed the
AEC to indulge in unrestrained technical frivolities without precedent
since the building of the Pyramids—because, charged with promotion as it was, and given a blank check by Congress, the AEC was
able to coast along quite some way on our childlike awe of the
miraculous achievement of the Manhattan Project. Money had
bought us one miracle—why not more?

High priests of religion ran the affairs of men in the days when
no limits existed over man's belief in magic. It took the new priests
of science and technology, whose bewitching power could be more
readily demonstrated, to capture the imaginations of men and thus
emasculate the old priesthood forever. And so at least until very
recently the scientist and the engineer enjoyed a position of infallibility in men's minds unequaled since the power of the Church
before Galileo. Accordingly, even the sky was no limit as the AEC
found not only its legitimate programs but even its harebrained

schemes rolling in research millions. Soon billions would be thrown away on schemes so foolish they should never have gotten *on* the drawing boards, much less off. It wasn't until some spectacular failures that some AEC scientists and even Congress finally learned that the atom had its limitations after all.

The excuse made today that "the mysteries of science have to be probed to their depths first before we can judge what ideas are foolish" simply doesn't apply to everything. The one thing in common among all the failures is that not one of those programs would ever have been considered seriously by a private corporation with its own capital up at risk. The reasons are simple. Each fiasco could be seen at the start either to have utterly unsolvable technical difficulties or to be so ill-conceived that even if the technical problems could be made to vanish the thing would still be too dangerous or expensive to use; for only in the make-believe world of government funding, where the reason for the existence of a project can have very little to do with the project itself, could those expensive ideas survive. Also, in every case it was obvious from the start that even if the most optimistic view turned out to be correct, the use of the atomic alternative could not provide much better all-around performance than the conventional methods already in use. But that's not how things run in government bureaucracies with blank checks; if a powerful bureaucrat likes an idea and identifies with it, he can promote his program through the secret labyrinths of internal acceptance and Joint Committee funding and then become the program director. Once started, his program can't be turned off unless his idea is so bad that even insiders come to voice active opposition and it is finally canceled. Predictably, then, only the most outrageous ideas have been turned off entirely, while the simply bad ideas drag on and on.

2 · SUPPOSE WE CAN BUILD IT— THEN WHAT?

BY ALL ODDS, the all-time worst idea was Pluto. That program was so bad it was actually canceled.

The military potential of the nuclear reactor was recognized even before the "atomic pile" had successfully sustained a nuclear chain reaction.[386] The nuclear alternative's chief advantage is its ability to provide power for long periods of time without refueling. Its military disadvantages have to do with its limited portability due to the great weight of the shielding required to protect its operators from atomic radiation. Another great disadvantage, although more important to the public than to the military, is the enormous hazard posed by the release of huge quantities of radioactivity in the event of the destruction of the nuclear reactor in combat or through accidental collision.

All things considered, the nuclear reactor is singularly suited to naval vessels and particularly the submarine. Nuclear power has provided the real advantage of decreasing the vulnerability of naval vessels in a way not possible by conventional means. At the same time naval nuclear power has not subjected our nation to greater risks from atomic radiation than the benefits (extra military security) provided by going nuclear. Accordingly, the Naval Reactor Program was a great success.

But that question is fundamental to all nuclear technology: suppose we can build the nuclear alternative, will it really be better than the conventional method already in use, considering the extra risk? That question has rarely, if ever, been addressed *honestly* by the AEC before it embarked on a new nuclear adventure. Invariably, when risk-benefit analyses are made of new atomic schemes, every assumption concerning the nuclear alternative is extravagantly optimistic, while developments in the conventional method already in use are assumed to remain static during the decade or so it might take to develop its atomic equivalent.

Probably the best example of bad decision-making in this connection is the flying nuclear reactor. An idea as formidable in its destructive portent and as insane (from the point of view of the risks that society must take in order to receive the benefits promised) as was Pluto is hard (though not impossible) to find.

Described by the AEC as "a nuclear ramjet propulsion system supersonic low altitude missile,"[387] Pluto was a nuclear edition of the pilotless V-1 German "buzz-bomb" of World War II. It had an atomic jet engine and carried a nuclear warhead up front. Independent of refueling stops, this flying atomic bomb was to cruise at very low altitudes (to avoid detection by enemy radar) and at very high speeds (faster than sound) all the way to its target across the world.

Technical difficulties with Pluto were serious but not insurmountable, providing all you cared about was getting the thing from one place to another. As a matter of fact, even today the AEC is fond of pointing out the fact that Pluto *worked,* after all. But that depends upon what you mean by "worked." Pluto worked as a method for carrying an atomic bomb to a target in the same way that a tightrope strung between two tall buildings works as a way to cross the street.

Pluto's nuclear jet engine was simply an open-ended nuclear reactor. The idea was to draw air through its intensely hot interior and expel the heated air through the exhaust. The radiation shielding problem (any nuclear reactor needs extensive shielding to protect people nearby from lethal radiation) was not so important with Pluto, since without pilots there was less to shield. But after hundreds of millions of dollars had been spent (the AEC spent $23 million in 1961 on this program alone),[388] Pluto was finally canceled in 1964. About all that is left of it today is a cluster of abandoned concrete buildings on a bleak windswept saddle overlooking the Nuclear Rocket Development Station in the Nevada desert.

The reason for canceling Pluto was not technical at all, since by that limited criterion Pluto actually worked. But Pluto was a success only in the laboratory; when the time came to bring Pluto out into the real world, the project directors had to address themselves to the hazards which would be created by actually flying an open-ended nuclear reactor spewing millions of curies of fission products, and little pieces of the reactor itself, behind it wherever it went, to say nothing of the additional risk of carrying an atomic bomb aboard a missile cruising at greater than the speed of sound and at altitudes one to two thousand feet above ground. However bizarre to contemplate, those risks had to be multiplied by many hundreds of times, since Pluto was not intended to be a single weapon but rather an airborne armada. Furthermore, the fallout produced by the explosion of Pluto's atom bomb would be increased immeasurably by the simultaneous destruction of its nuclear-reactor engine, thereby endangering not only the enemy but ourselves as well.

Thus Pluto was perhaps the best example of a nuclear fiasco that never would have happened if responsible people in the atomic establishment had first asked the simple question "Suppose we *can* build it—then what?"

3 · IT WILL NEVER GET OFF THE GROUND

IT HAS ALWAYS been the case that the development of an atomic fiasco had to proceed to a point where the promoters themselves could see no way out of their technical dilemma before they would finally kill the program themselves. As absurd as some of the atomic gadgets are (especially those already canceled), no word of rebuttal has ever appeared in testimony before the Joint Committee on Atomic Energy. No Congressman has realistically scrutinized these mad ideas; the congressional watchdogs of the AEC simply rubber-stamped every funding request made of them and, in many cases, even forced excess funds into programs which for technological reasons actually required less money. Only the President himself and his Office of Management and Budget has ever attempted to foil the

Joint Committee funny money men, and even they have had only limited success.

But as ill-conceived as Pluto was, at least it "worked." There was another giant fiasco which not only never worked but its failure was predicted in advance. Between 1946 and 1961, over one and a half *billion* dollars was spent in an attempt to develop an atomic airplane.

Called the ANP (for Aircraft Nuclear Propulsion), the atomic airplane was to be, like Pluto, simply an open-ended nuclear reactor. It was obvious from the very beginning that there were formidable problems involved; most of them were, and still are, insurmountable. Herbert York, the Director of Defense Research and Engineering in 1958 and the man who inherited jurisdiction over the atomic-airplane program, said of those early days:

> . . . optimism was not borne out by the initial findings of the researchers. A number of very difficult problems very soon became evident. It turned out that there were then no materials available which would (1) stand up to the high-intensity nuclear radiation which necessarily existed throughout the interior of the reactor, (2) resist corrosion by the very hot air which passed through the reactor at great speed, and (3) be guaranteed not to leak any of the highly radioactive fission products into the exhaust airstream.[389]

Today, over twenty-five years later, advances in materials have not yet solved one of these problems.

Although it was not obvious from the start that the problems would be so difficult to solve, there was one problem which was clearly insurmountable from the very beginning, and that was how to shield pilots from the intense radiation produced by the nuclear reactor when it was known that the necessary shielding would make the nuclear engine too heavy to fly. The scientific laws governing radiation shielding were the same then as they are today and will be tomorrow: that the more powerful a reactor is, the more shielding it requires, and that shielding materials are not discovered by chance but are chosen on the basis of their atomic structure. Accordingly, all the good radiation shields were known then as now, and none is light enough to shield the radiation produced by enough nuclear power to get it off the ground.

But that didn't stop the atomic promoter, who, like most functionaries, concentrated on solving those problems which had obvious solutions while ignoring those that clearly had none. After all, where was industry's motivation to find flaws in a program which was supplying just one of its contractors with over $100 million each year?[390]

When the shielding problem arose inevitably, a quick search was made for a lighter shielding material, but this is much like trying to find a lighter backstop for a rifle range; using any material in the world, you can make it just so light before the bullets start coming through. When it was realized that it was the laws of physics that were stopping them, they gave up the search and suggested several alternate ways of reducing the need for so much shielding.[391] Some bizarre proposals arose. "One which was discussed quite seriously was that older men . . . should be used as pilots so that genetic damage from radiation would be held at a minimum and because older people are generally more resistant to radiation than younger ones."[392] The only advantage ever claimed for the atomic airplane was that it would not require constant refueling, a dubious benefit considering the advanced state of conventional in-flight refueling techniques available at that time.

Even if the atomic airplane were possible, the real chance of an air crash and the simultaneous rupture of the reactor itself was never addressed. After running for only one year, a reactor of the size contemplated for use in the atomic airplane would contain inside itself fission products equivalent to the fallout produced by twenty bombs of the size dropped on Hiroshima. A single crash would disperse the lethal fallout over a wide area. But although the amount involved might be equivalent to twenty atomic bombs, the fallout danger created would be far more intense than twenty times the fallout around Hiroshima. This is because the heat created by an atomic explosion carries much of the fallout high into the stratosphere; an ordinary air crash would not do this. Thus, the fission products released from inside the reactor by a crash would remain concentrated, close to the ground, so that even cleanup crews could not come near enough to reduce the danger.

Gloomy predictions from the research laboratories concerning the future of the atomic airplane had no dampening effect on the project's strongest and most powerful supporter, the Joint Committee on Atomic Energy, which called for a "crash effort" on the program in 1954. Just after Sputnik was launched in 1957, the AEC and the Joint Committee called for an immediate "flight test" as a "means of increasing American scientific prestige" and "as a psychological victory to counteract the effects of Sputnik," but the "flight test" was to be as phony as the rest of the program, because the nuclear reactor, unable to propel an aircraft on its own, was to be simply a passenger aboard a conventional airplane which, as if to downplay the absurdity of it all, was called a "testbed."[393]

Possibly the most disgraceful aspect of this program was how fraudulent "intelligence reports" of a Russian atomic airplane were concocted, perhaps by the industrial contractors themselves, and leaked to the kept technological press, and how this "intelligence" served to convince Congress that the Soviets had already developed a nuclear airplane. A story in *Aviation Week* for December 1, 1958, stated flatly: "A nuclear powered bomber is being flight tested in the Soviet Union. Completed about six months ago, this aircraft has been observed both in flight and on the ground by a wide variety of foreign observers from communist and non-communist countries."[394] Hysteria mounted until, ten days later, President Eisenhower, who presumably had access to better intelligence reports than had *Aviation Week*, said, "There is absolutely no intelligence to back up a report that Russia is flight-testing an atomic-powered airplane."[395]

When all else fails, the ace in the hole of the boondoggle promoter has always been the Soviet bogeyman.

Finally the Department of Defense and the President lost enthusiasm for the atomic airplane, just after completion of a new $8-million ground-test plant in Idaho.[396] The squeals of bureaucratic recrimination rose from all sides, predictably the group most responsible for the huge fiasco, the Joint Committee on Atomic Energy, squealed the loudest, pointing the finger elsewhere: the atomic airplane, the committee said, "received a serious setback from the Undersecretary of Defense and the President on March 5 [1958]. For a while . . we thought the ANP was getting on the right track . . . the ANP program remains as a colossal monument of maladministration by the Defense Department."[397] By 1961, the Aircraft Nuclear Propulsion program was officially junked (but it lives yet; see below).

It might be expected that a great lesson was learned from the nuclear-airplane fiasco: *that not only must the nuclear alternative be better than conventionally available techniques in order to be worthwhile, but, considering the greatly increased risks involved, it must confer advantages absolutely unavailable elsewhere.* But even if the ANP could be made to work, its advantages *are* available elsewhere; the best that could be said is that the nuclear jet engine would avoid in-flight refueling, hardly an advantage great enough to counterbalance the tremendous risks involved.

Remarkably enough, the lesson was not learned at all. The Air Force is now engaged in a new examination of nuclear aircraft propulsion,[398] and today the National Aeronautics and Space Administration (NASA) spends a quarter of a million dollars *each year* on "in-house" nuclear-airplane studies but concedes the "difficult task of overcoming the subjective response of the public toward nuclear powered airplanes."[399]

Perhaps most hard to believe is that in 1971 the Navy actually awarded a new contract to Lockheed Aircraft to develop concepts to modify the giant C-5A airplane into a nuclear-powered seaplane.[399] All forty-seven of these airplanes were grounded by the Air Force in late 1971 after an engine "spun to the ground" when the pilot applied full power during a pre-takeoff check.[400] It developed later that cracks were found in the engine mount of at least one other C-5A which had only five hundred hours of flight time.[401] Consider how fortunate we are that the Navy's program for a nuclear-powered C-5A had not progressed very far in 1971, for in the dropping off of engines it is far better to clean up gasoline than atomic fallout.

Lockheed's C-5A is the same airplane which has been plagued with more than *$2 billion* in cost overruns on an eighty-one-airplane contract. Lockheed itself is the company which has prompted Senator Proxmire to seek an investigation into its mismanagement and "improper practices and what appears to be collusion with the Air Force to receive credit and payment for work on aircraft which has not been accomplished."[402] It seems appropriate that America's most mismanaged airframe company should be heavily involved in pursuing the elusive fantasy of the atomic airplane. In 1971, Lockheed's vice-president for airline requirements and product planning, said that "Lockheed is investigating a nuclear powered airplane that will carry 600 passengers in comfort at just under the speed of sound, non-stop to any city in the world."[403] It's a high price to pay indeed just to avoid a few refueling stops, but there's not too much to worry about. With Lockheed at the controls, it will never get off the ground.

4 · HOW DO YOU TURN OFF THE MONEY FAUCET?

PLUTO is gone. A new generation of Congressmen has come up, naïve to the failure of the ANP program a decade ago. And so the atomic airplane still lives, but barely. It is used as an ornament in appropriation requests before gullible congressional committees—if for nothing else, to show that those planners requesting funds are really on the ball, erudite and conversant with each new miracle the future holds for our society.

But there is another fiasco that still lives, kept alive by pork-barrel politicians who make no secret of the fact that it is not the program itself but rather the lost jobs and money already spent on that program that impresses them.[404]

Going by many names (ROVER, NERVA, the Nuclear Space Program), the nuclear rocket, first conceived of by the Germans,[386] has other things than misplaced values in common with Pluto and the ANP. The power plant is the same open-ended nuclear reactor, but instead of breathing air the NERVA (Nuclear Engine for Rocket Vehicle Application) carries a supply of liquid hydrogen along as a propellant. The hydrogen is squirted through the intensely hot reactor core and expelled through the exhaust along with radioactive fission products and many pieces of the nuclear-fuel elements themselves. As with the ANP and Pluto, materials capable of withstanding the heat (four thousand degrees Fahrenheit) and pressures inside the NERVA reactor as well as the chemical reactivity of the propellant itself have not been found, although improvements have been made.

But improvements are to be expected, considering the enormous cost of the program. To put that cost into perspective, the Manhattan Project of World War II, which culminated in the development of the first atomic bomb and involved building the enormous gaseous-diffusion plants at Oak Ridge, the huge plutonium production facilities at Hanford, Washington, and the secret weapons laboratory at Los Alamos, New Mexico, cost $2.2 billion.[405] The nuclear rocket has already cost the U.S. taxpayer over $1.5 billion, and the promoters themselves admit that the rocket engine alone will cost the taxpayer at least another billion dollars.[406] Furthermore, this estimate does not include many expensive extras such as a scrubber system to reduce the amount of radioactivity released during engine tests,[407] and the enormous additional expense of developing the rocket spacecraft itself, likely to cost at least as much as the engine and probably more.

But the Manhattan Project was a technical gamble that paid off; many haven't. Money alone doesn't guarantee success. The tombstones in the graveyard of canceled programs make interesting reading: the F-8, the B-70, the Skybolt, the Dynasoar, the Manned Orbiting Laboratory, and literally hundreds of others.[408] All were justified on the basis of national defense, the same justification used to keep secret much of the information necessary for legitimate debate concerning their practical worth, but the nuclear-rocket program has only seldom been touted as having any military use whatever. Even the manager of the whole project is "not aware of specific military applications."[409] So far, only the industrial contractors have been so boldly preposterous as to suggest that nuclear rockets could "intercept potentially hostile space vehicles."[410]

Although the program "began with a goal to develop a propulsion system for an ICBM,"[411] its main purpose has always been to provide power for space travel. It was first touted as a power plant for a moonship, until it was realized that chemical rockets could do the job far better. Even former AEC Chairman Seaborg feels that NERVA is too dangerous to "be launched as a primary rocket from the surface of the earth."[412] The ultimate use of the nuclear rocket is now expected to be for "deep space probes," to Mars and beyond, although the development of a space platform could very well make conventionally powered rockets the best choice again.

Since national defense is not at issue, then the practical worth of a nuclear rocket is a public question. But with checks and balances long gone, debates in Congress take place between AEC and NASA officials who support their laboratories from these funds, industrial contractors who receive over $100 million *each year* to design and build the atomic engines, and Congressmen from the states where the money is finally spent who make no effort to conceal the fact that it is not the rocket which is important, it's the jobs the rocket creates.[404] As a consequence, the debate not only is not a public question, it is no question at all. Like the atomic gadgets before, the nuclear-rocket program has turned into a very expensive welfare program for nuclear scientists which no one will turn off.

But let's examine the basis for continuing the development of the nuclear rocket. The technical reason the nuclear rocket was developed in the first place does have a somewhat sounder basis than the reason for developing the engine of either the ANP or Pluto. Because NERVA uses hydrogen as a propellant, the nuclear rocket can theoretically achieve twice the efficiency of either Pluto or conventionally powered rocket engines,[413] but the less technical questions involving an evaluation of whether the benefits to be gained by a nuclear-rocket program are worth the cost, was made without public participation because the true costs were never revealed.

For example, consider the health risks involved. From 1959 through 1969, thirty-one nuclear-rocket-engine ground tests have released airborne radioactivity detected well beyond the test-range complex in Nevada.[414] Radioactivity from some of the tests was detected well into Utah and California,[415] and *particles torn from the fuel rods themselves* were found over eighty miles away from their points of release.[416] Although strontium 90 and cesium 137 were also detected,[417] the principal contaminant detected was iodine 131 in milk.[418] Reminiscent of the days of atmospheric nuclear-weapons testing, *it was felt* that the dose to the infant thyroid gland was below fourteen percent and the whole body exposure below twelve percent of the "radiation protection standards for a population sample."[414]

Now, while NASA and AEC officials responsible for these tests regard these doses as "acceptably small,"[419] they are hardly the people who should have been left in sole charge of that judgment, especially considering the fact that an excellent alternative has always been available to reduce this unnecessary radioactive contamination, though they have never made use of it. The Los Alamos Scientific Laboratory devised plans for a cryogenic charcoal-silica-gel scrubber which would absorb virtually all of the harmful radiation that the rocket tests spew into the air. Despite the fact that its cost was about one percent of the total investment in the nuclear-rocket program so far,[407] the officials rejected the idea.

An insight into the values of these men who spend so much of the public's money, but arrange the release of information so that they are not answerable to the public, can be found by considering that about the same time that they rejected the scrubber idea they spent well over one million dollars simply to reinforce a rocket-test platform to withstand an expected increase in earth tremors from the atom-bomb testing site nearby. The weapons testers believed that the precaution was unnecessary, but the nuclear rocketeers overruled them, as they felt that even this small risk to their equipment was unacceptably large. Subsequent measurements demonstrated that the extensive reinforcing wasn't needed after all, but they were taking no chances. There is only one reason why similarly scrupulous attention is not applied to the problem of off-site radioactive contamination from these rocket tests, and that is that the public is unaware of the hazard it has been subjected to for twelve years and also unaware of how simple it would be to avoid that contamination in the future—and the nuclear-rocket promoters aren't about to tell them.

Furthermore, while each test produced off-site radioactive doses that they consider "acceptably small," nuclear rocketeers have never considered the total impact of all the tests in the past or all the tests they plan to conduct in the future. For if they did, surely a scrubber to eliminate the unnecessary radioactive pollution that each test produces would be the least they could do for the man who pays their bills. But the engineer is running things here, and his motto is familiar by now: "Get the job done—safety can wait."

In 1971 NASA, the customer for the nuclear rocket, decided that it didn't need the nuclear engine just yet. Since NERVA is too dangerous to launch from the surface of the earth,[412] it must first be placed into earth orbit by the space shuttle and started up in space. The space-shuttle concept involves a space station in orbit around the earth, with a reusable spaceship-airplane craft shuttling between earth and the space platform. NASA's chief testified, "NERVA needs the shuttle, but the shuttle does not need NERVA. For that reason we are proceeding with the shuttle development before the NERVA development."[420] Wernher von Braun said, "Since we cannot yet fund [NERVA's] payloads, it would be hard to justify the speedy development of a viable NERVA engine at this particular time."[421] Even Milton Klein, the director of the Space Nuclear Systems Office, the projects developer, said, "The program currently is at a stage where all the design that is worthwhile doing . . . has essentially been done."[422]

Accordingly, NASA decided to put its efforts into the development of the space shuttle, and to reduce its NERVA commitment to a "holding action." Since the customer wasn't buying, the AEC had to reduce its support of NERVA as well.[423] What this amounted to was a budget cut from over $100 million *each year* to $30 million for

1972, enough money to keep NERVA alive until there was a use for it, according to its promoters.

What followed was a singularly American phenomenon, a joint congressional hearing concerning that budget cut, where Congressmen from the affected states, industrial contractors themselves, and even the AEC engaged in lies, distortions, threats and other pressure tactics (see below), finally forcing NASA to reinstate the program at previous funding levels even though it was technically the wrong thing to do. This illustrates a unique problem for a democracy: when a technical development itself demands a delay or even a termination of its own program, how do you turn the faucet off? For the only thing that seemed to worry people at that hearing was that jobs, at least temporarily, would disappear.

Congressman Robert L. Legget (D., Cal.), strongly identifying with "his" contractor, said, *"We at Aerojet* in Sacramento have about nine hundred employees there. . . . There will be probably five hundred people in thirty days that will be out delivering milk and tending bar . . . ,"* and went on to say he thought that "the failure to include funds for the NERVA program amounts to almost a *national crime against the American people."** Senator Alan Bible of Nevada complained about the demoralization of the employees at the nuclear-rocket development station in his state while suggesting that all that is needed to complete the program is just *another billion dollars* (added to the $1.4 billion already spent). Nevada's other Senator, Howard W. Cannon, made his threat very clear: "This year's budget request for NASA totals $3.27 billion. Of that amount only $9.9 million has been requested for NERVA engine development, which, as I have said, virtually kills this program. . . . I know this committee, when we start our hearings in a few weeks, will look *very closely** at the remaining $3.26 billion."[424]

Even though one quarter of the initial money request was granted, along with the commitment to reinstate funding at higher levels just as soon as there was a requirement for NERVA, the case was

* Emphasis added.

strongly made by all that this was enough to kill the program *forever*. Senator Anderson spoke of the wasted $1.4 billion already spent on the rocket engine; Klein spoke of how layoffs would "result in a loss of about 12,400 man years of experience in the nuclear-rocket program," and, as if to underscore the irretrievability of the effects of the budget cut, Aerojet's man, Representative Legget, actually described the men who would be laid off as "nuclear engineers that the colleges are simply not turning out at the present time," an obvious falsehood.

Of course, the "Soviet threat" was not left out. Then head of NASA, George M. Low said, "If you look at 1970 alone, [the Russians launched] about eighty-eight payloads into space, while we only launched thirty-six." Representative James G. Fulton of Pennsylvania (homeland of Aerojet's primary subcontractor, Westinghouse Electric's Astronuclear Laboratory), speaking of the old days, said, "The comparative disability of the United States without power in space . . . was tremendously emphasized by Russian successes . . . I look at [NERVA] as one of the prime programs in space. We in the United States *must have it*. To me, and I say it very succinctly, *power in space is power*."[425]*

Unlike NASA, the AEC was used to working on projects which have no apparent reason to exist. Directors at the AEC have never accepted the idea that there has to be a legitimate use for the end product of their researches. Commissioner Ramey complained about the "requirements merry-go-round," which he defined as the "tendency to hold back the development of nuclear hardware until a specific mission or requirement is formally established by the agency that would use the hardware." To wait for a requirement is "highly inefficient and expensive," he complained, saying, "I believe that without the requirements problem, progress to date could have been accomplished sooner . . ."[411] There is no question but that without "requirements," progress can be accelerated, but at what cost? So typical of the bureaucrat who has had a blank check for so long, Ramey by now ignores the real world. *Legitimate requirements are*

* Emphasis added.

the only reliable way of distinguishing between good ideas and bad ideas. To avoid use of such criteria in favor of criteria established by the promoter himself would leave only a short time before the entire national budget would be committed to wild schemes, because when it comes to spending money, science and technology have no built-in limits at all.

Harold Agnew, the director of the AEC's Los Alamos Scientific Laboratories, in his zeal to see NERVA's funding restored, actually tried to blame the cancellation of a rocket test on the budget cut, when the fault was actually something quite different. According to Space Nuclear Systems Office officials, Pewee II, the latest experimental rocket, was set for a test in Nevada in early February of 1971,[426] well before the budget cut was to go into effect and only a few weeks before Agnew testified. In that test, like all the others before it, no provision was made to reduce the radioactive pollution produced (by capturing the radioactivity, for example, in some sort of a scrubbing device). The difference between this test and all the others was that it was the first nuclear-rocket test to take place after the National Environmental Policy Act (NEPA) went into effect.[427] Under that law, the "responsible officials" at the AEC and NASA were obliged to file a timely "environmental-impact statement" for the Space Nuclear Systems Office, which they did not do.

The reason for this was that the officials of the Space Nuclear Systems Office never prepared an environmental-impact statement for the AEC and NASA to file, simply because they felt it was unnecessary. This casual arrogance is normal for Space Nuclear Systems Office officials. Due to the original bureaucratic bungle they have two masters, the AEC and NASA, and serve neither. Accordingly, even AEC pressure was ineffective in moving them to file an environmental-impact statement. Finally, as has been the case so many times before, pressure forcing the radiation polluter to comply with the law had to come from outside the system. I sued the director of the Space Nuclear Systems Office, the chairman of the AEC and the administrator of NASA in federal district court in Denver to delay that test until the rocketeers complied with the law.[428] In his reply brief, the U. S. attorney said, "If, as it seems, it was plaintiff's purpose in bringing this suit to make certain that the AEC would issue an environmental statement before conducting their test, they have achieved their purpose."[429]

But because they started so late (only in response to my suit), the officials could not produce a final environmental-impact statement. On January 15, 1971, the AEC submitted a draft environmental-impact statement to the President's Council on Environmental Quality.[430] Comments began coming in to the Council a month later[431] and continued right up to the last minute.[432] "The last minute" in bureaucratese means June 30 of any year, or when the fiscal year ends. At that time, any unspent money allocated to any program has to be returned; any new money must come from the next year's appropriation. But since the budget cut was to reduce the fiscal 1972 money (the only money the Pewee II test could legally use after June 30), it looked as if Pewee II wouldn't be tested after all. So it wasn't budget cutting that killed Pewee II, as Los Alamos Director Dr. Harold Agnew tried to make Congress believe (see below) There was plenty of money and time to conduct the test if they had been able to follow their original plan. But because of the arrogance of the administrators, who refused to follow federal guidelines until they were forced to do so by a citizen's court suit, a delay fatal to the program had occurred (the court suit), and Pewee II had to be taken apart again, untested, and returned to Los Alamos.

That's why Peewee wasn't tested in 1971, but four months before the cut would take place Agnew tried to get the Congressmen to believe that it was the budget cut that was responsible:

SENATOR CANNON: . . . If this proposed budget takes effect, it will not be tested?
DR. AGNEW: It will not be tested.
SENATOR CANNON: The Peewee II will not be tested, period.

Only when Senator Cannon pressed the issue, complaining, "That does not give much of an answer," did Milton Klein give him more information: "We are waiting for the filing of the Final Environ-

mental Impact Statement before the reactor is to be tested."[433] But
mention alone wasn't enough. The false impression was made and
remained that Pewee II, with all the work that went into it, stands
useless because the budget was to be cut—and so Congress had
better not cut the budget.

And who there was qualified to present an alternate view? There
are few easier ways to cover up error and incompetence than to
have a congressional committee scrutinize a complex technical matter. Even if a committee member isn't overwhelmed by the technical arguments and raises a question or two, there are other ways
to silence him. A recent example illustrates how Holifield and his
followers who run the Joint Committee on Atomic Energy feel that
they are above normal procedure—even their own. Senator Stuart
Symington, (D., Mo.), a member of the Joint Committee on Atomic
Energy, is a long-time foe of another expensive nuclear bauble, the
Navy's CVAN-70 nuclear aircraft carrier. Because of its huge expense
(see Chap. II), serious questions have been raised over its practical
worth. In May 1971, on the Senate floor, Senator Symington complained that the Joint Committee had issued a report in the name of
all the committee members in praise of the CVAN-70. He testified:

... neither I nor my staff saw this testimony or report prior to its publication, nor was a copy of the printed document delivered to my office.
. . . The report contains conclusions and recommendations purportedly
made by members of the committee, but as a member of that committee I was never asked to comment. . . . In all the years I have served
in the Senate on various committees I cannot recall any committee of
which I was a member releasing a report of committee recommendations without first obtaining the permission of the members involved.[434]

With such power, and abuses of power, working to keep nuclear
boondoggles alive, it's no wonder that our nation is saddled with
so many of them. So Congress, in opposition to Administration requests, restored the cut funds, and the nuclear-rocket program steams
on as before. But Pewee, so important to the nuclear rocketeers, before Congress, lost its importance very quickly when the funds were
finally restored. For, according to their plans, testing during 1972
is limited to the "nuclear furnace," whatever new wonder that is.[435]

5 · NUCLEAR-POWERED MERCHANT SHIPS

THE GREAT MILITARY ADVANTAGES of naval nuclear power simply do not apply to merchant ships. There is just no reason for freighters and tankers to be independent of ports. On the contrary, their role is to proceed as fast as they can from one port to another, where they not only load and unload cargo but take on fuel as well.

Certainly atomic power will never provide a cheaper fuel than oil, not even in the distant future. Conventional ships use the most inexpensive fuel in use today, while naval reactors not only are still enormously expensive but very likely always will be. Furthermore, they require specially trained crews and expensive and different port facilities to service these unique vessels.

Despite the obvious lack of advantage of the atomic alternative, the keel of the nuclear ship *Savannah* was laid in 1958 (by Mrs. Richard M. Nixon). Twelve years and many millions of dollars later, President Nixon decided to deactivate the ship, and in his budget message for 1971 he *specifically provided* almost $2 million for that purpose. The *Savannah* was being subsidized at a $3-million yearly level[436] and had just about fulfilled her mission. That mission was to increase American prestige around the world, although there was some doubt that any such thing was accomplished. Because Japan and Turkey have unlimited-liability laws in the case of a nuclear accident (we have the Price-Anderson Act, a law limiting liability in the case of a nuclear accident to $560 million), the *Savannah* was denied entry into ports in those nations. None of the maritime nations was convinced that the nuclear merchant ship was practical, including Germany, whose nuclear ship *Otto Hahn* had also been going on cruises to nowhere.

Speaking on the House floor in opposition to the continued sub-sidized operation of the nuclear ship *Savannah,* Representative Craig Hosmer, a long-time member of the Joint Committee on Atomic Energy, observed that "the Germans wish that instead of the *Otto Hahn* they had bought a ten-foot pole not to touch it with."[437] As a final indignity, the Maritime Administration received a proposal from a Los Angeles firm "for use of the vessel as part of a fish pro-tein concentrator,"[438] but she still sails.

6 · NUCLEAR BATTERIES, OR HOW TO SPEND $100 MILLION AND GET TO THE SAME PLACE YOU STARTED FROM

BOMBS, jets and rockets are clearly impressive: they make noise. But the AEC would like its public to believe that there is another side to the peaceful atom just as exciting: dedicated men in labora-tories are discovering the many medical miracles of nuclear energy[439] (although scant mention is ever made of the not infrequent irre-sponsible uses of radioactivity in medicine[440]). But as with most things atomic, the supposed advantages of the nuclear alternative seldom live up to their original promise. Just before he stepped down as chairman of the AEC, Glenn T. Seaborg candidly admitted that in the early years of the commission's existence industrial, medi-cal and space applications of radioactive isotopes were "perhaps overworked in citing the benefits of nuclear energy."[64, 441] Today only a few radioisotopes are used in the treatment of cancer; their only extensive use has been in the field of medical diagnosis and research, but even here nonradioactive (heavy) isotopes could al-most certainly have achieved many of the same results if equivalent attention had been given to their development and promotion.

But atomic promoters still imply that the medical atom is suffi-cient justification for the whole atomic program. For example, Dr. Harold Agnew says, "I'd like to ask the 'Ban the Bomb' people if they want to ban life for victims of heart disease. Those pace-makers that keep some of them alive are powered with plutonium 238 and we [at Los Alamos] are the only people who can make plu-tonium pure enough for use in pacemakers."[442] (Cardiac pacemakers are tiny battery-powered devices which are surgically planted under the skin and are wired to the heart and stimulate its beat by a rhythmic electric pulse.[443])

Dr. Agnew thereby deduces that to "ban the bomb" is to ban plutonium, and to do that, he implies, is "to ban life for victims of heart disease." His illogic aside, an examination of Dr. Agnew's rather extravagant statement calls attention to some interesting facts. And these facts suggest that the nuclear cardiac pacemaker is just another atomic frill that should never have been developed in the first place.

Contrary to what Dr. Agnew implied, there are several hundred thousand cardiac pacemakers already in use throughout the world today powered by conventional batteries, while plutonium-powered pacemakers, despite six years of research[444] and many millions of dollars, are only in the earliest experimental stages; the first im-plantation in a human took place in France only four months before Dr. Agnew made his remarks.[445]

Since then, only three additional nuclear-pacemaker implants were made in humans;[446] interestingly, none of those operations took place in the United States. Perhaps it is our more stringent tradition against human experimentation that has prevented them so far, because there has not been anything like the countless animal experiments usually required to justify human use of experimental drugs, to support the use of nuclear-powered energy sources within the human body. The 1969 AEC progress report gives a feeling for the primitive state of the art when it says: "A 16-watt source was implanted in a dog for 26 months prior to its death in October 1969, from unknown causes. A larger 24-watt source has been implanted in a second dog since May 1968, and the animal remains in apparent good health."[447] By the beginning of 1970 our National Institutes of Health had made only a total of seven implants in dogs, but testing in *only two dogs* had "resolved the heat and radiation question" for the French.[448]

The most recent assessment of AEC progress in the field appeared in the AEC's annual report of 1970: "Since May 1968, eight of the nuclear-powered pacemakers have been surgically implanted in dogs. . . . during 1970, six of these units failed . . ." Three failed because of electronics, two because of the nuclear battery, and one because of both.[449] But if medical people have been slow and conservative in applying the invention, the AEC has been bold in developing it as its old "body-in-the-morgue approach" is seen again. The AEC first develops a technology and only later addresses itself to the question of the various hazardous side effects and whether they are serious or not. When they turn out to be serious, atomic establishmentarians find themselves out on a limb, thereby protecting a technology that is already an accomplished fact by unjustly minimizing the hazards involved. If those hazards were considered at the outset, the project would be doomed at the start if any private corporation, independent of assistance from the AEC, had been bold enough to have attempted the stunt in the first place.

Even Dr. Agnew's statement that "we are the only people who can make plutonium pure enough for use in pacemakers" is far from true. Not only do several nations produce plutonium suitable for pacemakers,[450] but the most advanced American pacemaker uses a French nuclear battery.[451] Furthermore, some months before he spoke, the Australian Atomic Energy Commission announced its choice of what is considered a better and less dangerous energy source, promethium 147,[452] and at least one American effort is directed toward this non-plutonium alternative.[453] The reason plutonium is losing favor among the pacemaker promoters is that as the plutonium battery ages, internal pressures (due to helium gas production) build up inside the battery, and, because of the accumulation of radioactive-decay products, the external radiation increases. This, of course, was predicted from the start, but plutonium enjoys a special position among the radioisotopes and is often used when other radioactive elements might do the job better (see Chapter 7).

But the irony of this turn of events is that if promethium 147, a safer source of nuclear energy, is used, the lifetime of the battery is reduced from ten years to only five, while today's conventional batteries can already last almost that long. Currently available pacemakers are guaranteed for two years,[454] while newer available models are advertised as lasting more than three years,[455] and manufacturers are already producing units for researchers which they call "certified cells" which last for five years.[456] Thus, the story is repeated: the nuclear alternative, once full of promise, becomes more disappointing the closer it is scrutinized, while conventional developments, assumed to have remained static, move ahead and overtake the atomic alternative.

But the cardiac pacemaker raises an issue far larger than the self-serving statement made by an atomic promoter. The crucial question is, what benefit does society gain from such a development and what risk does it take in the bargain? Let's look at those risks and benefits. As far as society at large is concerned, there is no benefit from a nuclear pacemaker whatever. Ordinary pacemakers already do the job well, they are getting very much better all the time, and if nuclear-powered pacemakers were never developed at all there would still be plenty of conventional devices to go around. They would benefit another promotional group, however: the pacemaker manufacturers. The projected price of a nuclear device is at least four times the existing price of a conventional model,[451] and the new business represents at least a $40-million market.[448]

But society does take a risk, and that risk is never mentioned by the promoters. There are about 100,000 Americans[457] and at least that many Europeans using conventionally powered pacemakers, for a total worldwide market of at least 200,000 devices. If nuclear-powered pacemakers entirely supplant the conventional variety (and that would be the only reason for funding such a research effort), society is faced with the danger of hundreds of thousands of potentially hazardous plutonium sources moving uncontrolled throughout the world. So the real question is, how would a plutonium battery hold up in an airplane crash, accidental cremation, or other accidents?[446] Manufacturers are sensitive to this question, and even intend to conduct experimental testing for pacemaker damage after a fall from an airplane or a gunshot wound.[458]

Consider how dangerous one such plutonium source might be. Presently the nuclear-powered pacemaker contains between two hundred[459] and five hundred milligrams[460] of plutonium 238 (future models will contain somewhat less) in a capsule carefully fabricated to prevent leakage. This is crucial because of the terrible toxicity of plutonium and its pyrophoric nature (it burns on contact with the air—see Chapter V).

If a single plutonium-powered pacemaker should rupture and burn, there is an excellent chance that all the plutonium inside would be oxidized to fine white plutonium-oxide smoke. Assuming the pacemaker contains 350 milligrams, or six curies, of plutonium 238, it would make available to the air 375 million doses equal to the maximum permissible lung burden established by the AEC for use as a plutonium-exposure threshold for workers in atomic plants.[461] Assuming that ten to a hundred of these "safe" limits in a person's lungs is enough to insure lung cancer (less will do), there would still be made available to the air three to thirty million doses sufficient to cause lung cancer.

Now this, of course, is a so-called worst-case analysis for a "maximum credible accident," and accordingly it gives only an idea of how bad it can be. In actuality all the plutonium smoke isn't likely to find its way into people's lungs any more than all the cyanide spilled along the road after a truck accident is likely to kill all the people in the world just because there's enough of it there to do the job. But the fact remains that it is awfully dangerous to anyone who happens to be nearby. Extraordinary measures will have to be taken to prevent problems which are obvious even now. For example, fire departments would have to know just where all the plutonium sources are in their community in order to know when to evacuate the area near a fire until the plutonium can be located and recovered.

But as sensitive as manufacturers are to the problem of accidental rupture, there has been no attention given to the greatest threat of all: the disposal of burned plutonium to the air by normal cremation after the death of the nuclear-pacemaker user.

Cremation is employed increasingly in the world today; the nationwide average in the United States is five percent,[462] with many nations' much higher. What doesn't go up the chimney might be scattered from an airplane over the sea, a growing practice today accounting for over thirty "burials" each day in southern California alone.[463] Therefore if the nuclear alternative displaces conventional pacemakers, several thousand plutonium batteries will be on their way to the crematoria each year. The question that doesn't seem to have an answer is, How do you track down and remove all those pacemakers in time?

There is no answer yet, and there is not likely to be one, because, consistent with its tradition, the AEC seems to be waiting until the technology is developed before addressing itself meaningfully to the hazards. Typically, it has all but ignored the problem, although on an unofficial level even AEC people worry about the ultimate disposition of the plutonium, suggesting that new legislation may be needed "to recover each pacemaker when it is no longer needed."[464]

However, the European Nuclear Energy Agency has taken the lead and "a joint group of experts has been established to draw up safety guidelines for pacemakers and to examine the technical, legal, and administrative problems arising from their use."[446] (Fortunately the United States *is* represented at these meetings.)

Other risks are associated with the heart patient himself: he will have an atomic battery inside his body generating electricity through nuclear heat. In addition to heating slightly the tissues in contact with the device (with unknown side effects), it subjects the nearby tissue to a radiation dose of about three millirem per hour, or over 150 times greater than the dose permitted under the present federal radiation guides, thereby increasing his chances for radiation-induced cancer. But since the danger of exposure to radioactivity increases with the length of time of the exposure, and since the average pacemaker user (sixty-five years old) has most of his lifetime already behind him, the increased risk is not judged to be important. And from the point of view of the patient, the extra radiation is not necessarily in violation of the philosophy behind radiation protection standards, which say that "there should not be any man-made radiation exposure without the expectation of benefit . . ."[465]

But what are the benefits? There is only one. While the conventional battery has to be changed every three years, the plutonium battery is expected to last for ten years (but won't). What this means to the patient is that instead of three or four skin-flap operations for a battery change each decade, he will require only one or two. The question of methods other than atomic to accomplish the same or better results has never been addressed by the AEC; the justification made is that the AEC is required by Congress to promote atomic energy alone, not other technologies.

An alternate and equally unconventional cardiac pacemaker has achieved about the same level of development as the nuclear pacemaker but without the massive funding and promotion of the AEC. This device requires no batteries at all; it converts variations of blood pressure into electrical energy by the use of piezoelectric disks.[466] These disks convert pressure directly into electricity and operate on the same principle as the old crystal radio set, which did not require batteries, either. Other new methods, such as charging pacemaker batteries by radio waves, without breaking the skin, are being developed as well.

The atomic establishment's one-sided promotion goes beyond the Joint Committee walls to the Senate itself. Without benefit of an explanation of the risks produced by the program, the Senate, thinking itself supporting an unassailable cause, doubled the 1971 appropriation of the cardiac-pacemaker program to $1 million.[467] Even the National Heart and Lung Institute, in a recent request for research leading to long-lived implantable cardiac pacemakers, included radioisotopes as one of the energy options in which it was interested.[468] But the first sign of a more measured approach occurred only weeks later, when the Institute "wished to rethink the pacemaker, this rethinking to include lower energy (non-atomic) sources," and abruptly canceled its original request for more research into the matter.[469]

So it can be seen, from a consideration of the benefits and risks of starting up a nuclear-pacemaker industry, that the decision to go ahead with the venture in the first place isn't at all clearcut. Many people consider that the risks to society at large far outweigh the marginal benefits provided the individual heart patient. Surely such an important decision ought to have been made with much public participation, but it wasn't.

The atomic establishment, because of its extensive funding of research and development efforts and its involvement of many private companies[470] in its venture, has already made that decision for us all.

7 · MORE NUCLEAR BATTERIES AND HEAT SOURCES

HOWEVER disproportionate are the risks and benefits of the cardiac pacemaker, there are far worse applications of the atomic battery. "Manpack thermoelectric generators" are now being designed for the military which will provide between sixty and one thousand watts of electricity from nuclear heat.[471] The risk of this convenience is the uncontrolled use of quantities of plutonium hundreds and thousands of times greater than contained in the pacemakers. Furthermore, they will be used in a combat environment, where destruction and abandonment of equipment is common. Even if one "manpack" plutonium generator were blown apart, it could easily make large areas dangerously contaminated for generations to come. Strontium 90, thought by some to be a better radioisotope for this purpose, would present an even worse hazard. As if this weren't bad enough, newspaper science columns gaily tout that "within three to five years, campers . . . might find themselves equipped with similar generators."[472]

In terms of the sheer numbers of uncontrolled alpha-emitting sources like plutonium, the proposed nuclear wristwatch is hard to beat. At a meeting of the American Society of Mechanical Engineers in 1969, the Bulova Watch Company announced that it is working on such a device which may be ready in thirty years.[473]

The AEC has produced plutonium-heated "long johns" for the Navy. Designed to be worn under a diver's suit, they contain about *one thousand grams* of plutonium 238, the heat from which keeps Navy divers warm at depths down to six hundred feet. This amount of plutonium is about sixteen thousand curies, or one trillion maximum permissible lung burdens.[474] One accident involving the loss, rupture or abandonment of one diving suit and the "No Swimming" sign goes up forever.

Monsanto Research Corporation, which operates the laboratory where the plutonium diving suit was developed, has some ideas of its own. Among other nuclear-powered gadgets for the future, Monsanto decribed the nuclear-powered coffeepot. Powered by one fifth of an ounce of plutonium 238, the pot will perk for more than a hundred years on its own self-contained heat supply. What is not mentioned is that one fifth of an ounce is about ten million lethal doses of plutonium.[475]

Not exactly a nuclear battery but too good to leave unmentioned is the petition to the AEC by a Boston company for permission to manufacture uranium cufflinks, citing as their main utility the fact that "their unusual weight prevents cuffs from riding up." The AEC denied the request,[476] pointing out that "the use of radioactive materials in toys, novelties and adornments may be of marginal benefit."[477] The AEC does not apply that admonition to itself, however: the main lobby of the AEC's headquarters at Germantown, Maryland, has only recently been paved with irradiated plastic wood.[478] While it is true that no residual radiation remains in the wood, much high-energy radiation was employed to produce that product, along with the accompanying industrial exposures. Accordingly, one might well question whether the production of irradiated wood (which has never been practical) is itself anything but an adornment.

8 · FOOD IRRADIATION

Beginning in the late 1950s and primarily at the urging of the Joint Committee on Atomic Energy, the AEC has been involved in a $16-million effort to apply atomic energy to the preservation of foods.[479] Similar to the canning process, where heat is used to sterilize food, the AEC's food irradiation program uses high-energy atomic radiation in an attempt to do the same thing, but it never did work out.

Any treatment capable of sterilizing food (killing all living microorganisms and spores) is bound to produce a profound change in the food as well. It's just a fortunate accident that the change produced by the heat and pressure sterilization used in the canning process is familiar to everyone: it's called cooking. But in order for atomic radiation to sterilize food as well as that, so much energy has to be used that unpleasant, unfamiliar and dangerous degradation products are formed in the food itself which make the product unacceptable. Therefore, less radiation than that required for complete sterilization had to be used even at the very beginning of the program. This immediately reduced the best hope for the method from long-term preservation in the normal sense (canning) to *possibly* increasing only slightly the "shelf life" of foods.

But this knowledge didn't stop the nuclear hucksters from exaggerating out of all proportion the alleged benefits of the atom in the supermarket. As early as 1959, the Joint Committee on Atomic Energy held what later became an annual event, its much publicized "Irradiated Food Luncheon." In 1967 a truck-mounted food irradiator built by the Atomic Energy Commission began a "cross country schedule of visits to private farms to demonstrate the benefits and commercial potential of food preservation by irradiation."[480] But the limitations of the method were never clarified by the promoters: it was widely represented and believed that the next miracle to come from old Mr. Atom (the friendly cartoon character used by the AEC in its promotional literature for children) was a new method of food preservation which would do away with cans, canneries, frozen food and freezers forever.

In 1968, a bombshell was dropped on this exuberant program by the U.S. Food and Drug Administration (FDA), and at least for a while the high-pressure tactics abated. FDA Commissioner Banes advised the Army that its irradiated ham had *not been shown* to be safe and furthermore listed some of the adverse effects it might produce:

1. Highly significant effect on the reproductive process.
2. Apparent production of antinutritional factors.
3. Apparent effects on mortality, body weight gain, red blood cell count and hemoglobin.
4. Possibility of increased risk of cataracts and tumors.[481]

Members of the Joint Committee were worried. Speaking of the "Irradiated Food Luncheons," Representative Bates asked, "I think it was 1959 that we first had that meal, was it not, Mr. Secretary of the Army?"

REPRESENTATIVE HOSMER: . . . He is gone now.
REPRESENTATIVE BATES: He is gone and the question is, are we going to be gone?
REPRESENTATIVE PRICE: We were guinea pigs.

But at least one Senator had better sense. Senator Aiken said, "I sent my bacon to the leading radiologist in the state. He ate it, and so far as I know he is still doing business. I didn't eat it myself. It might be all right, but why take a chance when you have a good radiologist to take a chance for you?"[482]

The AEC and the Army withdrew their Joint Food Petition (fish this time) from before the FDA soon afterward,[483] in favor of "more realistic target dates allowing additional time for completion of data gathering."[484] The next year, because of the requirements of the FDA and the Department of Agriculture, the AEC decided to drop its program for the radiation pasteurization of fresh red meat.[485]

There was strong opposition from both the Joint Committee and AEC Commissioner Ramey at this turn of events. Ramey felt he was making a strong point when he interpreted the FDA decision "not to indicate that irradiated food is harmful" but, as if to minimize its importance, "merely that there was not conclusive proof that irradiated ham was safe."[481] Thus Ramey's insensitivity blurs his ability to appreciate the real problem. What was going on was the familiar clash of philosophies between an engineering organization and public-health officials. The engineer, applying his views to public health, wants first to see obvious harm (the "body in the morgue") before he is convinced of the need for preventive action, while the philosophy of public-health people is that simply a real possibility of harm is sufficient cause for preventive action. Thus, public-health departments routinely condemn entire shipments of canned goods, for example, if only one tainted can is found; they do not wait until more people get sick before taking action. It is fair to expect that if the AEC were running the Food and Drug Administration, we might expect that the rest of the cans in a spoiled lot would be sold anyway, on the theory that an unopened can is not considered poisonous until proven otherwise.

Furthermore, Commissioner Ramey and the Joint Committeemen were indignant and refused to accept the fact that a small-scale Army program, completed years before the FDA was asked for its review, would not be sufficient to justify acceptance of the food irradiation process by the FDA. Remarkably, Ramey and the Joint Committee felt that way despite the fact that the FDA would have to take the Army's word for its study—the Army *lost its data* and presented only conclusions. As the Joint Committee put it, "the Army was *not able to retrieve laboratory records* to clarify the differences [between] investigators [the Army] and reviewers [the FDA] ten years after the studies were conducted."[481]*

Thus, like so many other atomic adventures, the food irradiation

* Emphasis added.

program—pushed into existence by the Joint Committee in the first place, and nurtured by that body long after its legitimate lifetime was over—attains a degree of the ridiculous not ordinarily found in real life. The foolishness of the whole affair was not lost on the scientists and technicians in the program itself. It's one thing to sit on the Joint Committee, ordering up an irradiated luncheon from a menu of fantasies of your own design; it's quite another thing to make it all work. Accordingly, in early 1970 the Army's plan to terminate entirely its food irradiation program[486] was announced. Ramey and the Joint Committee pulled out all the stops this time, and the Soviet "threat" was unleashed. Ramey noted that because of this cutback and the FDA policies, "he expected the U.S.S.R. may try to take over the leadership in this field."[487] Congressional coercion was used again when the House Committee on Armed Services recommended $1.8 million for the Army program in 1971, while the Army recommended zero. The committee's action was couched in terms wherein it "strongly urges" the Army to continue its food irradiation program; the Army indicated to the committee that the language was strong enough for it to "get the message."[488]

And so we are presented the same dilemma again: a technical program, brought into existence by politicians having no understanding of its problems, kept alive by various vested interests, finally becomes a demonstrable proven failure—but the funding goes on. How can we turn off the money faucet when checks and balances are gone?

9 · PLOWSHARE

PLOWSHARE, or the Division of Peaceful Nuclear Explosives of the AEC, has tried unsuccessfully to find constructive uses for atomic explosions since the division began in July 1957.[489] Conceptually, Plowshare began during World War II at Los Alamos, where weapons scientists like John Von Neumann, and Harold Brown later at Livermore, became interested in the possibilities of using nuclear explosions for peaceful purposes.

The main attraction of nuclear explosives is that they are much cheaper and more compact than conventional explosives, although this comparison is true only when the explosion is more than the equivalent of one or two kilotons of TNT. For example, a small, ten-kiloton nuclear explosive costs $350,000, while the equivalent amount of TNT costs over $4.5 million. Furthermore, while conventional explosives cost twice as much for twice the explosive power, the cost of nuclear explosives does not increase very much with increased explosive yield. Less than twice the cost of the ten-kiloton explosive will buy a very big blast from the AEC—two hundred times larger, or the equivalent of two megatons of TNT. That cost, $600,000, can be compared to $920 million for an equivalent explosion produced by TNT. Furthermore, that quantity of TNT represents four years' production of the entire American chemical industry.[490]

Size comparisons are also impressive. The two-megaton nuclear charge would fit into a forty-inch-diameter drilled hole, while the same amount of TNT would be a cube almost three hundred feet on each side. The newly developed "Diamond" nuclear explosive specifically designed for "underground engineering" (see below) can put eighty kilotons of explosive power into a device less than eight inches in diameter. An equivalent amount of ordinary explosives would occupy tens of thousands of cubic yards.[491]

For these reasons, nuclear explosives have tempted technologists for many years to use that new form of energy for gigantic earth-moving projects such as harbors and canals. But, as always with the atomic alternative, there are serious disadvantages. The big blasts are so big they can't be used anywhere near people, because of the dangers of the explosion itself. But more importantly, the radioactive fallout produced by even the smaller explosions is a serious concern. Nevertheless, Plowshare began by devoting virtually all of its energies to the new technology of creating large craters using atomic blasts. This choice was made despite the fact that in the whole world there are only two sites for sea-level canals (the Isthmus of Kra and the Isthmus of Panama) and about a dozen sites for harbors which fulfill the criteria of remoteness and practical value, and none of these sites (save one in Alaska) is in the United States.

Thus, the risks of nuclear digging aside for the moment, while cratering technology might eventually benefit men elsewhere, the $150 million already spent on Plowshare cannot be justified on the basis of providing any real technical improvements within the United States. The question then arises: How can the AEC justify this great expense? The answer lies not in the technology but elsewhere. The only meaningful support for the excavation program was never technical, it was political from the start, which might account for its ultimate failure.

In 1957, President Eisenhower ordered a new assessment of the steps required to improve the present Panama Canal, including the study of a sea-level canal (a canal without locks). After the study was under way, it was decided to include the possibility of using nuclear explosives to do the job.[492] Nuclear excavation was later established as a national policy in a charge from President Kennedy to the chairman of the AEC in 1964. The whole purpose was to provide a bargaining tool with the government of Panama. There were riots in Panama at that time, and one of the demands the Panamanians were making was that we renegotiate the treaty under which the Panama Canal was operating. The United States was in an extremely poor bargaining position, so what President Kennedy wanted at the time was some kind of alternative whereby a canal could be built in another country. The Isthmus of Tehuantepec in Mexico was considered, but the best route appeared to be through Colombia, the Atrato-Truando route.

But although nuclear explosives are indeed far cheaper in terms of yield, their use in the Isthmus of Panama would carry some serious side effects.[493] Large numbers of people would have to be relocated until the blasting was completed and the local radioactive fallout had decayed to safe levels. This could take a few years and would involve great expense, as would the repayment for damage done to property even after the inhabitants had been evacuated.

Extensive and expensive pre-shot and post-shot meteorological studies would have to be made in order to predict accurately the behavior of the fallout cloud after each explosion so as to minimize the harm to man. Not only would there be airborne fallout, but the radioactivity trapped in the craters would eventually enter the biosphere after the canal was flooded. Perhaps the most formidable obstacle of all would be the public's reaction, because it would be very difficult to make the case that a new transisthmian canal could justify adding so much more radioactivity to the environment. Besides, since the Limited Nuclear Test Ban Treaty of 1963 forbids any nuclear explosion which would cause "nuclear debris" to cross any international border, the project couldn't take place until that treaty could be amended to permit nuclear excavations, and that isn't very likely to have happened then or now.

Accordingly, between 1964 and 1970 a committee was formed called the Atlantic–Pacific Interoceanic Canal Study Commission, whose job it was to provide a political, military, economic and technical assessment of the various alternatives. But by the time the commission issued its report in 1970, the government in Panama had changed and the whole issue of the renegotiation of the treaty was resolved. The final report of that commission was an anticlimax. It recommended that conventional explosives be used to widen and improve the existing canal for two-way ship traffic, which, from a technical point of view, was the conclusion that everyone wanted in the first place.[494]

And so, by 1969, Plowshare's emphasis shifted to "underground engineering": the technology of creating large underground caverns for many uses. Some of the uses suggested are the permanent storage of dangerous wastes, the temporary storage of fuels such as liquified natural gas and the crushing of large volumes of rock underground to facilitate the release of natural resources such as gas, oil and minerals.

But the Plowshare concept involves the joint sponsorship of each of its ventures by the AEC *and* an "industrial partner" (although clearly the AEC's "partner" in the nuclear excavation program was a political partner). Superficially, this seems to be a good idea: the financial involvement, and therefore approval, of an industrial partner might be expected to guarantee the practical value of any Plowshare experiment and thus provide a brake to the fantasies of government visionaries. While it is true that a businessman might be more practical than an AEC bureaucrat, his goal is profit and not technical correctness; the two do not always go together.

Since Plowshare is so tied to the industrial user of the nuclear explosive, the first direction which the Division of Peaceful Nuclear Explosives took after abandoning nuclear digging did not turn out to be the best. Clearly the most obvious use for the "peaceful" nuclear explosion is to create large caverns deep underground for the permanent deposition of dangerous wastes. There would be small inconvenience to the public, since only a few waste caverns would be required nationwide. More importantly, though, the nuclear debris produced by the explosion itself would remain in the hole, and since the location and depths of those caverns would be chosen for the specific criterion of being able to immobilize dangerous wastes for millions of years, the nuclear debris produced by the explosion would constitute no problem. But there is a very small market throughout the United States for such waste depositories, too small to interest an "industrial partner."

Industry is interested in something else: There is a great deal (about a dozen years' supply) of natural gas around the country in "tight" formations. When conventional techniques are applied, gas from those wells comes to the surface, but only very slowly, too slowly to be of economic value. However, nuclear explosions can be used to shatter rock in such wells in order to cause a "stimulation" of gas flow. Since *many thousands* of wells would be involved, industry is interested in developing this technology because of the larger work volume involved, although, as we shall see, gas stimulation is far from the best application of "underground engineering." One industrial user of Plowshare nuclear services for gas stimulation told me quite candidly that even though waste storage might be a better application for nuclear explosions, the market (a few dozen caverns) couldn't keep his company in business while the much larger potential market for gas stimulation could.[495] Corroborating the dilemma from the other side of the fence, the director of the Plowshare division of the AEC's Lawrence Livermore Laboratories, Glenn C. Werth, told me, "Find us an industrial sponsor and we'll dig you a waste disposal cavern."[496] Thus, for lack of an industrial sponsor, Plowshare's best application remains neglected.

Let's examine some of the drawbacks of the gas stimulation program.[497] Unlike waste disposal caverns, gas stimulation caverns must be reentered and the gaseous contents brought to the surface and eventually piped around the country and used. But that gas has been made radioactive, contaminated with some of the products of the nuclear explosion. Although, by dilution, the radioactivity in the gas can be reduced to below AEC-established health standards,[498] it still carries with it enough radioactivity to render it, perhaps for aesthetic reasons alone, less than acceptable by the consumer.

There is the additional problem of public acceptance, generated by the fact that in order for gas stimulation to be a viable technology, and make all the research worthwhile, thousands of detonations will have to take place at many locations throughout the country. In addition to inconveniencing the public by causing a great deal of structural damage from the earth shocks produced, there will be left behind, deep underground, thousands of hardened puddles of radioactive glass, the "fallout" from the atomic explosives themselves. Since the criterion for where these puddles end up is the presence of natural gas and *not the ability of the rock formation to contain the wastes for very long time periods,* the chances are that sooner or later the wastes will contact an underground water supply and, through fractures, be brought to the surface and enter the biosphere. Although atomic promoters find this inconceivable, so did they find the Grand Junction indoor radon problem "difficult to conceive." The next gas stimulation experiment, Project Rio Blanco, is scheduled to take place in Colorado in 1973. Accordingly, Coloradoans are asking, If the radioactive waste puddles should turn out to be a serious problem in 1990, will the AEC then say the problem is the responsibility of the states and not its own, as it did for the uranium tailings problem in 1971?

But the nuclear stimulation technique does not need public opinion to kill it; it will die on its own, because it just isn't that good. Two experiments have taken place already, one in New Mexico (Project Gasbuggy in 1967) and one in Colorado (Project Rulison in 1969), and the results have been disappointing. The best that can be said for the ability of a nuclear explosive to free natural gas from tightly held formations deep underground is that the gas production is increased by five to ten fold.[499] This is hardly enough of an increase[500] to justify further development of the technique by the AEC or its further employment by industry.

It's ironic that after wasting billions of dollars on crackpot schemes, the AEC, finally on the threshold of doing something good with a nuclear explosion, finds itself unable to do so because industry just isn't interested. For with respect to Plowshare alone the AEC is a prisoner of industry: if industry is not interested in pursuing that particular use of the nuclear explosion which is technically best, the AEC can't do a thing about it, as its role is simply to provide nuclear explosives for suitable projects conceived by industry. That is why so vast an amount of effort has gone into gas stimulation and so very little into the technology of waste disposal in deep caverns. If bureaucratic bungles were a natural resource, surely the mother lode must be at the AEC.

VII
THE REAL
PROBLEMS WITH
ATOMIC ENERGY
TODAY

[The people in this country] are going to have their
electricity and they are going to shut up about eco-
logical conditions. They are all comfort seekers.
　　　　　—REPRESENTATIVE CRAIG HOSMER,
　　　　　Joint Committee on Atomic Energy[501]

1 · THE JOB ISN'T BEING DONE WELL
AND THERE'S NOWHERE TO GO

AMERICA is running out of conventional fuels. With two dozen years
of proven reserves left, natural gas and oil are already used up, from
the point of view of the long-range energy planner. Sunlight, the
only new form of energy worth considering, has far too many drawbacks to be ready in time to solve America's impending energy crisis.
The environmentalists cry for reducing our population, and each of
us working to conserve electricity is simply not realistic, as it is based
upon a misunderstanding of why we use so much power.[502] The only
conventional fuel left is coal, and even those reserves are finite: they
will last a couple of hundred years. Therefore sooner or later, and
like it or not, America will be powered by nuclear energy.

And so there is a serious job to do, to develop and supply nuclear power for America's future. But how can we expect that the job will get done properly when the exclusive responsibility for accomplishing it lies in the hands of demonstrable incompetents? Although that seems like a harsh word, in the most meaningful sense it is true. The long history of the AEC's technical blunders aside for the moment, it must be admitted that the AEC *has* accomplished the hard (and exciting) parts of its two main jobs: it has brought the nuclear power reactor into existence and it has provided us with a mighty arsenal of nuclear weapons. But, as might be expected from its history, the AEC has all but ignored the unglamorous aspects of both technologies, aspects second in importance only to bringing the technology into existence in the first place. They are the problems of radioactive waste disposal and the development of emergency methods to handle the worst type of accident likely to happen to a nuclear reactor, the loss of its coolant fluid. Thus I would define organizational competence as the ability to do the *whole* job, not just part of it. The AEC has failed in this respect not just once, but in *both* of its two major endeavors.

As to the political aspects, the Joint Committee on Atomic Energy has taken sides, protecting the AEC and joining it in a closed loop of values, judgments and decisions, with the public very deliberately and conspicuously left out. This arrangement is becoming increasingly intolerable as the public, realizing that it has been denied its rightful voice, expresses its frustration by attempting to stop virtually every nuclear-power reactor in the country. Add to this the undisguised contempt for the public's intervention on the part of the men who run atomic energy in the United States, and it is no wonder that, denied a legitimate outlet, the tensions and pressures have built up to the degree we observe today. Nuclear reactors are widely regarded by the public as being even more dangerous than they really are, with the result that, tarred with the same brush, even the good that nuclear energy can bring us could be denied to our society. And if that happens, it will be due to no more than the insolent and inflexible behavior of those old-timers in the AEC and on the Joint Committee who refuse to accept the fact that what they conceive of as the public's interest cannot be entirely correct, as the increasingly effective campaign against the nuclear-power plants ought to have indicated to them by now.

2 · THE AEC'S PRIORITIES ARE REVERSED, AND WHY

POSSIBLY the best testament to the misplaced values of the American atomic establishment is its history of doing everything backwards. Two decades of boiling radioactive wastes were produced by the weapons program before the AEC addressed itself in any meaningful way to solving the problems of waste disposal. Reactors have been on line for over a decade and the AEC is just beginning to direct itself to the emergency core cooling system, the only way thought of so far to arrest a core melt-down accident before it goes too far. The nuclear-rocket program steams along without a scrubber to capture the radioactive effluents produced by each experiment, while pork-barrel politicians whine that unless another *billion dollars* is poured into that totally unneeded nuclear-rocket program a "national crime" will have taken place.

Compare the AEC's attitude toward the testing of its products for the military and the civilian markets. Nuclear-weapons tests simulated on computers simply won't do for the military; even the smallest design changes must be subjected to an actual test. Accordingly, the underground explosions go on and on, since the military does not tolerate uncertainty. It's an open secret that Cannikin, the five-megaton test that took place under Amchitka Island, Alaska, in late 1971, provided almost no information not already known, but when it comes to weapons the AEC cannot be too sure. On the civilian side, however, everything is just the opposite. None of the existing twenty-three nuclear-power reactors, or the fifty-four already under construction, has ever been tested for the accident that the nuclear engineer worries about most: the loss of cooling fluid and the subsequent melt-down of the reactor core.

In late 1966 the AEC organized a task force to study that problem. Completed the next year, the Ergen Report (named for the task-force leader, the late Dr. W. K. Ergen) described the sequence of events to be expected in the event of a loss-of-coolant accident at a nuclear-power reactor. In little more than one minute the temperature of the reactor core would reach well over three thousand degrees Fahrenheit, causing "core collapse" and melt-down of the core material, which would accumulate at the bottom of the reactor vessel. The report goes on: "Pressure-vessel melt-through might be expected to take from 20 to 60 minutes." Ralph Lapp described it this way:

The behavior of this huge, molten radioactive mass is difficult to predict, but the Ergen report contains an analysis showing that the high-temperature mass would sink into the earth and continue to grow in size for about two years. In dry sand, a hot sphere of about 100 feet in diameter might form and persist for a decade. This behavior projection is known as the China syndrome.[503]

The "China syndrome" is the nuclear engineers' half-serious description of where the molten blob would head for as it melted its way through our planet.

Instead of developing the emergency core-cooling system *before* the reactors went into service all across America, the AEC put it off. The *first test* of a prototype safety system won't take place until 1974. Unlike its weapons development, what the AEC has done here is to rely upon a computer program which *simulates* an actual accident, but that turned out to be a pipedream, too. One experiment on a non-nuclear, electrically heated "reactor core" was held at the AEC's National Reactor Testing Station in Idaho in November of 1970. In that test, the main cooling line was broken deliberately, thus permitting the regular cooling water to escape and causing the emergency core-cooling water to flow. But instead of cooling the "core," the emergency core-cooling water merely went out of the same hole in the line. R. Kingsley House, the man in charge of that test, admitted that the computer analysis had not predicted that un-expected result.[504]

Thus, what little evidence exists today indicates that a rupture of a main cooling line, by accident or sabotage, is *all that is needed* to cause a reactor-core melt-down, the nuclear engineer's idea of the worst accident imaginable. And sabotage is not a farfetched worry, either; it almost certainly has happened already. Consolidated Edison's new Indian Point No. 2 nuclear reactor (an 873-megawatt plant) is only forty miles north of New York City. Late in 1971 it was hit with a fire of suspicious origin which caused nearly $5 million worth of damage. Daniel McMahon, the Westchester County sheriff said, "We have not altered our view that the evidence in our possession indicates that it was arson."[505]

Repeating history, it took an independent scientific group to bring the dangers of the lack of an emergency core-cooling system to pub-lic attention and finally to galvanize the AEC into quicker action. In its first report on the subject, the Union of Concerned Scientists said that the AEC's safety systems were "substantially inadequate and, we believe, cannot even add marginally to the presently narrow, or possibly non-existent, margin of safety in a loss-of-coolant acci-dent."[506] In the scientists' second report they concluded that "the gaps in basic knowledge concerning the effectiveness of the safety features of large power reactors, the surprising scarcity of adequate tests—amounting nearly to a total lack—has astonished our group, especially in view of the large number of apparently hazardous de-signs that are already operating."[507]

History demonstrates clearly that every major AEC effort has in-volved at least one monumental blunder. It would seem that a re-actor-core melt-down after loss of coolant at a large civilian electric-power plant will be the next blunder to be expected. It is as sure to come, sooner or later, as fires come to old wooden factory buildings unprotected by sprinkler systems. When that happens, public pres-sure will not only force the precipitous liquidation of the Atomic Energy Commission itself, it will also spell the end of nuclear power in America for a very long time, with everybody the loser.

Those acquainted with the way the AEC ranks its priorities are inevitably astonished at its lack of sensible planning and how that could have been permitted by its "watchdog" in Congress, the Joint Committee on Atomic Energy. But the reason behind all those wrong decisions is really very simple. In any technical adventure, there are exciting parts and there are dull parts. An analysis of every AEC blunder to date indicates clearly that the AEC has accomplished the exciting aspects of every job with competence, expertise and dispatch. But as with individuals, organizational competence isn't defined as doing exclusively just what pleases and satisfies. There's also the dull but inescapable part of any job which must get done, too, like cleaning up the mess after a job is over.

The breakdown of checks and balances which occurred when the Joint Committee set aside its watchdog responsibilities left the AEC like a child without parental supervision. Accordingly, without anyone to answer to, the AEC's priorities were permitted to degenerate into atomic trivia and glamour, far less difficult and dangerous than trying to contain a molten reactor core, and far more exciting than nuclear garbage. It is for this simple reason that the AEC had too much freedom to do what it pleased, and could ignore what was dull and boring; that caused it to become the incompetent agency it is today. Because to do half a job well is not enough, the whole job must be done competently or it might be better left not done at all.

The AEC promoter, freed from having to contemplate the unattractive aspects of his product, found the sky no limit for his fantasies. He became the "question man," an old vaudeville routine where instead of answering questions the question man provided the answer first; the question came later, along with the laughs. But the answer was always the same—it was atomic energy. Everything from power so that cheap electric meters would be obsolete to nuclear-powered airplanes that would never have to land—all of it would come from atomic energy.

And if anyone cared to dispute those promises, he was treated with scorn, abuse and the "Soviet threat." While that threat was true during the development of the hydrogen bomb, it hasn't been true since. The Russians haven't flown a nuclear airplane (and presumably haven't wasted a billion dollars trying), despite the "authoritative reports" printed by the kept technological press. The Russians haven't developed a nuclear rocket (and presumably haven't wasted $1.5 billion trying), despite the warnings of the AEC/NASA industrial contractors. The Russians haven't taken over the international irradiated-food business (and presumably haven't wasted millions trying) despite the warnings of AEC Commissioner Ramey.

What seems never to have been suggested is that perhaps it would be better, in a chancy technology not demonstrably vital to national defense, if we would just let the Russians do it first. Let them waste their money, and if it turns out that they are successful we will have had the hardest question answered for us free: Can it be done at all? Once that is known, we can catch up with them quickly, as history has already shown. The Soviets took far less time to develop an atomic-weapon capability because, from our lead, they knew just which way to go and thereby saved a lot of their time, effort and money. Likewise, we developed our rocket technology far faster than they did (and even surpassed them) because they did it first and thereby helped us in just the same way.

But it's easy to get carried away with atomic pie-in-the-sky schemes, imagining Ivan at the door with a bigger and better atomic mousetrap. The facts are that nuclear waste is dull and can't compete with the glamorous blasts that caused such an accumulation of waste; and reactor-core melt-down prevention is dull (and dangerous) and can't compare with the glamour of producing cheap and limitless electricity for mankind from a totally new source of energy.

3 · TURNING ON THE LIGHTS, AND TURNING OFF THE PUBLIC

PREDICTABLY, in the development of nuclear reactors, the arrogance of the atomic promoters became the root cause (and even the source of motivating energy) for widespread, dedicated public opposition to nuclear-power plants. The Joint Committee and the AEC were no strangers to bending or even breaking the law when democratic tradition and due process of law threatened to slow down what they conceived of as being the "orderly development of nuclear energy." Accordingly, they cut a lot of legal corners to get the nuclear reactors out of the laboratory and on line at the power plants across America.

If there ever was a key point in the development of nuclear-power reactors it was December 1963, when the Jersey Central Power and Light Company announced that it was going to build a boiling-water nuclear reactor at Oyster Creek, New Jersey, with no *direct* government subsidy. It was optimistically predicted that cheap, competitively priced nuclear electric power could be produced, and it seemed as though the civilian nuclear power reactors had come of age. The cost of electricity delivered from the plant (including construction and operation costs) was estimated to be about 3.5 mills per kilowatt hour (in the same ball park then as conventionally produced electricity). But projections made in 1969 showed plants running twice that figure, causing the drop in orders for nuclear plants that year.[508] In 1971 AEC officials were estimating 8.2 mills nuclear and 8.3 mills coal-fired,[509] but these AEC figures do not take into account the heavily subsidized nature of the whole nuclear-reactor business, from free insurance (the Price–Anderson Act)[510] to government programs to handle nuclear waste. But since it is the taxpaying public and not the utility which pays for the hidden extras, 1971 saw an increase in reactor orders.

In order to make the nuclear plants more economical, they have been scaled up sharply in size, with strong side effects for both the public and the electric-power industry. While the reactors in operation in 1966 ranged up to 265 megawatts electric power, those on the drawing boards had already far surpassed that size. Those ordered in 1966 averaged eight hundred megawatts, and today plant orders run to over a thousand megawatts. The cost too has skyrocketed. The price now ranges to even more than $500 million for each plant.

Though these big plants do indeed bring an economy of scale, they also make an electric-power industry particularly vulnerable to breakdown. If one of a large number of small plants breaks down, then others can temporarily handle the extra load. But when New York City's Big Allis, a 1,000-megawatt oil-fired generator, broke down on July 21, 1970, it knocked out fully fourteen percent of the city's electrical capacity.[511] Such is the stuff of brownouts and blackouts.

And what does the sharply increased size of the new plants mean for the electrical industry itself? It means that the big get bigger and the small get squeezed out. In this case, the small are generally the tiny rural cooperatives and city-owned electric-power plants. Most of the rural cooperatives supply power to the scattered farms and villages of America, averaging about two customers per mile of power line (while the big, privately owned power companies average thirty to forty).[512] These little companies can't find a banker or float bonds or organize the finances for a $500-million nuclear reactor. Even if they could raise the money, they cannot find enough customers for a plant which produces one thousand megawatts. Therefore they (and their customers) are shut out from the benefits of nuclear energy by the economics of scale. As William C. Wise, a lawyer for the Mid-West Electric Consumers' Association, Inc., told the Joint Committee, ". . . if our member cooperatives and municipal electric systems are not given the opportunity to obtain the necessary share of the low-cost power and energy to be generated by the large nuclear plants, they will be forced out of business and absorbed by the investor-owned electric utilities before the end of this century."[512]

The move to bigness swept across the whole electric-power industry, and, as a consequence, the small electric utility was indeed shut out. In this way, the situation rapidly approached a "combination in restraint of free trade," or, in other words, a violation of antitrust laws. But the Atomic Energy Act foresaw this; it was the intent then, as now, to provide everyone with the benefits of atomic energy, since everyone paid for the development of that new form of energy. Until 1970, there was even a legal requirement binding the AEC to submit any application for the construction of a nuclear-power reactor to the Justice Department to see if it would "tend to create or maintain a situation inconsistent with the antitrust laws." If a reactor could be developed and looked as if it might be a commercial success, the AEC would formally send a letter to the President saying that the reactor had "practical value." Then the commercial licensing would begin, subject to the antitrust review.

But to be licensed as a commercial reactor would make the electric utility companies subject to antitrust laws. Then they couldn't squeeze out the smaller utilities by building increasingly larger nuclear reactors. The electric companies were interested in expansion (bigger reactors) *and so was the AEC*. Accordingly, the AEC gave a very big present to all those electric utility companies who wanted to build big nuclear reactors. The AEC decided that the nuclear reactors had *no* "practical value"!

Surely, the Oyster Creek announcement in 1963 made it apparent that the big reactors had practical value. But the AEC "shut its eyes to the reality of commercial feasibility," as Senator George Aiken, Vermont Republican and Joint Committee member, noted in a speech to the Senate on March 4, 1970. The AEC refused twice, after hearings, to license them as commercial reactors. Though there may have been a rush to go nuclear, the AEC continued to license "every new plant . . . as a research project under the *medical therapy* section of the law."[513]* Such "experimental" licenses were good for forty years, a rather long "experiment."

The situation clarifies when it is seen for what it really is: a conspiracy by the AEC and the utilities to evade antitrust laws. "The failure of the AEC to make any practical value finding naturally pleases the utilities and their friends, because it leaves them free from antitrust legislation," Senator Aiken said. The reactors were certainly producing electric power and selling it, and plenty of the plants were on order. The utilities are sensitive about antitrust laws and for good reason, since they are very actively trying to consolidate and enlarge their markets. For an indication of their success, consider the fact that the total number of electric utilities has dwin-

* Emphasis added.

dled in number from one thousand corporations in 1945 to three hundred today.[514] "Economics of scale" gave the big utilities a convenient handle to force the smaller competitors out of the market while the AEC ducked its responsibility and covered it all with the absurdity of a forty-year "research" project. But what about motives? The AEC was paid off by the great support given to its nuclear-reactor program by industry, both before Congress and before the public. Industry, on the other hand, benefited enormously since that section of the act that licensed the nuclear reactors as "experiments" specified that there would be "a minimum amount" of regulations as well.

The Joint Committee, after two years of effort by Senator Aiken, took the bull by the tail, not the horns, and simply wiped out the "practical value" part of the law, softened the antitrust review sections and gave the industry one more present: it exempted the seventy-three nuclear reactors under construction or completed at the time. They will *all* be "experiments."

But the "experimental" label is a fake. There is nothing magical about reactors; there is very little in physics to distinguish them from the first controlled nuclear experiment which took place on December 2, 1942, in a squash court under the west stands of Stagg Field in Chicago. In that experiment cadmium control rods were drawn out of the fuel, thereby causing the first sustained nuclear chain reaction ever to take place.[515] Today's most modern commercial reactor works on the same principle. Former Senator Albert Gore, a member of the Joint Committee for many years, noted, ". . . we are really still proceeding with relatively primitive reactor concepts."[516] The men who invented the "experimental" sham did so because they were dissatisfied with the legal strictures binding them to the "orderly development of nuclear energy." Like all zealots, they knew what was right and found convenient justification for their questionable practices in their belief that the quick development of nuclear energy was worth it all.

Another point where, if not the principle of due process of law, certainly fair play was abused is the AEC's licensing process. Although that procedure is represented by the AEC as providing the opportunity for meaningful public participation all along the way, this is not so.

The first step in the licensing process occurs when the utility applies for an AEC construction permit. The issuance of that permit is determined by the AEC's own regulatory staff and the AEC's Advisory Committee on Reactor Safeguards (also appointed by the AEC). Although they review the application with great care and dedication, there is no public participation at all. It is only after both of those groups approve the construction permit application that a mandatory public hearing takes place, and this is heard before a three-man panel of the AEC's Safety and Licensing Board. Unless there is an intervenor, the only parties at the public hearing before the AEC's board are the utility applicant himself and the AEC's regulatory staff, whose role it is to defend its conclusions already arrived at in private. Since there is no mechanism for public participation until the AEC regulatory staff has already made its decision, the fact is that the position of the regulatory staff is frozen long before the public has ever had a chance to participate. Therefore, the regulatory staff *always* finds itself aligned against any intervenor representing the public at those hearings.

Anyone from the outside wanting to be heard in protest has only a few weeks in which to prepare his case, while the AEC has been carefully considering its own position for a year or two. "Requests for postponement of the hearing are strenuously resisted by the AEC staff and the applicant [the utility], since delay will interfere with the applicant's having new power capacity on line when scheduled and needed," Harold Green noted. "The hearing itself is a strange, hybrid affair, part town meeting and part legal proceeding, with the parts interspersed." The objector and his lawyer are required to sit through endless proceedings, day after day, and even though most of the action does not concern them, they are required to be present anyway. "The entire proceeding is reminiscent of David versus Goliath," Mr. Green said. "The intervenor's counsel, sitting alone, usually without adequate technical assistance, faces two or three

AEC attorneys, two or three attorneys for the applicant, and large teams of experts who support the AEC and applicant's attorneys."[517]

In 1971 I accepted an invitation to testify on behalf of the intervenors in the case of the proposed Shoreham (nuclear) station of the Long Island Lighting Company in New York. According to AEC rules, my testimony was prepared in written form and was in the AEC's hands months in advance of my scheduled appearance. Furthermore, I was informed that my testimony would be restricted to what I had written, and at my appearance I would not be allowed to add to it or elaborate upon it in any way, once it had been submitted to the AEC in written form months before.

Now, the AEC has a blatantly self-serving rule: it will not rule upon the admissibility of testimony unless the witness is present at the time of the ruling. This is true despite the fact that during the months the AEC has any written testimony in hand, there can be (and were in my case) many opportunities (hearing days, when representatives of all sides are present) to rule upon the admissibility of such testimony. On the surface this seems to be a good idea: a safeguard so that the witness's testimony is not judged in his absence, so that he may confront those who seek to disallow his testimony and rebut their arguments. But this isn't so. The witness must be present, all right, but during the deliberations on admissibility he must stand mute and therefore *cannot* defend himself or his testimony. Therefore, no legitimate purpose is served by requiring the witness to be present at that time.

But there is a nonlegitimate purpose in requiring the witness to be present, though mute. It is to accomplish exactly what the AEC has accomplished in my case: to discourage a witness from "testifying" at another hearing, when that witness must travel across the country as I did; for what witness would do so if he knows in advance that his testimony may be disallowed at the pleasure of the AEC ruling board?[518] If his testimony is favorable to the AEC, he can reasonably expect no worries at all; if it is damaging to the AEC, he now knows that his chances of being heard at all are small, since it is the AEC board itself which makes the ruling.

Techniques such as this violate not only due process of law (a constitutional guarantee to which the AEC is not bound) but fair play, common sense and even enlightened self-interest as well. Remarkably, after freely indulging in this nefarious hypocrisy, the AEC still wonders why it is being "persecuted" by the public.

The real vice as I see it [Harold Green said] lies in the assumption that scientists and engineers are omniscient and possess almost infinite capacity to solve problems and permanently to fix leaky faucets. Our society has permitted these experts to play God: to assess benefits, to define risks, and to determine what risks the public must assume, cheerfully, just as it pays taxes, in exchange for benefits which the experts think the public should have.

What is more, under the carefully nurtured myth that judgments as to nuclear safety can be soundly made only by these experts, we have permitted these experts to decide these risk–benefit questions largely behind closed doors and in the esoteric, obfuscatory jargon of their disciplines. . . .

What is needed is to drag the entire process out into the open so that the public will have a full opportunity to comprehend the risks and benefits. The establishment tells us that the licensing process takes place today in a goldfish bowl. Perhaps this is true, but the bowl is opaque with vision permitted only through the opening at the top.[517]

But despite all the obstacles, interventions in nuclear-power-plant licensing proceedings have increased sharply in the last few years. The Joint Committee's Craig Hosmer, for one, would like to see procedures made more efficient by getting rid of the public intervenors. Speaking to the American Nuclear Society in May 1971, he said:

Tossing aside the antitrust and power preference hanky-panky and forgetting the newly imposed environmental determinations for the moment, there remains just one ultimate question the licensing procedure has to answer and that is: Is there a reasonable assurance that this reactor is designed and will be constructed and operated so as to prevent accidents from happening and to mitigate their consequences if they do? Yes or No?

The decision is the AEC's, he said, "not the applicant's, nor the public's nor the intervenor's," adding that he wasn't sure the presence of "a lot of environmental dilettantes and their hovering legal eagles has ever contributed much to nuclear safety or ever will."[519]

But all of the elaborate safety precautions, the safety research, the insurance coverage so huge that the federal government has to provide the financial protection lest a loss bankrupt the insurance industry, the concern over radiation safety limits, the gigantic steel and concrete reactor vessels and buildings, the double-safe emergency control systems for operating reactors, the extreme precautions needed for handling atomic waste—all of it is a frank testament to the dangers involved in the nuclear reactors. It is too big a responsibility to leave to Representative Hosmer and the others like him on the Joint Committee, or to Milton Shaw and the rest at the AEC. They have demonstrated already that they cannot handle easier jobs than this without outside help. Now they need that help more than ever.

4 · THE PRIMA-DONNA PROBLEM

ONE very strong reason, often overlooked, why the AEC has so frequently found itself clinging desperately to a technically discredited plan has to do with the sponsor of that plan, how powerful he is within the AEC, and how able he is thereby to promote his plan. It's no accident, for example, that plutonium has always held a special position in the dreams of the atomic promoter, at least since Glenn Seaborg became the chairman of the AEC. "The ornery element," as he calls it, received undue attention as the isotope of choice when other radioactive elements would almost certainly be better suited for the job (see Chapter VI). Seaborg has a special attachment to this element because he is plutonium's co-discoverer, a fact of which his audiences are frequently reminded. Consider his personal identification with the stuff: "This is the element to which

I had devoted many of my younger years,"[520] and "there is also the significant place plutonium occupies in my own life."[227] He regards the element much as his own child: "Born on a humble research budget and cradled in a cigar box, [plutonium] will have become the energy giant of the future,"[224] and "I am so well acquainted with plutonium's early childhood that I am inclined to view it as one might consider a 'bad' child."[227]

It is not generally appreciated (although obvious on reflection) that the discoverers of technical advances have an irresistible tendency to exaggerate the importance of their discoveries. Consider Seaborg's words: "If Brigham Young would have gazed down upon the first visible amount of plutonium and would have anticipated its future as he had done with his valley of the Great Salt Lake, I think he would have exclaimed, 'This is the element!' instead of the now famous 'This is the place!' . . . No other element has commanded such caution, carefulness and respect."[520]

It would be impossible to discover today just how far Seaborg's personal power was responsible for what many regard as the AEC's overreliance on an element whose unimaginable toxicity might vitiate any benefit it could otherwise provide. Our nation is now committed to the development of the breeder reactor, a program which could easily provide at least as many risks from plutonium as benefits, and a program for which all the value judgments concerning those risks have already been made, in ignorance of their actual magnitude, and in secret, by the program's promoters.[521]

When a powerful bureaucrat in the AEC sticks his neck out as far as Milton Shaw did when he attempted to commit our nuclear wastes to what must be the only wet salt mine in the country (see Chapter V), it takes a lot to make him, and therefore the AEC, admit to error. Shaw not only has great political power inside the atomic establishment, but he is a forceful, able man as well. A nuclear-reactor company official says of Shaw:

Even those who don't especially like him think he's highly competent. He went to school under Admiral Rickover in the Navy reactor program—and he soaked up a good deal of that quasi-Prussian, autocratic tradition. But you can take it as axiomatic that government projects succeed best when the project manager is smarter and tougher and meaner than the private industry people he's dealing with. And Shaw is all of those things.[522]

But Shaw can also make mistakes, and he made a big one in March of 1971. Unfortunately, all of those fine abilities of his can and are being used to gloss over the seriousness of that error and then some. For example, Shaw is also the administrator responsible for the nondevelopment of the emergency core-cooling system to prevent a reactor-core melt-down accident; a *New York Times* story on the subject could not include Shaw's comments on the subject, because repeated "attempts to contact Mr. Shaw by telephone were fruitless."[504]

Perhaps even more serious is how mistakes made by the AEC are permitted to influence the attention paid to the development of new technical advances related to those mistakes. About the same time as the Lyons salt-mine fiasco, a plausible alternative to salt-bed disposal was put forward by scientists at the AEC's Lawrence Livermore Laboratory in California. They proposed to store high-level radioactive wastes in a cavern created by a nuclear explosion detonated six thousand feet underground. Unlike the Kansas mine, which sits atop a water-bearing layer in the earth, this "Plowshare method," as it is called, would provide a far deeper cavern that would be well below available water-bearing rocks. Perhaps more important, the new method would avoid the transportation hazards of the single-dump concept. The Kansas plan calls for carrying the hot wastes from all over the country to Lyons, with the real possibility of a roadside radioactive spill. Under the Plowshare plan, one cavern near each of three nuclear fuel-reprocessing plants could contain all the electric industry's nuclear waste until the turn of the century.[523]

Ordinarily, a plan like this would have received considerable support from the AEC, especially since the Plowshare method is so sensible, but it did not coincide with AEC party line. The AEC was committed to salt-bed disposal for radioactive waste, and to support anything else would be for the AEC to admit to what everyone concerned already knew—that the AEC had made a fool of itself over the Lyons, Kansas, proposed atom dump. Accordingly, pressures against the Plowshare method began building inside the AEC. A critique of the method was prepared which itself is a monument to bureaucratic trivia. The document sniped at small points, even criticizing the distribution list (". . . there seems to be no point in providing AEC technical reports to *him*"), but failed to raise a single technical objection.[524]

The project sponsors were obliged to adopt a "low profile" posture on the matter. This is AEC jargon for keeping something quiet though not secret; publicity was discouraged and press releases were avoided. The reason given to the Lawrence Livermore Laboratory by AEC headquarters for all of this (according to a scientist close to the situation), was that "waste policy is established and this proposal [the Plowshare method] is contrary to that policy and therefore will only confuse and impede the orderly implementation of our [AEC headquarters] policy of radioactive-waste disposal in salt." Again, no *technical* objections to the novel approach were raised. It will be an interesting paradox (but historically consistent) if the very technique which finally solves the radioactive-waste problem has to do so over the objections of the AEC itself.

In the promotion of nuclear energy, the AEC and the Joint Committee have never lacked for men of self-righteous zeal. But such devotedness carries drawbacks as well. Consider the case of former AEC Commissioner Francesco Costagliola. On May 7, 1969, he wrote to Kenneth S. Pitzer, president of Stanford University,[525] and Howard W. Johnson, president of the Massachusetts Institute of Technology,[526] warning that he would withdraw $40 million worth of nondefense AEC research grants if those universities were to "cave in to campus dissidents," as Costagliola described it himself in an interview a month later.[527] He wrote to Cornell,[528] Johns Hopkins,[529] and the University of Minnesota[530] as well; even though there was no trouble at those universities, he called attention to the amount of AEC support each university was receiving and enclosed a "reprint which reflects some of my views regarding the academic community."[531] In retrospect, it seems barely believable that a man could so flagrantly use his influence as an AEC commissioner to force universities to accept, along with their other obligations under their AEC contracts, his own personal solution to the political problems of the day. Interestingly, no voice was raised in the AEC against Costagliola's vulgar impropriety.

At one time the long arm of the AEC could reach well beyond the president of a university; it influenced events down at the faculty-meeting level as well. In 1959, Dr. William O. Pruitt, Jr., worked under an AEC grant to the University of Alaska. A biologist, Pruitt studied the mammals of the Cape Thompson region of Alaska in connection with an AEC-supported ecological study of the area for Project Chariot. That was the AEC's plan to use nuclear explosives to excavate a harbor well north of the Arctic Circle, about thirty miles southeast of Point Hope, on the shores of the Chukchi Sea.

Pruitt's research findings were unfavorable to the AEC's plan (Project Chariot never did come off) and led him to the conclusion that the several nuclear explosions would be detrimental to the life of the area, particularly to the Eskimos.[532] A dispute arose in which University of Alaska officials maintained that Pruitt's reports were unsatisfactory. Countercharges were made, suggesting that AEC pressures to edit Pruitt's findings were responsible for the university's displeasure and Pruitt's subsequent departure from his post.[533] Pruitt then applied to the department of zoology at the University of Montana for a position. Because of the controversy in Alaska, more than the usual attention was paid to his application in Montana. After an investigation, it was the zoology department's unanimous recommendation to hire Dr. Pruitt.

The Montana zoologists were surprised to be told that their deans "were rejecting the unanimous recommendation from the zoology staff to employ Dr. William Pruitt." At a zoology staff meeting in 1963, Dean Abbott told how he was "advised to contact Dr. John Wolfe of the AEC. This Dean Abbott did by phone and he obtained an unfavorable report on Dr. Pruitt from Dr. Wolfe. . . . Dean Abbott explained to the zoology staff that on the basis of unfavorable impressions he had obtained about Dr. Pruitt from these conversations with Dr. Wolfe . . . he was rejecting Dr. Pruitt's application."[534] Dr. E. W. Pfeiffer, a professor of zoology at the University of Montana and one of those present at the 1963 meeting, recalled those days recently; he said, "The actions of the University of Montana administration in assisting the AEC's blackballing of Pruitt over the unanimous wishes of the Department involved constituted an unprecedented event at this institution."[535]

There is still a dispute, of course, concerning the reasons for Pruitt's departure from the University of Alaska. His competence, at least, is not in question, especially considering Pruitt's unanimous approval by Montana's Department of Zoology. AEC people tell me today that the reason was that Pruitt's final report was technically incomplete. But for whatever reasons the university and the AEC were dissatisfied with his study, one thing is clear. If Pruitt's conclusions were favorable to the AEC, those differences would have been resolved without Pruitt having to leave the University of Alaska: scientific reports are routinely rewritten for any number of reasons. Likewise, the blackballing of Pruitt at the University of Montana would not have occurred had his conclusions been favorable to Project Chariot. Assuming the worst, that Pruitt had indeed submitted an incomplete report, even that seems scant justification for going through what must have been a lot of trouble to convince the University of Montana to overrule its own people in "an unprecedented event" at that institution.

I have personally observed a more recent attempt at intimidation by a highly placed individual in the AEC. In 1970, the Colorado Committee for Environmental Information, a group of scientist-critics,[536] produced a study proving that there was far more plutonium in the soil around the fire-prone Dow-AEC Rocky Flats weapons plant (just outside Denver) than plant officials had admitted to until then.[537] The AEC was very concerned, because it realized, correctly, that the plutonium study would cause it a great deal of embarrassment. Accordingly, on February 10 the AEC convened a meeting in Denver between senior officials from the AEC and Dow and the members of the Colorado Committee for Environmental Information.[237]

During the luncheon break, Dr. Martin Biles, director of the AEC's Division of Operational Safety, approached two of the Colorado Committee scientists and questioned them closely as to who their employers were and where the plutonium study was done. The men answered that they both worked at the Department of Commerce's laboratories in Boulder, and that the study was done at the National Science Foundation-supported National Center for Atmospheric Research. Dr. Biles then said, "You won't mind if I bring this matter up with the appropriate officials of the Department of Commerce and the National Science Foundation." He added that he had a "personal hangup about one federal agency engaging in activities critical of another federal agency."[538] Even though Biles was informed that the two federal employees were on annual leave that day, and that the National Center for Atmospheric Research, where the plutonium study was done, "is a private, independent, nonprofit, university-affiliated corporation," Dr. Biles repeated his charges at the meeting after it resumed.[539]

Dr. Seaborg, regarding the incident as an "unfortunate situation," stated that "it is not an AEC objective to try to restrict freedom of expression by individuals."[540] But of course, although true, that's not the problem. Don Price said that "the most tyrannical political systems are built not on corruption, but on self-righteous fanaticism."[541] Accordingly the question is, how can the AEC escape breeding a cadre of arrogant zealots like Costagliola, Shaw and Biles when that agency, having lost contact with its public purpose, devotes its main energies to serving itself?

5 · BREAKING UP THE AEC

FOR SEVERAL YEARS there has been talk of "disbanding" the AEC. There is widespread agreement that there has been disproportionate attention given to atomic energy, at the expense of development of other forms of energy. After all, energy from the atom is just one source of energy among the many required now and in the future. The present situation, wherein oil, gas, coal and nuclear energy compete with each other for the favors of the public and the politicians, is neither useful nor productive. The winner will not necessarily be the best, for the outcome of the race will be determined by which promoter spends the most money on his publicity campaign. In this respect the AEC, in its promotion of atomic energy, clearly has an unfair advantage. Unlike the others, it pays no taxes and is not subject to unrealistic price controls like the natural-gas industry. But most unlike the others, the AEC has never had to earn the money it so lavishly spends on promoting itself; the taxpayer takes care of that matter.

Obviously the AEC is not alone in having outlived its usefulness in its present form. The same is true, more or less, for almost every other governmental agency. Addressing himself to that question, President Nixon called the attention of Congress to the sad state of inefficiency and unresponsiveness of the Executive Department of the government.[542] He could have been (and was to some degree) talking about the atomic-energy bureaucracy.

Of course, the President had something in mind. On April 5, 1969, Mr. Nixon had announced the appointment of a President's Advisory Council on Executive Organization. The eighth major study of executive reorganization since 1937, the group became known as the Ash Council, named for its chairman, Roy L. Ash, president of Litton Industries. The Ash Council recommended that many governmental departments and agencies be regrouped into four new departments, one of which is to be a Department of Natural Resources.[543] Legislation establishing the new Department of Natural Resources has already been prepared by Senator Charles H. Percy (R., Ill.).[544]

Contrary to what is commonly supposed, the new plan does not break up the AEC. Only about twenty percent of that agency's responsibilities will be moved over to the Department of Natural Resources.[545] They are to be uranium raw materials and enrichment and the "policy and funding" of civilian nuclear-powered reactors and Plowshare. "Operations" of both the AEC's civilian nuclear-power program, Project Plowshare, and the fusion-reactor program will remain at the AEC, contrary to the Ash Council's recommendation.[546]

The only other time in its history that the AEC was threatened with a reorganization directed by outsiders was in 1961 (see Chapter I). Then the agency anticipated the move and reorganized itself to suit itself, thereby blunting the attacks of its intended reformers by presenting them with an accomplished fact. Nothing much more was done then to change things, except that Harold L. Price's title was changed from director of licensing and regulation to director of regulation. Ten years later the AEC, faced with another reorganization threat, reacted in just the same way. The main difference in 1971 was that the threat was more potent and so the AEC's internal reorganization was much more extensive. Presidential prestige was behind a total reorganization of the entire Executive Department of the United States government, and the AEC could see what was coming. Consequently, on December 7, 1971, well before any of President Nixon's recommendations could even be debated by Congress, R. E. Hollingsworth, the AEC's general manager, announced sweeping organizational changes in the Atomic Energy Commission.[547] Nine general program areas were reduced to six (but the total number of divisions remained about the same.)

The AEC's internal reorganization was widely reported to have been in response to public pressure for a reorientation of the AEC's priorities. One AEC source discussed the changes as "a top management shake-up and a major reorientation of the AEC's objectives."[548] For example, one new program area is called Environmental and Safety Affairs, but a closer look reveals that the same old divisions (Operational Safety, Waste Management, etc.) are found under that catchy title.

Another reason given for the reorganization has to do with making the agency more efficient. AEC Chairman Schlesinger said that "the realignment of the agency staff—the first broad reorganization in ten years—essentially pulls together various related programs which previously had been scattered, and streamlines our staff organization."[547] While there can be no doubt that an organizational change every decade can streamline the staff and create increased efficiency, the main reason for the sweeping changes at the AEC seems to be something quite different than either public pressure or a desire for increased efficiency.

In addition to the reasons already mentioned, the 1971 reorganization of the AEC was apparently designed not only to anticipate the conclusions of the Ash Council and the subsequent recommendations of the President (all of which involved only twenty percent of the AEC) but to anticipate the eventual total disassembly of the entire Atomic Energy Commission. All of the AEC programs which have been selected for inclusion in the Department of Natural Resources have been grouped together in two divisions to facilitate their easy transfer to the new agency ("Energy and Development Programs" and "Production and Management of Nuclear Materials"). More significantly, though, all defense-oriented programs have been collected into one division ("National Security"), all scientific programs in another ("Research"), and all environmental matters in still another ("Environment and Safety"). This arrangement greatly simplifies the eventual transfer of the "Environment and Safety" division to the Environmental Protection Agency, the "Research" division (the laboratories) to the Office of Science and Technology, National Science Foundation, and "National Security" to the Department of Defense, where it belongs. With five divisions thus spun off to their more natural homes, requirements for managers by the overloaded staff of those other five agencies would absorb the personnel of the remaining division at the AEC: "Administration."

6 · A UNIQUE PROBLEM FOR A DEMOCRACY

IN OUR AMERICAN SYSTEM, when a governmental agency is shown to be incompetent and at the same time is under the protection of its congressional watchdog committee, it's extremely difficult to dissolve that agency and replace it with something better. If the arrangement is supported by organizational nepotism as well, the solution to the problem approaches the impossible.

It would be hard to find an agency which has abused its original purpose("to facilitate the establishment and maintenance of an efficient national transportation system") more so than the Interstate Commerce Commission (ICC). Consider its most glaring failure: America is the only advanced nation in the world today without a passenger-railroad system. Yet the ICC goes on and on, invulnerable to change and protected from attack by its friends in Congress and industry.

While the Atomic Energy Commission can't begin to approach the ICC's corruption of original purpose, the problem with the AEC is, paradoxically, even harder to solve. Because not only are the same insurmountable obstacles present as with the dissolution of any ordinary agency (such as the ICC), but the technical complexities of atomic energy itself make the problem extraordinary, complicating the solution to the problem immeasurably. It is realistic, then, to consider the possibility that there are *no* established mechanisms left in our system to solve the basic problem of atomic energy in the United States: How can we get the job done when the only way is blocked and there is nowhere to go?

In the normal course of government, when built-in correction mechanisms fail, other forces eventually take over in an attempt to solve the problem. A necessary prerequisite, however, is an aroused public. That is the case today with the AEC (but not with the ICC).

The main mechanism left to the legislative branch of government to control the AEC is an across-the-board funding cut (and this has been seriously proposed). Sensing a safe issue, the rest of Congress could override the recommendations of the Joint Committee on Atomic Energy and just cut the AEC's budget. A nonspecific funding slash would surely create competition for money, and it is naïvely believed that the most competent individuals and programs within the AEC will "percolate to the top" and survive. Of course, nothing could be further from the truth. What would happen is exactly the reverse. The atomic bureaucracy got into its troubles because of the misplaced values of its leaders. A simple cut in funds without at the same time replacing the bureaucrats who control that money is simply to give the same leaders who created the problem in the first place the power to solve it. Instead of firing themselves and their own pet programs as they ought to do, they would end up weeding out the younger, less powerful bureaucrats (who are presumably more competent; they could hardly be less) and thus *increase* the overall fraction of incompetence at the AEC.

The executive branch of government has different remedies. It is, of course, the most powerful force capable of controlling the AEC. As discussed in the previous section, the President can simply split up any executive department almost at his pleasure, although in the case of the AEC, he would encounter strenuous objections from the Joint Committee on Atomic Energy. Those committeemen, now as in the past, "are not ready to preside over the dismemberment of a prestigious and bountiful fiefdom."[549] But the Joint Committee notwithstanding, the mechanism for just such a reorganization is being worked out. However, the mischief which may result from redistributing AEC personnel among the several other organizations has not been considered at all.

Of course, there is some justification for using the same AEC people to do the same jobs but in other agencies: they have the necessary expertise and experience. Responsibility for the regulation of an esoteric and complex technology like atomic energy just can't be dropped into the laps of naïve bureaucrats today any more than the problem of uranium wastes could be left up to the health departments of the uranium-mining states twenty-five years ago. On the other hand, as bad as it might be to hand over the problems of atomic energy to officials outside the atomic establishment, worse problems could be created by scattering AEC personnel among several other agencies as intended by the President's reorganization plan. It would be highly unlikely that any new agency would ever adopt a position contrary to AEC policy if the very people whose responsibility it was to make the key decisions in the new agency were themselves the authors (or cronies of the authors) of the original policies when they were employed by the AEC. We already have had a small taste of what that could be like when a dozen AEC people, transferred to the Environmental Protection Agency, put the protection of the AEC's reputation above sound public-health policy in the dispute over the indoor radon problem in Colorado (see Chapter V).

Furthermore, technical polemics between the AEC and other agencies have appeared in the public record until now; a consolidation of functions (and personnel) would hide these differences from public view. Assume that the AEC announced that its researchers had discovered that Pike's Peak contains a three-hundred-year supply of granite for tombstones, and that because of an impending tombstone shortage it was going to be necessary to fracture that mountain with nuclear explosives in order to exploit that natural resource. Until now, there always has been another federal agency to consult on the AEC's evaluation of such a plan. (The analogy is half serious:

AEC arguments for using nuclear explosives for natural gas stimulation are almost as specious as any which might support the existence of a "tombstone shortage" and the use of nuclear explosives to
solve it.) But with the Department of the Interior and key promotional elements of the AEC in the new Department of Natural Resources together, the "tombstone" polemic (or natural-gas stimulation, or railroad and highway cuts using nuclear explosives, or any
other technology using atomic power) would take place behind closed
doors without public participation or knowledge. By the time the
public found out about it, another questionable project could be an
accomplished fact.

A situation analogous to the sellout by the Environmental Protection Agency over a public-health issue in Colorado could develop
at the new Department of Natural Resources over technical issues.
For example, the Department of the Interior was a co-sponsor, along
with the AEC and the natural gas industry, of Project Rulison, the
second Plowshare experiment designed to free natural gas underground, using nuclear explosives. After Rulison, Interior declined
to co-sponsor Project Rio Blanco, the third experiment in the series,
because of its differences with the AEC and the Joint Committee
over the policy connected with the new technology.[550] Since the two
agencies were in no other way connected, the Department of the
Interior was able to abandon its formal involvement with gas stimulation while the AEC continued its own efforts in that direction.
The new Department of Natural Resources (which is to be centered
around the Department of the Interior) collects the same people
into one agency. Therefore future policy, concerning this particular
technology at least, will not reflect differences in opinion, since only
a unified view will be released to tne public. Which view prevails
will be only partially determined by the correctness of the technology; as before, it is the power of the promoter that decides the issue,
only this time the deliberations will be conducted in secret.

Another route the President has by which to change the AEC is
to appoint a new chairman. In most cases, a new leader for an old
organization quickly finds himself so restricted by tradition and red

tape that he might as well be the prisoner of his own palace guard. Consider the remark of Pope John XXIII shortly after he assumed the papacy in 1958: "I'm in a bag here." While AEC traditions certainly are not as formidable as those faced by Pope John, they are strong nevertheless. Glenn Seaborg resigned as chairman of the AEC in 1971, after a ten-year tenure which has been described by insiders as a period with "no chairman at all." While Seaborg was absorbed with his pet scientific projects, the palace guard at the AEC was indeed able to shape that agency to its own tastes without a chairman to hinder its progress.

Thus, whoever was to fill Seaborg's post not only would be walking into a "bag" at the AEC but would have there on his desk, his first Monday morning on the job, a decade's worth of undone work to clean up. But, instead of appointing another malleable drudge like Dr. Seaborg, President Nixon's choice was James Rodney Schlesinger, a man of impressive credentials,[551] who just may go a long way before his progress is finally stopped by the nuclear industry, the Joint Committee and the head of the palace guard himself, Commissioner Jim Ramey.

Chairman Schlesinger surprised the press[552] and, particularly, industry in his "first formal expression of views" three months after he assumed the leadership of the AEC.[553] He clearly delineated the role of the AEC, whose responsibility it was, he said, "to develop new technical options and to bring these options to the point of commercial application." Of course, this has always been the real function of the AEC, but it was never willing to limit itself strictly to that position until today, under fire as it is from all sides.

Dr. Schlesinger went even further, describing what the AEC's role is *not*:

From its inception the Atomic Energy Commission has fostered and protected the nuclear industry. . . . You should not expect the AEC to fight the industry's political, social and commercial battles. . . . It is not the responsibility of the Atomic Energy Commission to solve industry's problems . . . that is industry's responsibility. . . . The AEC's role is a more limited one, primarily to perform as a referee serving the public interest . . . the AEC should be officially neutral.

But no head of any federal regulatory agency ever got very far in Washington by being honest. Luxuriating in illegitimate largesse for years, industry is not likely to accept Chairman Schlesinger's new views without a real fight.

Industry isn't all that Schlesinger alienated in that first speech of his; he even went so far as to say, "I believe broadside diatribes against environmentalists to be not only in bad taste but wrong," a remark sure to earn him the enmity of Chet Holifield and Jim Ramey, the prideful authors of most of those distasteful diatribes and the men who run atomic energy in the United States today. Typically vulgarians mind less being wrong than being accused of bad taste.

Surely many of the AEC's troubles today can be blamed on its last chairman. Understandably, Dr. Schlesinger has said, "I have no desire to justify prior policies or any AEC actions prior to the time I joined the Commission."[554] On the other hand, things have gone wrong far too long for any one chairman, however competent he may be, to set them right again. After all, in order to do so he needs the help of the very people who made the mistakes in the first place. They haven't admitted to them so far, and they're not likely to do so in the future, for that would require them to put the good of their agency above their own self-interest, and that is simply an unrealistic expectation.

The judicial branch of government provides the route most available to the public to control the AEC. Accordingly, many citizens and groups have gone to the courts seeking to define the limits of the AEC's powers (*Northern States Power Co. v. Minnesota*[555]), to enjoin the AEC from conducting experiments at the Nevada test site (*Metzger v. Klein, Seaborg and Low*[428]), to stop other nuclear experiments in other states (the Rulison case—*Crowther v. Seaborg et al.*[210]), to force the AEC to comply with the National Environmental Policy Act (*Scientists' Institute for Public Information v. Seaborg* et al.[556] and *Calvert Cliffs Coordinating Committee v. AEC*[557]), and even to challenge the constitutionality of the source of the AEC's powers, the Atomic Energy Act itself (*Conservation*

Society of Southern Vermont, Lloyd Harbor Study Group, et al. *v. AEC* et al.[558]).

The many suits have served at least one purpose: they have delayed the AEC's experiments and thus provided an opportunity for public review and an even graver consideration of the consequences of each experiment by the AEC itself. But by far the most successful efforts have taken place after the passage of, and in connection with, the National Environmental Policy Act of 1969 (NEPA).[427] Before then, the AEC argued that although its mandate included the regulation of only those radiological hazards "considered important by the Commission," it had no authority to consider the broader environmental impact of its operations.

Consider the following dialogue in 1966 between Senator Edmund Muskie and AEC General Counsel Joseph Hennessey, concerning the uncontrolled release of uranium wastes (tailings) from the several AEC-licensed mills:

SENATOR MUSKIE: Good housekeeping is not a responsibility of the Commission?

MR. HENNESSEY: No, sir. Aesthetics are not within our jurisdiction.

SENATOR MUSKIE: Well, you know, in state after state we require now, in our forestry practices, that harvesters of these forests should clean up the slash and debris they leave behind. It would seem to me [that the AEC] license could be so interpreted that these [tailings] piles should be stabilized and controlled. . . . Would you consider that to be so far outside the authority [of the commission] that you could not require that as part of the license? . . .[559]

The philosophy behind Mr. Hennessey's answer, that the AEC had no further responsibility (except for that which it chose to accept), thus justified the radium pollution of the waters of the Colorado Plateau, the radioactive air pollution of the mill towns there, and the indoor radon problem in Grand Junction, Colorado—all an object lesson in what is meant by "environmental impact."

But the passage of NEPA changed all of that. While not establishing environmental protection as an exclusive goal, Congress imposed a specific responsibility on federal officials to *reorder their priorities* so that the environmental costs and benefits will assume their proper place along with other considerations. But, typically, the AEC either ignored NEPA completely[428] or interpreted it so self-servingly as to make, in the court's opinion, "a mockery of the Act."[557]

In the *Calvert Cliffs* decision, pointing out that environmental protection is now a part of the mandate of every federal agency, the court said that "the Atomic Energy Commission, for example, had continually asserted, prior to NEPA, that it had no statutory authority to concern itself with the adverse environmental effects of its actions. Now, however, its hands are no longer tied. It is not only permitted but compelled to take environmental values into account." The court, obviously miffed at the AEC's "crabbed interpretation" of NEPA, asked:

What possible purpose could there be in the Section 102(2)(c) requirement [of NEPA, that a "detailed statement" accompany proposals through the agency review process] if "accompany" means no more than physical proximity—mandating no more than the physical act of passing certain folders and papers, unopened, to reviewing officials along with other folders and papers? What possible purpose could there be in requiring the "detailed statement" to be before hearing boards if the boards are free to ignore entirely the contents of the statement? *NEPA was meant to do more than regulate the flow of papers in the federal bureaucracy.** The word "accompany" in Section 102(2)(c) must not be read so narrowly as to make the Act ludicrous.[557]

Thus, as late as 1971, arrogant and isolated, the AEC still felt it could write its own ticket.

At the time, it appeared that the AEC would appeal the court's decision;[560] that surely would have been the case if Glenn Seaborg had not just resigned as AEC chairman. But with James Schlesinger in the post, the AEC seems to have gotten the message. In a very uncharacteristic move, it decided to accept the judgment of the court (and therefore, Congress) and not appeal the *Calvert Cliffs* decision.[561] Consider the pressures that Schlesinger was under to do otherwise; he said, "Finally—and let me underscore this point—it

* Emphasis added.

is not the AEC responsibility to ignore on your [industry's] behalf an indication of Congressional intent, or to ignore the courts. *We have had a fair amount of advice on how to evade the clear mandate of the federal courts.** It is advice that we did not think proper to accept."[553]

And so how can the AEC be changed? It seems that every solution carries with it the seeds of its own defeat. The President's reorganization plan may accomplish far more harm than good in the end. No one chairman of the AEC can rehabilitate that agency, as the increasing pressures on Dr. Schlesinger will demonstrate. Congress can only increase the problem with an across-the-board budget cut, and relief through the courts is slow, inefficient and expensive (although, paradoxically, except for NEPA it has been the only responsive branch of government so far).

But the interesting thing about a system as inefficient as our own is that all of these things can and do work at the same time, amid great confusion, along with what can almost be properly considered a fourth branch of government today: public opinion. While public opinion can be (and has been) led into error occasionally, when it comes to technology the public seems to have been less gullible than our Presidents, Congress or the courts, as a reading of recent history demonstrates. It's no wonder that the AEC finds public opinion so disagreeable. After all, it was the public which led the government out of its fallout blunder, and it was the public again, ten years later, which brought reality to the politician dazzled by the pipedream of a supersonic transport (SST).

Industry is maddened by the increase of public intervention in its plans as well. It too has good reason: the completion of many multi-million-dollar nuclear electric-generating plants has been delayed while public objections are aired through extended agency hearings and the courts. But that is a small price to pay in order to decrease significantly the chances of a serious atomic accident somewhere across America. It is also a small price to pay for the preservation of

* Emphasis added.

our individual liberty, which the federal functionary so zealously (though unintentionally, perhaps) tramples upon in the name of technical progress.

For it is a fact that few federal bureaucrats or politicians understand America's newfound dissatisfaction with established institutions such as the AEC. Most atomic establishmentarians truly feel that they are doing the best job technically possible—naïvely believing that that's all there is to it. Few of them realize that technical possibility is not a guarantee of political and social acceptance. Fewer yet appreciate the fact that because the AEC is an old organization, having indulged in secrecy and self-regulation for too long, it has developed many bad habits—habits which by now cannot be corrected. On top of it all, the AEC has become irreversibly entrenched as well, invulnerable to change through the normal system of checks and balances.

The bureaucrat is insensitive to this for two reasons: in the first place, the slip into self-interest happened so gradually as to be imperceptible to him, and secondly, the self-serving nature of the atomic establishment benefits its members grandly, thereby depriving internal critics of the necessary motivation to seek change. After all, where else can an executive be paid $36,000 annually (GS-18 scale, common at the AEC) without *ever* being required to produce anything more concrete than an encouraging progress report filled with the promise of things to come?

But for the average citizen, the story is quite different, for without make-work schemes and job security to hypnotize him into the unquestioning approval of crazy technical adventures, he can afford to look at things somewhat more critically—especially since he is paying for everything. But when he does become involved, his motives are challenged and his legitimate questions are treated with scorn and derision by the Joint Committee, by the atomic industry, by the AEC itself and its kept experts at the universities. When the citizen seeks redress through establishment channels, such as hearings concerning nuclear-power reactors, he finds that self-regulation over the years has produced a system of administrative review so unfair and one-sided as to render meaningful public input next to impossible. His frustration turns to anger and he is thereby radicalized. And so it is the atomic establishment *itself* which provides the motivating force for that modern version of the pamphleteer of Revolutionary War days, today's citizen with his Xerox machine in the cellar.[562] Such is the stuff of which citizen intervenor suits are made.

Public opposition to nuclear-power plants through intervenor suits had become so effective by 1972 that the government resorted to extraordinary measures. In keeping with the tradition that democracy is fine only so long as things go according to plan, the Nixon Administration, in order to avoid a threatened power shortage, asked Congress for special legislation to circumvent the normal provisions and procedures of NEPA.[563] This meant that environmental-impact statements, public hearings and the like would be suspended in order to facilitate the construction of future nuclear-power plants.

But that means leaving everything up to the AEC again, at a time when it needs advice from the outside more than ever before. For without such guidance, the AEC will surely have its next big blunder in connection with a core melt-down accident somewhere at a big civilian nuclear-power plant. Certainly, vast public involvement in technical questions can delay progress, but since it is the public that pays the bills, receives the benefits and suffers the risk of any new technology, public involvement is both appropriate and necessary. Considering the record of government, the public could hardly do worse. We're fortunate today that an informed public is involved early enough in the nuclear-reactor game, before the AEC gets its chance to finish the job of sweeping the dull and dangerous parts of its responsibilities under the rug again.

Thus, the most immediate danger is not technical but political: when nobody is looking, the public will have its right of participation in public decisions taken away by someone in Washington.

REFERENCES

Congressional committee prints referred to in the following pages are available in libraries or directly from the Superintendent of Documents, U.S. Government Printing Office, Washington, D.C. 20402.

Similarly, AEC press releases and reprints are available from the Division of Public Information, U.S. Atomic Energy Commission, Washington, D.C. 20545.

Also, Atomic Energy Clearing House reports are found in libraries or are available directly from Congressional Information Bureau, Inc., Colorado Building, Fourteenth and G Streets N.W., Washington, D.C. 20005.

ABBREVIATIONS USED IN THE REFERENCES

AEC	Atomic Energy Commission
DOD	Department of Defense
DPNE	Division of Peaceful Nuclear Explosives
EPA	Environmental Protection Agency
FRC	Federal Radiation Council
HASL	Health and Safety Laboratory (USAEC)
JCAE	Joint Committee on Atomic Energy
NVOO	Nevada Operations Office (USAEC)
PHS	Public Health Service
USAEC	U. S. Atomic Energy Commission
USDHEW	U. S. Department of Health, Education and Welfare

1. *The Life of Reason,* by George Santayana (1905), Vol. I.

2 Interview with Rep. Chet. Holifield by Anthony Ripley of the *New York Times,* June 1970.

3. *The Nature of Radioactive Fallout and Its Effects on Man,* JCAE hearings, Parts I and II, May–July 1957.

4. *Radiation Standards, Including Fallout,* JCAE hearings, Parts I and II, June 1962.

5. Dr. Glenn T. Seaborg on NBC's *Meet the Press,* reported by the *Washington Post* News Service, as seen in the San Francisco *Chronicle,* Aug. 9, 1971. See also "AEC Pays Pentagon's Atomic Weapons Bill," by John W. Finney, *New York Times,* as seen in the Denver *Post,* Aug. 5, 1962.

6. *Atomic Energy Legislation through the 91st Congress, 2nd Session* (Joint Committee on Atomic Energy, January 1971).

7. *The Scientific Estate,* by Don K. Price (Belknap Press of Harvard Univ. Press, 1965; also Oxford Univ. Press paperback, New York, 1968, p. 172). Also *op. cit.* ref. 5, "AEC Pays Pentagon's Atomic Weapons Bill."

8. *The Joint Committee on Atomic Energy: A Study of Fusion of Governmental Power,* by Harold P. Green and Alan Rosenthal (Na-

tional Law Center, George Washington Univ., Washington, D. C., 1961), pp. 296-306.

9. *Ibid.,* p. 35. Also Jackson, "Congress and the Atom," *Annals of Congress, 290,* 77 (1953).

10. "Feud Deadlocks Appointments to AEC," by John W. Finney, *New York Times,* as seen in the Denver *Post,* July 30, 1962. Also see "JFK Reportedly Set to Fill Jobs in AEC," UPI dispatch as seen in the Denver *Post,* Aug. 5, 1962.

11. *Change Hope and the Bomb,* by David E. Lilienthal (Princeton Univ. Press, Princeton, N. J., 1963).

12. Green and Rosenthal, *op. cit.* ref. 8. Also see *Congressional Record, 91,* 9888 (1945).

13. *Annual Report to Congress of the Atomic Energy Commission for 1970* (U.S. Gov. Printing Office, January 1971).

14. *Major Activities in the Atomic Energy Programs, January–December 1969,* USAEC (U.S. Govt. Printing Office, January 1970).

15. *Radiation Exposure of Uranium Miners,* JCAE hearings, Parts I and II, May–August 1967, pp. 716-20.

16. Letter to Sen. Mike Gravel from Dr. Philip Handler, Aug. 12, 1970.

17. A scientific paper submitted to a "refereed journal" is sent out to other scientists in the same field for pre-publication review. The article is accepted for publication, sent back for rewriting or rejected outright on the basis of the critiques prepared by the reviewers, who remain anonymous. As might be predicted, the pre-publication review process has thus served as an ideal place for other scientists in the same field to squelch those scientific papers which, for any number of reasons, are not to their liking.

The suggestion that scientific pub-

lications are thus censored not only shocks editors and reviewers, but, paradoxically, is often rejected by the very authors who find that they are forced to delete parts of their scientific papers because of the political or ideological bias of anonymous pre-publication reviewers. This widespread practice usually concerns scientific questions (such as a rival theory), but in the case of the USAEC, offensive parts or even complete reports were suppressed simply because what was said ran counter to AEC "party line."

The most clear-cut case of AEC censorship in the open scientific literature is described in Chapter III. Harold Knapp's 1963 report was suppressed for over a year while the AEC tried frantically to discredit his results. Martell's iodine fallout data was treated similarly then and five years later he was subjected to a repeat performance. Martell had prepared an article critical of the AEC's nuclear excavation program and submitted it to *Science* magazine (a publication historically vulnerable to fashion and fads in science and politics). Martell states that his article was successfully blocked from publication in *Science* by Philip Abelson, an old AEC stalwart (it finally appeared in *Environment,* April 1969).

In addition to the open scientific literature, there are publications which, although sponsored by the AEC, are represented as being independent from ideological controls. One of these, *Nuclear Safety,* invites authors to submit "interpretive articles which will be reviewed for technical accuracy and pertinency." Unmentioned is that they are also reviewed and rejected for nonconformance with AEC "party line." This is accomplished with controversial scientific reports by the simple expedient of picking as the anonymous reviewers those scientists who are on the other side of the controversy in question. For example, an article once submitted to *Nuclear Safety* contained an estimate of the mortality resulting from radiation exposure. Now, at the time it was against AEC "party line" to put any number, however small, on how many cancers might be expected to arise from a given dose of atomic radiation. In-house AEC reviewers were picked to judge that article and they found reason to postpone its publication for over a year and a half.

Even more strict censorship occurs with the in-house AEC laboratory publications. Many examples (like the AEC's attempted suppression of the "Plowshare method" for radioactive waste disposal, described in Chapter VI), indicate that AEC in-house publications are reviewed *primarily* for ideological and political content. Dr. Gary Higgins, a division director at the Lawrence Radiation Laboratory at the time, was in Minneapolis in the summer of 1959 to give a speech before the American Society of Mechanical Engineering. His paper concerned an analysis of the use of nuclear explosives for excavation purposes. At the last minute, the AEC found an offensive passage: Higgins had made mortality estimates in connection with the amount of radiation which was expected to be released during the nuclear-assisted construction of a trans-isthmusian canal. Higgins was informed of this by telephone on the evening before the day he was to deliver his paper in Minneapolis. He was obliged to rewrite his talk, deleting the offensive mortality estimates. His paper appeared in *Mechanical Engineering* in January 1960, thus bowdlerized.

The most ironic result of an AEC attempt at censorship concerned Dr. Ernest J. Sternglass, the "Controversial Prophet of Doom", who predicted that 400,000 babies have died due to radioactive fallout from atmospheric weapons tests (Boffey, *op. cit.* ref. 109). Assigned the task of discrediting Sternglass' work, Dr. Arthur R. Tamplin, of the Lawrence Livermore Laboratory, published "A Criticism of the Sternglass Article on Fetal and Infant Mortality" in 1969 (Internal Document UCID-15506). Tamplin found that the excess mortality reported by Sternglass was due to "differing social-economic conditions," but he went on to say "At the same time, the existing experimental data indicates that fallout radiation probably did contribute to infant and fetal mortality by way of lethal mutations but nowhere near the effect suggested by Sternglass. The effect is most likely at least a factor of 100 smaller than he proposes."

In other words, an AEC scientist in an AEC laboratory, while disagreeing with Sternglass' estimate of 400,000 fetal and infant deaths due to fallout, had acknowledged a number of deaths 100 times smaller, or 4,000 deaths. Pressures were brought against Tamplin to delete the offensive passage from his paper. As mentioned before, it is against AEC "party line" to assign any number to the mortality to be expected from atomic radiation. AEC scientists are required to state that radiation-induced mortality is "low" and to leave it at that.

There is a twofold irony in that story. Firstly, the AEC requested and expected from Dr. Tamplin a club with which to beat down Dr. Sternglass, and instead it got something even more unacceptable than Sternglass: a choice between Sternglass, an outside scientist-critic charging responsibility for 400,000 deaths, and Tamplin, its own acknowledged inside expert, who admitted to 4,000 deaths. Secondly, AEC pressures on Dr. Tamplin (which were unsuccessful in convincing him to delete the offensive passage) radicalized his opinion of the AEC and made of him, along with Dr. John Gofman, the most vocal of the in-house AEC critics.

18. *Improving the AEC Regulatory Process,* (JCAE, March 1961), Vol. I, p. 3.

19. *Ibid.,* pp. 4-5.

20. USAEC Press Release D-58, March 16, 1961, "Atomic Energy Commission Establishes Position of Director of Regulation."

21. *Radiation Safety and Regulation,* JCAE hearings, June 1961.

22. *Environmental Effects of Producing Electric Power,* JCAE hearings, Parts I and II, January–February 1970, Vol. I, p. 124.

23. "A-Tests in Nevada Face Hughes Suit," by Gladwin Hill, *New York Times,* March 31, 1969; "Rumbles Over Atomic Tests in Nevada," by Walter Sullivan, *ibid.,* April 6, 1969.

"Howard Hughes Raises New Questions About Atomic Test Blasts in Nevada" by Gladwin Hill, *New York Times,* April 18, 1969.

24. Lawrence and Oppenheimer, by Nuel Pharr Davis, (Simon and Schuster, New York, 1968). "Technically sweet" quote is also found in *Brighter Than a Thousand Suns,* by Robert Jungk (Harcourt Brace, New York, 1958), p. 296.

25. *The Oppenheimer Case,* by Philip M. Stern with Harold P. Green (Harper and Row, New York, 1969).

26. *Underground Weapons Testing,* hearing before the Senate Foreign Relations Committee, Sept. 29, 1969.

27. Q clearance is an expensive frill which the AEC has maintained as part of its secrecy apparatus. It is a leftover from its pseudo-civilian status in military affairs. Instead of having the military investigate and clear employees to handle secret documents, it uses the FBI for the more sensitive cases and Federal Civil Service for the rest. Although it might be expected that the security budget would decrease over the years, the AEC still spends about $7 million *every year* for security investigations which are constantly updated.

28. Personal interview with Gary Higgins, Ph.D., Lawrence Livermore Laboratory, 1971.

29. "Atom Leak Forces Hundreds to Flee Nevada Test Site," *New York Times,* Dec. 19, 1970. Also "Atomic Controls: Some Feel They Should Be Much Tighter," by Ralph Lapp, *ibid.,* Dec. 27, 1970.

30. Interview with Capt. E. Bauser, exec. secretary, and Colonel Schwiller, aide, JCAE, by Anthony Ripley, *New York Times,* June 1970.

31. *Op. cit.* ref. 22, p. 129.

32. "Vietnam's Economic Lesson: Peace Can Yield Fatter Profits Than War," interview with Pierre A. Rinfret by T. George Harris, *Look,* May 31, 1966, p. 44.

33. *Man and Superman,* by George Bernard Shaw (1903).

34. *Race to Oblivion,* by Herbert F. York (Simon and Schuster, New York, 1970), p. 17.

35. The two visitors were Jerome P. Cavanagh, then mayor of Detroit, and his assistant, Anthony Ripley, January 1966 (personal communication from Mr. Ripley).

36. *The Military Establishment,* by Adam Yarmolinsky (Harper and Row, New York, 1971).

37. Presidential press conference, Jan. 31, 1970.

38. Address to Missiles and Astronautics Div., American Ordnance Assn., Sept. 22, 1970, at Offutt Air Force Base. General Holloway is also head of the multiservice Joint Strategic Target Planning Staff, which suggests possible missile and bomb targets to the President.

39. Adm. Husband E. Kimmel and Lt. Gen. Walter C. Short were immediately recalled to Washington, where a special panel headed by Supreme Court Justice Owen J. Roberts investigated the matter for President Franklin D. Roosevelt and found "dereliction of duty" on the part of Kimmel and Short. Both retired from the service and were the subject of other wartime congressional investigations.

40. *Men Against Fire,* by S. L. A. Marshall (William Morrow, New York, 1947), p. 21.

41. *Atomic Shield, 1947–1952* (Vol. II of the official history of the USAEC), by Richard G. Hewlett and Francis Duncan (Pennsylvania State Univ. Press, University Park, Pa., 1969).

42. *There Will Be No Time: The Revolution in Strategy,* by William Liscum Borden (Macmillan, New York, 1946, L.C. No. 46-8052).

43. Hewlett and Duncan, *op. cit.* ref. 41, p. 183.

44. Statement by Congressman Henry M. Jackson, 1951, as reported in *The Weapons Culture,* by Ralph E. Lapp (Norton, New York, 1968), p. 52, Jackson also proposed a tenfold increase in the budget of the AEC; *New York Times,* Oct. 10, 1951.

45. Obituary of Sen. Richard B. Russell, *New York Times,* Jan. 22, 1971.

46. *A Thousand Days,* by Arthur M. Schlesinger, Jr. (Houghton, Mifflin, Boston, 1965), p. 506.

47. *The Ordeal of Power,* by Emmet John Hughes (Atheneum, New York, 1962), Ch. 5.

48. As quoted in *The Anti-Communist Impulse,* by Michael Parenti (Random House, New York, 1969).

49. *Totalitarianism and American Social Thought,* by Robert A. Skotheim (Holt, Rinehart and Winston, New York, 1971), p. 72. See also *Blueprint for World Conquest,* by William Henry Chamberlin (Human Events, Chicago, 1946).

50. *The New Mexican,* Santa Fe, N.M., Sept. 2, 1970.

51. "Nuclear Diplomacy: Britain, France and America," by Andrew J. Pierre, *Foreign Affairs,* January 1971, pp. 283, 301.

52. See press releases and letters dated Sept. 28, 1970, and Nov. 15, 1971, available from the American Security Council, 1101 Seventeenth St. N.W., Washington, D.C. 20036, John M. Fisher, president.

53. "American Security Council 'Scare Tactics' Charged," by William Beecher, Denver *Post,* Oct. 27, 1970; the story originated at the *New York Times.*

54. *Proving Ground; An Account of the Radiobiological Studies in the Pacific, 1946–1961,* by Neal O. Hines (Univ. of Washington Press, Seattle, 1962), pp. 165-69.

55. "AEC Studies Cut in Nuclear Arms," by Richard D. Lyons, *New York Times,* Oct. 18, 1971.

56. "Arms: Any Way You Add It, the Figures Are Quite Ominous," by Ralph Lapp, *New York Times,* Dec. 20, 1970.

57. Note: The exact number of tactical nuclear weapons is a military secret but the Dept. of Defense admits that there are 7,200 such weapons presently stored in Europe. From that estimate alone it would be conservative to estimate the total, including those stored elsewhere

around the world and at home, to be 30,000 to 50,000.

58. Associated Press report, Washington, D.C., April 27, 1970, and U.S. Navy News Bureau, Washington, D.C.

59. *Naval Nuclear Propulsion Program, 1970,* JCAE hearings, March 20, 1970, p. 198.

60. *Ibid.,* pp. 22-23.

61. Personal interview (previously unpublished) with Dr. York in La Jolla, Calif., by Anthony Ripley of the *New York Times,* May 1970.

62. *Op. cit.* ref. 59, p. 65.

63. "Safeguard ABM and SALT," testimony by W. K. H. Panofsky before the Disarmament Subcommittee of the Senate Foreign Relations Committee, April 13, 1970.

64. Hewlett and Duncan, *op. cit.* ref. 41, pp. 569-70; see also *Brighter Than a Thousand Suns,* by Robert Jungk (Harcourt Brace, New York, 1958), p. 301.

65. Personal interview (previously unpublished) with Dr. Hugh De Witt by Anthony Ripley of the *New York Times,* June 1970.

66. *New York Times,* July 16, 1970.

67. Nuclear design activities are carried out at Los Alamos and Livermore, while non-nuclear engineering and development work is done at the Sandia Laboratories at Albuquerque, N.M., and Livermore. There are nine other AEC-owned national laboratories. The 11 national laboratories cost $2.3 billion to construct, while an additional $900 million has been invested by the AEC in research facilities, such as Sandia, which it does not own.

68. Personal interview (previously unpublished) with Dr. Tesche at AEC headquarters, Germantown, Md., by Anthony Ripley of the *New York Times,* June 1970.

69. Titled "Test Ban Safeguards,

Investigation Report by Preparedness Program; Interim Report by Preparedness Subcommittee of the Committee on Armed Services, U.S. Senate, Senate Resolution 75, 88th Congress, 1st Session, on the: Military Implications of the Proposed Limited Nuclear Test Ban Treaty."

70. "Why We Test," remarks by Dr. Tape at the governors' briefing, AEC Nevada Operations Office, Las Vegas, April 1, 1969 (AEC Press Release S-10-69).

71. News Release No. 71-3-21 (2), "SAC 25," Directorate of Information, Offutt Air Force Base, Neb.

72. *Supplemental Appropriations Bill, 1971,* hearings before the Subcommittee of the House of Representatives Committee on Appropriations, Oct. 1, 1970, pp. 284, 296.

73. *Einstein: The Life and Times,* by Ronald W. Clark (World, New York, 1971).

74. *The German Atomic Bomb,* by David Irving (Simon and Schuster, New York, 1967).

75. *Alsos,* by Samuel A. Goudsmit (Henry Schuman, Inc., New York, 1947).

76. Stern, *op. cit.* ref. 25, p. 79.

77. *The New World, 1939–1946* (Vol. I of the official history of the USAEC), by Richard G. Hewlett and Oscar E. Anderson, Jr. (Pennsylvania State Univ. Press, 1962), p. 358.

78. *The Rising Sun—The Decline and Fall of the Japanese Empire, 1936–1945,* by John Toland (Random House, New York, 1970), pp. 764-65, 789, 794-98, 806-7; see also Jungk, *op. cit.* ref. 64, pp. 206-9.

79. *The Rising Sun* (ref. 78), pp. 798-99.

80. Hewlett and Anderson, *op. cit.* ref. 77, p. 394.

81. *Ibid.,* p. 404.

82. "Now We Are All Sons of

Bitches," by William L. Laurence, *Science News*, July 11, 1970.

83. *Functionaries*, by F. William Howton (Quadrangle Books, Chicago, 1969).

84. "UC Designs Nuclear Weapons," by Marti Keller, *The Daily Californian*, April 14, 1970.

85. Lawrence Radiation Laboratory memorandum, April 16, 1970, to Hugh De Witt from Eugene Goldberg, E. Division leader, experimental physics, copy to Edward Teller.

86. AEC News Release Index for January–December 1969, by Theodore F. Davis (USAEC, Div. Tech. Info. Extension, Oak Ridge, Tenn. 37830).

87. *Ibid.* for January–December 1970.

88. "New AEC Chief Pledges Discussion on Hazards," by Richard D. Lyons, *New York Times*, Aug. 20, 1971.

89. "On Misunderstanding the Atom," speech by Dr. Seaborg at National Press Club luncheon, Washington, D.C., March 22, 1971 (AEC Press Release S-4-71).

90. *AEC Authorizing Legislation, Fiscal Year 1972*, JCAE hearings, Part II, March 4, 1971.

91. *Ibid.*, Part IV, March, May 1971, p. 2313.

92. *Op. cit.* ref. 22, p. 1210.

93. Source: "Preliminary Report, 3rd National Cancer Survey, 1969 Incidence," prepared by the Biometry Branch, National Cancer Inst., National Institutes of Health, Bethesda, Md.

94. *Assuring Public Safety in Continental Weapons Tests* (USAEC, January 1953), "Fallout and Public Health" section.

95. Pamphlet, *Atomic Tests in Nevada* (USAEC), March 1957).

96. *New York Times*, Oct. 4, 1951.

97. "Who Should Judge the Atom," by Chet Holifield, *Saturday Review*, Aug. 3, 1957.

98. *Science*, Oct. 31, 1969.

99. "Hiroshima/Nagasaki, Atomic Bomb Casualty Commission Perseveres in Sensitive Studies," by Philip M. Boffey, *Science, 168*, 679 (1970).

100. "Cancer in Japanese Exposed as Children to Atomic Bombs," by Jablon *et al.*, Dept. of Statistics, Atomic Bomb Casualty Commission, Hiroshima, Japan, *The Lancet*, May 8, 1971.

101. *AEC Authorizing Legislation, Fiscal Year 1971*, JCAE hearings, Part I, February 1970, p. 59.

102. "Background Information on Nevada Nuclear Tests," Appendix C, Claims Arising from Nevada Tests, Nevada Test Site Organization, NTS, Mercury, Nev. Prepared by the Office of Test Information, USAEC, Las Vegas, Nev.

103. Report of the UN Scientific Committee on the Effects of Atomic Radiation, 24th Session, 1969 (United Nations, New York), XXIV-Supplement 13.

104. "Summary Statement of Findings Related to the Distribution, Characteristics and Biological Availability of Fallout Debris Originating from Testing Programs at the Nevada Test Site," by K. H. Larson, J. W. Neel, *et al.*, UCLA under contract with the USAEC (Report No. UCLA-438, Sept. 14, 1960), p. 4.

105. "Late Somatic Effects of Ionizing Radiation," by Charles D. Van Cleave, prepared under the auspices of the Div. of Technical Information, USAEC (TID-24310).

106. See *Effects of Nuclear Weapons* (McGraw-Hill, New York, 1964, prepared for the AEC and DOD), and: *Radioactive Fallout from Nuclear Weapons Tests*, AEC Report CONF-765, November 1965, p. 411. The total of fission explosions from all atmospheric nuclear tests to

date is about 205 megatons. The best published figure for the first 100 megatons of this contamination yields an average dose rate of 2.86 millirem/year (see above). Multiplying this number by the ratio of the total yields gives the average yearly dose of radiation to the population due to radioactive fallout, which is 5.7 millirem/year. (Dr. Gary Higgins, Lawrence Livermore Laboratories, personal communication, June 1971.)

107. "A Suggested Guideline for Low-Dose Radiation Exposure to Populations Based on Risk–Benefit Analysis," by Jerry J. Cohen, Lawrence Radiation Laboratory UCRL-72848, June 1971. Cohen's literature review is reproduced below:

MORTALITY RISK DUE TO
RADIATION EXPOSURE

AUTHOR	Estimated Probability of Death/Man-Rad
W. L. Robison and L. R. Anspaugh, "Assessment of Potential Biological Hazards from Project Rulison," UCRL-50791, December 1969.	.001
J. J. Cohen, "Plowshare: New Challenge for the Health Physicist," *Health Physics, 19*, 633 (November 1970).	.001
J. W. Gofman and A. R. Tamplin, "Low-Dose Radiation, Chromosomes, and Cancer," GT-101-69, presented at IEEE Nuclear Science Symposium, San Francisco, October 1969.	.001
H. J. Otway, R. K. Lahrding and M. E. Battat, "A Risk Estimate for an Urban Sited Reactor," *Nuclear Technology*, October 1971.	.0007
P. J. Barry, "The Siting and Safety of Civilian Nuclear Power Plants," *CRC Crit. Rev. in Env. Cont.*, June 1970.	.0001
A. P. Hull, "Radiation in Perspective: Some Comparisons of the Environmental Risks of Nuclear- and Fossil-Fueled Power Plants," *Nuclear Safety, 12*, 3, 185 (May 1971).	.0001
J. B. Storer, "Late Effects: Extrapolation to Low-Dose Rate Exposures," *Health Physics, 17*, 3, January 1969.	.0001

Not included in Cohen's table is:

". . . on this basis, the theoretical increase is one cancer per 7000 man-rem," testimony of William D. Ruckelshaus, EPA administrator, in "AEC Licensing Procedure and Related Legislation," JCAE hearings, Part 1, June and July 1971, p. 190.   .00014

108. "Genetic and Somatic Effects of Carbon-14," by Linus Pauling, *Science, 128*, 1183 (1958).

109. Using the UN estimate (ref. 103) that each human being worldwide receives 140 millirem from fallout as his integrated dose, and assuming a global population of 3 billion (see "World Facts and Trends," Center for Integrative Studies, State Univ. of N.Y., Binghamton, N.Y. 13901), multiply the numbers to get the total man-rem:

$$(140 \times 10^{-3} \text{ rem}) (3 \times 10^9 \text{ man}) = 420 \times 10^6 \text{ man-rem.}$$

Assuming "one statistical death" for every 1,000 man-rem (ref. 107), multiply this by the result above:

$$(4.2 \times 10^8 \text{ man-rem}) \left(\frac{1 \text{ statistical death}}{10^3 \text{ man-rem}} \right) = 420,000 \text{ "statistical deaths."}$$

This is about the same number arrived at in a series of detailed studies by Ernest J. Sternglass, professor of radiation physics at the Univ. of Pittsburgh. See his articles "Infant Mortality and Nuclear Tests," *Bulletin of the Atomic Scientists*, April 1969, p. 18, and "The Death of All Children," *Esquire*, September 1969, p. 1a. Sternglass' results are the subject of a lively polemic which is reviewed in "Ernest J. Sternglass: Controversial Prophet of Doom," by Philip M. Boffey, *Science, 166*, 195 (1969). Also see *op. cit.* ref. 17.

110. Speech at 7th Annual Indus-

trial Health Conference, Houston, Tex., Sept. 23, 1954.

111. Hewlett and Duncan, *op. cit.* ref. 41, p. 499.

112. *13th Semi-Annual Report of the AEC* (to Congress), Jan. 28, 1953.

113. W. F. Libby in *Science, 123,* 657 (1956).

114. *Science and Survival,* by Barry Commoner, (Viking, New York, 1967).

115. Ralph E. Lapp, in *Science, 137,* 756 (1962). Also see his series in *Bulletin of the Atomic Scientists:* November 1954 "Civil Defense Faces a New Peril"; February 1955, "Radioactive Fallout"; June 1955, "Radioactive Fallout III"; November 1955, "Global Fallout"; September 1956, "The 'Humanitarian' H-Bomb"; October 1956, "Strontium Limits in Peace and War."

116. H. M. Clark, in *Science, 119,* 619 (1954).

117. Of the 64 people exposed, several children suffered from serious growth retardation due to nodules and other thyroid radiation damage, and one woman contracted thyroid (papillary-follicular) cancer. See also *Some Effects of Ionizing Radiation on Human Beings—A Report on the Marshallese and Americans Accidentally Exposed to Radiation from Fallout and a Discussion of Radiation Injury in the Human Being* (USAEC, July 1956), Ch. III, "Skin Lesions and Epilation."

118. "Operation Crossroads: A Look Into the Abyss," by Neal O. Hines, Washington *Post,* July 25, 1971.

119. New York Sunday *News,* Mar. 20, 1955.

120. UN Scientific Committee on the Effects of Atomic Radiation, 1958 Report (United Nations, New York). See also *New York Times,* Aug. 11, 1958.

121. HASL-42, USAEC, October 1958.

122. Strontium Program Quarterly Summary Report, HASL, NYOO, USAEC, Feb. 24, 1959.

123. *Nuclear Information,* April 1959, November 1959, September 1962, June 1963; *Scientist and Citizen,* September–October, 1964, September 1965, April 1967. Note: The publication of the Greater St. Louis Citizens' Committee for Nuclear Information, St. Louis, Mo., was called *Nuclear Information* from 1958 to 1964, *Scientist and Citizen* from 1964 to 1968, and *Environment* from 1968 to the present. The address is 438 No. Skinker Blvd., St. Louis, Mo. 63130. A cumulative index for *Environment* is available from the Minnesota Committee for Environmental Information, P. O. Box 14207, University Station, Minneapolis, Minn. 55414. Back issues of *Environment* are available from Maxwell Reprint Co., Fairview Park, Elms Ford, N.Y. 10523, or on microfilm from Xerox University Microfilms, 300 North Zeeb Rd., Ann Arbor, Mich. 48106.

124. Testimony of Lauriston S. Taylor at hearings on S. 2067 before the Senate Commerce Committee, August 1967, p. 202.

125. The FRC was created in direct response to public interest in fallout; see FRC Staff Report, May 13, 1960, USPHS (a division of Mr. Cellebrezze's Dept. of HEW) press releases for Nov. 24, 1961, Feb. 20, 1962, May 24, 1962, July 17, 1962.

126. Executive Order 10831, Aug. 14, 1959, and Public Law 86-373, Sept. 23, 1959.

127. See ref. 124, p. 391, testimony of Dr. Paul C. Tompkins, exec. dir., FRC; also ref. 4, p. 462.

128. Memorandum to the President from the FRC, *Fed. Register,* May 18, 1960.

129. *Atomic Energy Law Journal,* 6, 256 (1964).

130. *Air Conservation,* Publication No. 80 of the American Assn. for the Advancement of Science (Washington, D.C., 1965), pp. 176-77.

131. *The Recommendations of the International Commission on Radiological Protection* (Pergamon Press, London, 1959).

132. FRC Report No. 2, *Background Material for the Development of Radiation Standards* (U.S. Govt. Printing Office, 1961).

133. FRC Staff Report No. 1, May 1960, and No. 2, September 1961.

134. *New York Times,* Oct. 18, 1962.

135. *Fallout, Radiation Standards, and Countermeasures,* JCAE hearings, Part I, June 1963, and Part II, August 1963.

136. *Science, 141,* 640 (1963).

137. UPI dispatch, Oct. 28, 1963; AP dispatch, Oct. 29, 1963.

138. "Thyroid Nodules as a Late Sequella of Radioactive Fallout in a Marshall Island Population Exposed in 1954," *New Eng. Jour. Medicine, 274,* 1391 (June 23, 1966).

139. "Thyroid Carcinoma in Man After Exposure to Ionizing Radiation: A Summary of the Findings in Hiroshima and Nagasaki," *ibid., 268,* 406 (Feb. 21, 1963).

140. "Nevada Radioactive Levels Soar," by Howard Simons, Washington *Post,* Aug. 17, 1963.

141. Los Angeles *Times,* Aug. 21, 1963.

142. FRC press release, Sept. 17, 1962, news article in *New York Times,* Sept. 18, 1962.

143. FRC Report No. 4, *Estimates and Evaluation of Fallout in the United States from Nuclear Weapons Testing, Conducted through 1962,* (U.S. Govt. Printing Office, 1963).

144. FRC Report No. 5 (1964).

145. *Scientist and Citizen,* (see ref. 123), April 1967, pp. 77-80.

146. *Op. cit.* ref. 22, p. 409.

147. "Tests Find Levels of Fallout Safe," *New York Times,* July 8, 1962.

148. *Op. cit.* ref. 135, p. 473.

149. *The Legacy of Hiroshima,* by Edward Teller and Allen Brown (Doubleday, 1962). See also *Our Nuclear Future,* by Edward Teller and Albert L. Latter (Criterion Books, New York, 1958).

150. *Nature, 202,* 534 (1964).

151. Washington *Post,* Aug. 17, 1963.

152. *Op. cit.* ref. 135, pp. 914-1082.

153. Washington *Post,* Aug. 21, 1963, p. A18.

154. "The Nuclear Plant Controversy—III: Radiation Risks," by Ralph E. Lapp, *New Republic,* Feb. 27, 1971.

155. *Op. cit.* ref. 4, p. 748-804.

156. S. Penn and E. A. Martell, in *Science, 143,* 126 (1964). Also *Jour. Geophysical Research,* July 15, 1963.

157. *AEC Authorizing Legislation, Fiscal Year 1965,* JCAE hearings, pp. 127-29.

158. Letter from Gary Higgins, Lawrence Livermore Laboratories.

159. See refs. 135, 3 and 4; for further opinions see "Comments on a Paper by S. Penn and E. A. Martell, 'An Analysis of the Radioactive Fallout over North America in Late September, 1961,' " by Elinor R. Reiter (CSU, Ft. Collins, Colo.), *Jour. Geophysical Research, 69,* 786 (1964). Two additional comments using the same title as the above are by L. Machta, R. J. List and K. Telegadas (U.S. Weather Bureau, Washington, D.C.), *ibid.,* p. 791, and by Luther B. Lockhart, Jr., U.S. Naval Research Labs, Washington, D.C., *ibid.,* p. 796.

160. AP dispatch, Oct. 24, 1956.

161. Television speech, Oct. 12, 1964.

162. E.g., A highly critical report on the U.S. Forest Service practice of clear cutting, prepared by six "inside" professionals and published by the U.S. Forest Service itself; the panel was headed by Carl M. Bernstein, head of the agency's experimental station in Fort Collins, Colo. (AP dispatch July 16, 1971). Or consider an Aug. 9, 1971, UPI dispatch, "SEC Chief Admits Agency's Failings," where it is reported that William J. Casey, chairman of the Securities and Exchange Commission, admitted that his agency was not doing "the sort of job we ought to be doing."

163. As reported in *United Mine Workers Journal,* Dec. 1, 1968, p. 12.

164. *Op. cit.* ref. 21, pp. 181-84.

165. *Ibid.,* p. 397.

166. "Atomic Science Fatalities" List No. 13, July 1, 1968, prepared by Leo Goodman, consultant, Energy and Natural Resources, UAW Washington office, 1126 Sixteenth St. N.W., Washington, D.C. 20036. (Note: The 148 total fatalities listed here include 31 uranium miners from the Colorado Plateau.)

167. (These figures exclude uranium miners.) See Studies in Workmen's Compensation and Radiation Injury, prepared by the USAEC (issued 1969), Vol. V.

168. *Operational Accidents and Radiation Exposure Experience within the U.S. Atomic Energy Commission, 1943–1967,* issued December 1968 by the Div. of Operational Safety, USAEC, Washington, D.C. 20545.

169. Not only will cancers not be recorded if they occur after the workers' retirement, but the Dow employees I have interviewed believe that if a worker receives an excess dose of radiation there, the Dow management induces him to resign his employment, either by early retirement or by simply making his job so unpleasant that he quits.

170. *The Plutonium Registry,* Hanford Environmental Health Foundation, P. O. Box 100, Richland, Wash. 99352.

171. Preface by Brian MacMahon, M.D., to *Radon Daughter Exposure and Respiratory Cancer: Quantitative and Temporal Aspects,* Joint Monograph No. 1, 1971, report from the Epidemiological Study of U.S. Uranium Miners by F. E. Lundin, J. K. Wagoner, and V. E. Archer, PHS, USDHEW.

172. Speech at a conference sponsored by the National Tuberculosis and Respiratory Disease Assn., Miami Beach, Fla., May 25, 1969.

173. The peak year of uranium mining in the West was 1958, with about 1,200 miners employed (from "The Uranium Miners Problem," a report prepared for the Radiological Health Subcommittee, Task Force on Environment, Colo. State Health Planning Council, by R. G. Beverly, director, Radiation and Pollution Control, Mining and Metals Div., Union Carbide Corp., April 1970.

174. *Op. cit.* ref. 15, pp. 993-1015.

175. Testimony of Jack Fisher, member of Local 2-708, Grants, N. M. (Kerr McGee mine), at "Hazards in the Industrial Environment," conference sponsored by Dist. 2 Council of the Oil, Chemical and Atomic Workers' Intl. Union, May 21-23, 1970, Salt Lake City, Utah, pp. 26, 28. Available through OCAW Legislative Dept., 1126 Sixteenth St. N.W., Washington, D.C. 20036.

176. From a 1971 telephone interview with Mr. Feay Smith.

177. F. H. Harting and W. Hesse, "Der Lungenkrebs, die Bergkrankheit in der Schnessberger Gruber," *Vierteljahrssehr. f. gerichtl. med. offen Sanitäts, 30,* 296 (1879; *31,* 102 (1879); *31,* 313 (1879).

178. "History of the Exposure of Miners to Radon," by D. A. Holaday *Health Physics, 16,* 547 (1969).

179. "Radioactivity and Lung Cancer: A Critical Review of Lung Cancer in the Miners of Schneeberg and Joachimsthal," by Egon Lorenz, senior biophysicist, National Cancer Inst., Natl. Institutes of Health, USPHS, in *Jour. Natl. Cancer Inst.*, 5, 1, 1944.

180. J. Lowy, "Über die Joachimsthaler Bergkrankheit" (vorläufige Mitteilung), *Med. Klin.*, 25, 141 (1929).

181. H. Sikl, "Über der Lungenkrebs der Bergleute in Joachimstahl," *Z. Krebsforsch, 32,* 609 (1930).

182. F. Behounek, "History of the Exposure of Miners to Radon," *Health Physics, 19,* 56 (1970).

183. *Proceedings, Second United Nations Conference on Peaceful Uses of Atomic Energy* (Geneva), *21,* 62 (1958).

184. "Sometime in 1947, the Health and Safety Laboratory of the N. Y. Operations Office, AEC, had taken radon samples in several mines, and the results showed radon concentrations high enough to arouse Mr. Beatie's [Ralph Beatie, safety engineer for the AEC Grand Junction Operations Office] concern" (from *Report on the Uranium Study,* by P. W. Jacoe, dir., Div. of Occupational and Radiological Health, Colo. State Dept. of Public Health, August 1964; also, personal interviews with Mr. Jacoe, 1970).

185. *Op. cit.* ref. 41, p. 147.

186. *Ibid.,* p. 173.

187. *Radioactive Water Pollution in the Colorado River Basin,* hearings before the Subcommittee on Air and Water Pollution of the Senate Public Works Committee, May 6, 1966; see p. 107 for a letter from the AEC containing response to questions raised by Senators Bartlett, Muskie and Moss, May 17, 1966.

188. "Radiation Hazards in Uranium Mines and Mills," speech delivered Sept. 16, 1959 (USAEC Press Release S-22-59).

189. *Op. cit.* ref. 15, p. 159.

190. Telephone interview with Norman Blake, December 1970.

191. Excerpt from several interviews with P. W. Jacoe, 1970, 1971.

192. Letter to D. E. Harrison, Vanadium Corp. of America, Naturita, Colo., from J. J. Parker, M.D., July 29, 1949.

193. Letter to P. W. Jacoe, from Harmon Kallman of the Denver *Post,* June 16, 1955.

194. Letter to Colo. Dept. of Public Health from Mrs. Alta J. Bischoff, Grand Junction, May 13, 1967.

195. From a telephone interview with Mr. Sundin, December 1970.

196. Letter to the Colo. Dept. of Public Health from H. D. Whipple, M.D., Health Div., Los Alamos Scientific Laboratory, Aug. 17, 1949.

197. *Radiation Hazards in Uranium Mining,* by H. N. Doyle, asst. chief, Occupational Health Program, Div. of Special Health Services, USPHS, Washington 25, D.C.

198. *Control of Radon and Daughters,* USPHS Bulletin No. 494.

199. *Employee Radiation Hazards and Workmens Compensation,* summary-analysis of hearings, JCAE, March 1959, p. 11.

200. *Governors' Conference on Health Hazards in Uranium Mining —A Summary Report,* USDHEW, PHS Publication No. 843 (Washington, D.C., 1961).

201. *Op. cit.* ref. 15, pp. 45-93, 728-50.

202. "$650 Million Uranium Stockpile to Be Sold," AP dispatch from Las Vegas, Nev. (NVOO, USAEC), Oct. 14, 1971.

203. By A. J. Breslin, A. D. George, and M. S. Weinstein (HASL-220, USAEC, N.Y.C. operations office, December 1969).

204. "A Review of Radium Toxicity Studies," BRH/DEP-70-5, Bur. of Radiological Health, USPHS, Rockville, Md., December 1970.

205. *Radiation Hazards and Control,* Bur. of Radiological Health, USPHS, Rockville, Md., April 1967.

206. *Radioisotopes in the Human Body: Physical and Biological Aspects,* by F. W. Spiers (Academic Press, New York, 1968), p. 301.

207. Studies (in press) by Dr. William Brandon, Univ. of Denver, reported in *Cervi's Journal,* Denver, Colo., Oct. 14, 1971.

208. *Op. cit.* ref. 15, p. 681.

209. "The Question of Safe Radiation Thresholds for Alpha-Emitting Bone Seekers in Man," by J. W. Gofman and A. R. Tamplin, *Health Physics, 21,* 47 (1971), and references therein. (Snyder, Archer, Parker, all from the 1967 JCAE hearings on miners, ref. 15). See also G. Hems, *Brit. Jour. Radiology, 40,* 506 (1967).

210. Testimony of Robley D. Evans in the "Rulison case," Civil Action C-1712, Crowther v. Seaborg *et al.,* U.S. Dist. Court, Denver, Colorado, official transcript, Vol. V, pp. 913, 918, Jan. 16, 1970.

211. *Op. cit.* ref. 15, p. 650.

212. *Ibid.,* p. 259.

213. "New Miner Radiation Curbs Delayed," by Thomas O'Toole, Denver *Post,* Dec. 25, 1970. The original article appeared in the Washington *Post.*

214. "Epidemiologic Studies of Uranium Miners," a report prepared for the Interagency Uranium Mining Radiation Review Group, Jesse L. Steinfeld, M.D., U.S. Surgeon General, chairman, Jan. 27, 1971.

215. "Radiation Hazards in Modern Industry," speech by Leo Goodman, atomic consultant, UAW, at the John Fogarty Memorial under the auspices of the American Public Health Assn. and the D.C. Public Health Assn., April 26, 1967, Washington, D.C.

216. *Radiation Standards for Uranium Mining,* JCAE hearings, March 1969.

217. *Ibid.,* p. 58.

218. Letter to H. Peter Metzger from Dr. Geno Saccomanno, June 2, 1970.

219. *Chronology of Uranium Mining Health Protection Activities,* Div. of Operational Safety, USAEC, November 1970, p. 16.

220. *Op. cit.* ref. 216, p. 168; also *Nucleonics Week,* June 5, 1969, p. 6.

221. *Fed. Register,* Vol. 35, No. 245 (Dec. 18, 1970).

222. *Ibid.,* Vol. 36, No. 101 (May 25, 1971).

223. Alvin M. Weinberg in *Review,* Oak Ridge National Laboratory, Oak Ridge, Tenn., Winter 1971.

224. "The Plutonium Economy of the Future," speech at the 4th International Conference on Plutonium and other Actinides, Santa Fe, N. M., Oct. 5, 1970 (USAEC Press Release S-33-70).

225. By weight, the carcinogenic toxicity of plutonium approaches the chemical toxicity of botulism toxin (botulin): The maximum permissible lung burden for plutonium is 16×10^{-9}g. Although it is probably incorrect, the AEC has suggested that there is a safety factor of 100-fold built into this standard. But assuming it to be right, then 16×10^{-7}g of plutonium in a man's lungs will insure the production of lung cancer. The lethal dose of botulin is 10^{-10}g/kg. body weight or 6×10^{-9}g for a 60 kg. man. Thus on this basis plutonium is only some 270 times less toxic than botulism toxin. But if the AEC's safety factor is wrong by 100, as many critics have suggested (see next ref.), then plutonium and botulism toxin are com-

parable in toxicity (within a factor of three).

226. "Plutonium and the Energy Decision," by Donald P. Geesaman, *Bulletin of the Atomic Scientists,* September 1971, p. 33. Also, Geesaman, "An Analysis of the Carcinogenic Risk from an Insoluble Alpha-emitting Aerosol Deposited in Deep Respiratory Tissue," UCRL-50387, Feb. 9, 1968, and "Plutonium and Public Health," GT-121-70, Lawrence Radiation Laboratory, Livermore, Calif.

227. "Plutonium: The Ornery Element," remarks by Dr. Seaborg at the Meeting on the Commercial Fabrication of Plutonium Fuel, Richland, Wash., April 3, 1964 USAEC Press Release S-6-64).

228. From *The Hazards and Characteristics of Plutonium and Uranium Contamination,* Nuclear Branch, Atomic Weapons Training Group, Field Command, Defense Atomic Support Agency, Sandia Base, Albuquerque, N.M., March 10, 1961, p. 4. In support of this quote, the following statement is made ". . . only about 0.003 percent of the plutonium that is swallowed is absorbed into the bloodstream." Assuming 10 kg. is enough to "go critical," then if a man could swallow so much he would absorb into his bloodstream: $(.003\%)(10kg) = 0.3g$. The maximum permissible body burden for plutonium is $4.0 \times 10^{-8}g$ (it is less, $1.6 \times 10^{-8}g$, for the lungs). Therefore, the amount required "in order for plutonium to be hazardous to an individual who swallows it" according to the publication above is overestimated by *7.5 million times!*

229. The half-lives (that time required for a radioactive element to lose half of its radioactivity) for radium and plutonium are 1,620 years and 24,000 years respectively. Ten half-lives will reduce radioactivity

to about ⅕ of one percent of the amount originally present. For this reason, 10 half-lives is the figure often used to estimate how long a given hazard will exist. However, this depends greatly on how dangerous the amount originally present was; 2 half-lives is sufficient to reduce the danger in some cases, in others a wait of 20 half-lives may be required.

230. "Nuclear Materials Safeguards: A Joint Industry–Government Mission," by Clarence E. Larson, commissioner, USAEC, October 1969 (available through Clearing House for Federal Scientific and Technical Information, Springfield, Va., as WASH 1147).

231. "Plutonium: Reactor Proliferation Threatens a Nuclear Black Market," *Science, 172,* 143 (1971).

232. "Basement H-Bombs," by Sheldon Novick, *Environment* (as *Scientist and Citizen*), 10, 243 (1968); "Do-It-Yourself," by Sheldon Novick, *Environment,* 11, 22 (1969); "The AEC and Do-It-Yourself H-Bombs," an AEC reply to "Basement H-Bombs" attributed to Dr. Glenn T. Seaborg, in *Environment, 11,* 25 (1969). Also "Laser is Stirring Imagination of Weapons Scientists," by Anthony Ripley, *New York Times,* Oct. 16, 1971.

233. "Atom-Age Trash," by Dennis Farney, *Wall Street Journal,* Jan. 25, 1971.

234. Fires are distinguished from conflagrations. Some famous conflagrations were the Cleveland Gas fire in 1944, the Chicago fire in 1871, the Peshtigo fire the same year, and the largest, the San Francisco earthquake of 1906 (where the loss was $350 million). The Dow-AEC fire of May 11, 1969, was unusual in that the monetary loss was so high while the structural damage was barely obvious, a situation possible only when much expensive equipment is de-

stroyed. The only similar fire in this respect was the NASA tracking-station fire in Florida in 1965; the loss there was $35 million. The largest fire until the Dow-AEC accident was the great GM fire at Livonia, Mich., where the loss was put at $50 million.

Because the AEC has released conflicting information, it is difficult to ascertain the exact cost of the Dow-AEC fire at Rocky Flats, Colo. According to the Denver *Post* (June 24, 1969), the AEC's asst. area manager there said that "earlier estimates of $50 million damage in the fire stand, but that only $45 million was asked for repairs because the Rocky Flats facility had $5 million on hand to begin the project." Furthermore, this and other news articles all state that "about $20 million worth of plutonium was involved in the fire." An AEC press release (see ref. 236) says that the value of the lost plutonium was not included in the large estimate. Thus the complete loss can be no larger than $70 million.

Complicating the issue is that most of the lost plutonium is recoverable but the cost for the recovery operation is unknown. Plutonium was valued at about $40 per gram (*Fed. Register*, Vol. 22, p. 395, June 6, 1957) but may be down to $10 per gram by now, making the total amount lost between 1,000 and 4,000 pounds, much of it dispersed throughout the fire site and therefore difficult and costly to recover.

So however much the plutonium recovery operation was, it would have to be added to the $50-million figure to get the total damage of this disaster. Furthermore, that figure would also be the amount by which the Dow fire exceeded the GM Livonia fire, as the largest total loss to date.

It must also be mentioned that because of the various biases involved in each fire, the GM estimate was likely to be high for their fire, and the AEC estimate likely to be low for theirs, both for self-serving reasons.

235. Remarks by General Giller on NBC-TV's *First Tuesday* program, Jan. 6, 1970.

236. "Report by the USAEC on the May 11, 1969, Fire at the Rocky Flats Plant Near Boulder, Colorado," Nov. 18, 1969 (AEC Press Release M-257).

237. "Secret meeting" between representatives of the AEC, Dow and the Colo. Committee for Environmental Information at the U.S. Post Office, Denver, Feb. 10, 1970.

238. Telephone interview with Mr. Erkins, Buhl, Ida., September 1970.

239. "Fire Cleanup Keeps Plutonium Plant Busy," by Lawrence E. Davies, *New York Times,* June 27, 1969.

240. "A-Waste Storage in Idaho Revealed by J. Shifferdecker," *Idaho Statesman,* Sept. 11, 1969.

241. "Radioactive Wastes Disposal Not Hazardous, AEC Claims," Idaho Falls *Post-Register,* Sept. 11, 1969.

242. Nat. Acad. of Sciences–Natl. Research Council, Div. of Earth Sciences, Committee on Geologic Aspects of Radioactive Waste Disposal: Report to the Div. of Reactor Development and Technology, USAEC, May 1966.

243. "Solon Asks U.S. Study of Wastes," by Tom Ochiltree, *Idaho Statesman,* Sept. 13, 1969.

244. *Congressional Record,* March 6, 1970, S-3131-3146.

245. "Comments on the Background of the May 1966 Report of the NAS Committee on Geologic Aspects of Radioactive Waste Disposal," unsigned, USAEC, March 1970.

246. "AEC Staff Analysis of *Wall Street Journal* Waste Article," unsigned, USAEC, April 1971.

247. "AEC Scored on Storing

Waste," by Bob Smith, *New York Times,* March 7, 1970.

248. *AEC Authorizing Legislation, Fiscal Year 1972,* JCAE hearings, Part III, March 9, 16 and 17, 1971, p. 1582.

249. "Dangerous Radiation in Washington Ducks," Hanford, Wash., UPI dispatch (Oakland *Tribune,* March 14, 1970).

250. Testimony of Nolan W. Hancock, financial secretary, Local 2-652, OCAW, Idaho Falls, Ida., at "Hazards in the Industrial Environment" conference (see ref. 175).

251. Progress and Problems in Programs for Managing High-Level Radioactive Wastes," a report to the JCAE by the Comptroller General of the U. S. (USAEC-164052, Jan. 29, 1971).

252. "A Radioactive Waste Repository Set," *New York Times,* Jan. 30, 1971.

253. "Project Salt Vault: A Demonstration of the Disposal of High-Activity Solidified Wastes in Underground Salt Mines," Oak Ridge National Laboratory Document ORNL-4555; final report: March 1971.

254. *Op. cit.* ref. 248, pp. 2209-19.

255. "Disposal of Solid Radioactive Wastes in Bedded Salt Deposits," report by the Committee on Radioactive Waste Management, Natl. Acad. of Sciences–Natl. Research Council, Washington, D.C., November 1970.

256. *Op. cit.* ref. 248, p. 1371.

257. *Ibid.,* p. 1508.

258. *Ibid.,* pp. 1448-49.

259. "The Radioactive Salt Mine," by Richard S. Lewis, *Bulletin of the Atomic Scientists,* June 1971, p. 27.

260. "Draft Environmental Impact Statement: Radioactive Waste Repository, Lyons, Kansas," by R. E. Hollingsworth, gen. mgr., USAEC, November 1970.

261. "Nuclear Waste: Kansans Riled by AEC Plans for Atom Dump," *Science, 172,* 249 (April 16, 1971).

262. *Congressional Record,* March 17, 1971, H-1678-90.

263. "Kansas Geologists Oppose a Nuclear Waste Dump," by Anthony Ripley, *New York Times,* Feb. 17, 1971.

264. "Water, N-Waste Potentially Lethal," by Fred Brown, *Denver Post,* Sept. 28, 1971, p. 51.

265. *Atomic Energy Clearing House Reports,* Oct. 4, 1971, p. 3.

266. "AEC May Abandon Lyons Plan," by Fred Brown, *Denver Post,* Oct. 3, 1971.

267. *Ibid.;* also see text of remarks by Rep. Joe Skubitz to KSTB-TV, Topeka, Kans., Oct. 28, 1971, available as news release from Rep. Skubitz, House of Representatives, Washington, D.C. 20515.

268. *Op. cit.* ref. 248, see pp. 1374-76.

269. *Nuclear Safety, 11,* 130 (1970).

270. *Op. cit.* ref. 187, p. 20.

271. George Santayana.

272. Report prepared for the Joint Economic Committee, U.S. Congress, by the Environmental Policy Div., Legislative Reference Service, Library of Congress, August 1970.

273. In 1969 the estimate for the total amount of uranium tailings in the United States was slightly over 90 million tons (see *Evaluation of Radon 222 Near Uranium Tailings Piles,* USDHEW, ECA, Bur. of Radiological Health, Rockville, Md., March 1969). Uranium is still being milled for industrial purposes today and so the piles have been growing since 1969. Current estimates indicate that the 100-million-ton mark is already passed.

274. *Disposition and Control of Uranium Mill Tailings Piles in the Colorado River Basin,* USDHEW, Fed. Water Pollution Control Ad-

min., Region VIII, Denver, Colo., March 1966.

275. "Uranium Mill Tailings," a presentation for an "AEC Pollution Meeting" by the Div. of Operational Safety, USAEC, September 1967.

276. *Op. cit.* ref. 187, p. 3.

277. *Radium-226 Exposure to a Population Downstream From a Uranium Processing Mill,* by J. Hickey and S. Black, USDHEW, Rockville, Md., presented at the Congrès International sur la Radioprotection dans l'Utilisation Industrielle des Radioelements (Health Physical Society international meeting), Paris, Dec. 13-15, 1965.

278. *Op. cit.* ref. 187, pp. 101-4: answers to questions submitted to the Fed. Water Pollution Control Admin. by Senator Bartlett.

279. Transcript of Conference on Interstate Pollution of the Animas River, held in Santa Fe, N. M., April 29, 1958.

280. *Waste Guide for the Uranium Milling Industry,* Technical Report W62-12, USDHEW, USPHS, Cincinnati, O., 1962. Also *Radiological Content of Colorado River Basin Bottom Sedimentation,* Report PR-10, USPHS, Region VIII, Denver, Colo., June 1963, and *Radioactivity In Water and Sediments of the Colorado River Basin 1950-1963,* Radiological Health Data and Reports, November 1964 (U.S. Govt. Printing Office, Washington, D.C. 20402).

281. *Op. cit.* ref. 187, pp. 97-101: answers to questions submitted to the Fed. Water Pollution Control Admin. by Senator Muskie.

282. Personal interview with the inspector, Mr. P. W. Jacoe, December 1970.

283. Letter to H. Peter Metzger from Stuart Loeb, M.D., 801 W. Maple, Farmington, N. M. 87401, Nov. 5, 1971.

284. "AEC Orders Licensees to Improve Safety of Mill Operation," AEC Press Release B-125, July 30, 1959.

285. Speech before the American Mining Congress, Denver, Sept. 16, 1959 (AEC Press Release S-22-59).

286. *Op. cit.* ref. 187, p. 42.

287. *Ibid.,* p. 106.

288. Farmington *Daily Times,* April 13, 1960.

289. Durango *Herald News,* Oct. 23, 1970.

290. "Environmental Hazards Associated with the Milling of Uranium Ore," HASL-40, USAEC, June 4, 1958.

291. Winchester Laboratory Report WIN-112, by Natl. Lead Co. for USAEC, Feb. 1, 1960.

292. Winchester Laboratory Reports WIN-124, WIN-125, by Natl. Lead Co. for USAEC, 1961.

293. Letter to Robert D. Siek, chief, Radiological Health Section, Colo. Dept. of Public Health, from Anthony Mastrovich, gen. mgr., Climax Uranium Co., Grand Junction, Colo., March 18, 1969.

294. *Evaluation of Radon 222 Near Uranium Tailings Piles,* USDHEW, USPHS, Bur. of Radiological Health, Rockville, Md. 20852, March 1969.

295. Letter to the Colo. Dept. of Public Health from G. F. Tape, acting chairman, USAEC, June 9, 1966.

296. Radiological Appraisal of the Monticello Project, IDO-12049, USAEC, Idaho Operations Office, Idaho Falls, Ida.

297. "Uranium Mining Health and Safety," speech before the Atomic Industrial Forum, Miami, Fla., by Robert J. Catlin, asst. dir. for health protection, Div of Operational Safety, USAEC.

298. *Status Report: Tailings Pile Situation,* by W. C. Gilbert, radiological health dir., Arizona Dept. of Health, Phoenix, November 1965.

299. Letter to Glenn T. Seaborg,

chairman, USAEC, from R. L. Cleere, M.D., Colo. dir. of public health, April 25, 1966.

300. H. L. Price in a statement before the JCAE, Feb. 11, 1966.

301. Letter from D. R. Chadwick, M.D., chief, Div. of Radiological Health, USPHS, to Dr. R. L. Cleere, Colorado dir. of public health, May 3, 1966. Also letter from James G. Terrill, Jr.

302. *Op. cit.* ref. 187, p. 17.

303. *Ibid.*, p. 20.

304. "Evaluation of the Radon Film Badge," by Robert N. Snelling, Southwestern Radiological Health Laboratories, USPHS, and Robert D. Siek, Radiation Hygiene Div., Colo. Dept. of Public Health, April 1968.

305. Interoffice memorandum, "Comparison of Chest X-Ray Exposure with Indoor Radon Type Exposure," by J. B. Baird, Colo. Dept. of Public Health, May 12, 1971.

306. "Warnings on Tailings Peril Set," *Rocky Mountain News,* Denver, Nov. 18, 1971.

307. "U.S. Agencies Want Out of Radiation Group," by Steve Wynkoop, Denver *Post,* Aug. 29, 1971.

308. "Report of Practicability Study and Cost Estimate: Removal of Uranium Mill Tailings from Under or Near Certain Residences in the Grand Junction, Colorado, Area," prepared for the USAEC September 1971.

309. *Hearings on the Use of Uranium Mill Tailings for Construction Purposes,* Subcommittee on Raw Materials, JCAE, Oct. 28, 29, 1971, testimony of Commissioner Clarence E. Larson.

310. *Ibid.,* testimony of Stanley R. Anderson, mayor of Grand Junction, Colo.

311. *Ibid.,* testimony of Robert Siek, asst. dir., Occupational and Radiological Health Div., Colo. Dept. of Public Health.

312. Letter dated Sept. 24, 1963.

313. Letter to H. Peter Metzger from Dr. Donald I. Walker, March 19, 1971.

314. Letter dated May 5, 1964, to Mr. Edwards from Lyall Johnson, acting dir., Div. of Materials Licensing, USAEC.

315. "Summarization of Cincinnati Meeting on Uranium Mill Tailings, March 10, 1964," prepared by Leo J. Dymerski, program dir., radiological health (Denver office), USPHS. This document, along with many others of Mr. Dymerski's records of that period, is on file in the office of Paul Smith, regional rep., Radiation Office, EPA, Lincoln Towers, Denver.

316. *Op. cit.,* ref. 187, p. 40.

317. Personal interview with Robert Siek.

318. Telephone interview with Mr. Westbrook, October 1971.

319. *Op. cit.* ref. 304. Siek's answer to Westbrook's claim (that it was the inaccuracy of the radon-film-badge technique which caused him to reject Siek's 1966 request to put the film badges in the schools) was related to me in an interview with Siek in October 1971. He said, "Our whole purpose in being in Grand Junction then was to test the film badge; neither Westbrook nor anyone else could have known whether it was a good technique or not, since it was a brand-new technique at the time. No one even knew about its existence but us."

320. Letter to Mesa County Valley School Dist. 51, 2115 Grand Ave., Grand Junction, Colo. 81501, from G. A. Franz III, industrial hygienist, Colo. Dept. of Public Health, 4210 E. 11th Avenue, Denver, Colo. 80220, July 17, 1970.

321. AEC's undated, unsigned "Comments on Indoor Radon Study";

cover letter to Dr. Martin B. Biles, dir. of operational safety, USAEC, from Harvey F. Soule, Materials and Control Branch, USAEC, April 11, 1969.

322. "Radioactive Colorado," a program in the *Hot Topic* series, appeared on KLZ-TV, Denver, Feb. 23, 1970.

323. "Files: Radiation in Houses at Uravan, Colorado," by Rafford L. Faulkner, dir., Div. of Raw Materials, USAEC, Jan. 21, 1970.

324. "Trip Report—Colorado Indoor Radon Study." (On February 10 and 11, 1970, I attended a meeting at the . . ."), by Harvey F. Soule, materials process engineer, Div. of Operational Safety, USAEC.

325. "Questions and Answers for JCAE Hearings February 2, 1970," prepared by the Div. of Operational Safety, USAEC; sent to me by Martin Biles, Ph.D., dir., Div. of Operational Safety, April 6, 1971.

326. "Indoor Radon Daughter and Radiation Measurements in East Tennessee and Central Florida," HASL-TM-71-8, Health and Safety Laboratory, USAEC, New York, N. Y. 10014, March 1971.

327. Colo. Dept. of Public Health: *Indoor Radon Progeny Exposure Evaluation Study,* 2nd quarterly report, February 1969, p. 3.

328. "Staff Report—Atomic Energy Commission: AEC Responsibilities Regarding the Mining and Milling of Uranium."

329. AEC letter claimed to have been sent to the states (March 7, 1961) and the mills (June 1961), signed by H. L. Price, dir., Div. of Licensing and Regulation.

330. Letter to Robert D. Siek, Colo. Dept. of Public Health, from Robert E. Sundin, dir., Section of Industrial Hygiene, Dept. of Health and Social Service, Cheyenne, Wyo. 82001, May 26, 1971.

331. Letter to Robert D. Siek from Marshall W. Parrott, dir., Radiation Sect., Oregon State Bd. of Health, Portland, Ore. 97201, June 4, 1971.

332. Memo to Robert D. Siek, from Donald C. Gilbert, exec. dir., Arizona Atomic Energy Commission, Phoenix, Ariz. 85012, May 24, 1971.

333. Letter to Robert D. Siek, from Donald G. Kurvink, chief, Environmental Science Services Program, So. Dakota State Dept. of Health, Pierre, S. D., June 17, 1971.

334. Letter to Robert D. Siek from Martin C. Wukasch, P.E., acting dir., Div. of Occupational Health and Radiation Control, Texas State Dept. of Health, Austin, Tex., June 2, 1971.

335. Letter to Robert D. Siek from Dennis R. Dalley, chief, Radiation and Occupational Health Sect., Utah State Div. of Health.

336. Letter to Robert D. Siek from Edward L. Kaufman, supervisor, Radiation Protection Unit, Health and Social Services Dept., Santa Fe, N. M. 87501, May 27, 1971.

337. Letter to Robert D. Siek from Arnold J. Moen, supervisor, Radiation Control Section, Dept. of Social and Health Services, Olympia, Wash. 98501, May 27, 1971.

338. Anthony Ripley in the *New York Times,* Sept. 27, 1971, city ed. ("Radioactive Building Sands Stirs Dispute"), and Sunday, Oct. 3, 1971, "News of the Week" sect. "Did Someone Make a Deadly Blunder?").

339. *Op. cit.* ref. 309, testimony of H. Peter Metzger, Oct. 28, 1971.

340. *Atomic Energy Clearing House Reports,* Oct. 18, 1971, p. 1.

341. Letter to H. Peter Metzger from Robert D. Siek, June 29 and July 14, 1971.

342. *Enemy of the People,* by Henrik Ibsen (1882).

343. Letter to Gov. John A. Love, from Howard H. McMullin, exec. v.p. and secy., Mutual Savings and Loan Assn., Dec. 22, 1969.

344. Grand Junction *Daily Sentinel,* Jan. 21, 1971.

345. *Ibid.,* Dec. 21, 1969.

346. *Ibid.,* Sept. 9, 1971.

347. "Tailings: Grand Junction 'Snickers,' EPA Worries," *Cervi's Journal,* Denver, Sept. 13, 1971.

348. "Aspinall 'Federalist' View on Junction Radiation Hit," by Tom Rees, *Rocky Mountain News,* Sept. 16, 1971.

349. "Town in Kansas Is Willing to Live with Atom Dump," by B. Drummond Ayers, *New York Times,* March 11, 1971.

350. *Op. cit.* ref. 171, see entire text.

351. "Recommendations of Action for Radiation Exposure Levels in Dwellings Constructed on or with Uranium Mill Tailings," by Jesse L. Steinfeld, M.D., Surgeon General, PHS, July 27, 1970.

352. "AEC Staff Analysis, PHS Recommendations of July 27, 1970, on Action Levels Associated with Uranium Tailings in Dwellings," Aug. 26, 1970; cover letter to Dr. R. L. Cleere, dir., Colo. State Dept. of Public Health, from Martin B. Biles, dir., Div. of Operational Safety, USAEC, Sept. 4, 1970.

353. Letter to Richard N. Gray, city mgr., Grand Junction, from Robert D. Siek, asst. dir., Occupational and Radiological Health Div., Colorado Dept. of Public Health, May 12, 1971.

354. Letters to Dale Hollingsworth, Grand Junction Chamber of Commerce, from Robert D. Siek, May 3 and 12, 1971.

355. "Order" by the Board of County Commissioners, Mesa County, Colo., July 12, 1971, County Court House, Grand Junction.

356. Minutes, "Colorado Indoor Radon Study, Sixth Meeting of the Joint Agency Working Committee, Aug. 24-25, 1971," available from D. M. Ross, DOS, USAEC, Washington, D.C.

357. Minutes of September meeting, *ibid.;* also available from Roween Danbom, public information dir., Colo. Dept. of Public Health, 4210 E. 11th St., Denver, Colo. 80220.

358. "Committee Recommends Uranium Tailings Action," by Tom Rees, *Rocky Mountain News,* Sept. 22, 1971.

359. "Panel Asks Removal of Junction Tailings," by Steve Wynkoop, Denver *Post,* Sept. 22, 1971.

360. "EPA Denies Two Officials' Views on Tailings Is 'Policy,'" by Tom Rees, *Rocky Mountain News,* Sept. 29, 1971.

361. "The President's Reorganization Plan No. 3, 1971."

362. AP dispatch, Washington, D.C., Oct. 29, 1971, as seen in the Boulder, Colo., *Daily Camera.*

363. Grand Junction *Daily Sentinel,* Sept. 15, 1970.

364. *Ibid.,* Sept. 4, 1971 ("Aspinall Douses Hopes Costs of Removing Tailings Would Be Borne by Government").

365. "Tailings Solution Doubted," Denver *Post,* Sept. 16, 1971, p. 3.

366. "Dr. Cleere Target of Hostile Quiz at Tailings Hearings," by Leonard Larsen, Denver *Post,* Oct. 31, 1971.

367. Grand Junction *Daily Sentinel,* Nov. 20, 1970.

368. *Op. cit.* ref. 187, p. 44.

369. "Love Nears Cleere's Stand on AEC," by Richard Tucker, *Rocky Mountain News,* Sept. 29, 1971.

370. Presidential Executive Order 11258, Sect. 1, Subsect. (3).

371. "Application for AEC License to Transfer, Deliver, Export, or Receive Uranium or Thorium Source Material," from Climax Uranium Co., P. O. Box 1901, Grand Junction, Colo., May 31, 1957.

372. Letters to the Div. of Licensing and Regulation, USAEC, from Edward G. Littel, asst. to the pres., Vitro Corp. of America, Aug. 7, 11 and 13, 1959.

373. Interoffice memorandum, Div. of Licensing and Regulation, USAEC, from L. R. Rogers, chief, Radiation Safety Branch, to Lyall Johnson, chief, Licensing Branch, Aug. 29, 1959.

374. "The Trouble with 90.5 Million Tons of Radioactive Tailings," by Roger Rapoport, *West,* the magazine supplement of the Los Angeles *Times,* April 12, 1970.

375. Casper, Wyo., *Star-Tribune,* March 4, 1971.

376. Telephone interview with Robert E. Sundin, October 1971.

377. Editorial, "Aspinall Handling of AEC Critics on Mill Tailings Rude and Wrong," Denver *Post,* Nov. 3, 1971.

378. Witnesses can expect to be insulted and harassed if they attack AEC "party line" before the JCAE. After abusing Minnesota Gov. Harold E. Le Vander, Rep. Craig Hosmer (R., Calif.) attacked the governor's scientific adviser, Dr. Ernest C. Tsivoglu. Hosmer was miffed that Dr. Tsivoglu had also served as a consultant to the Senate's Committee on Public Works (a "rival" committee also hearing testimony on radioactivity). Goading Dr. Tsivoglu, Hosmer suggested that the significance of Tsivoglu's consultantship to the Senate committee might be due less to technical competence and more to "political acceptability." Throughout the testimony, Hosmer addressed his witness as "Dr. Zhivago" (see "Congressmen Clash with Minnesota Governor Over Limits on Atomic Waste," by E. W. Kenworthy, *New York Times,* Jan. 28, 1970, also corroborated by telephone with Dr. E. C. Tsivoglu, Atlanta, Ga., Dec. 25, 1971).

Not surprisingly, the transcript of the hearings has been cleaned up, so that none of Mr. Hosmer's bad manners is preserved in the official record (see *Environmental Effects of Producing Electric Power,* JCAE hearings, Part II, January–February 1970, Vol. I, p. 1123. The JCAE is scrupulous in maintaining an accurate record of its proceedings, except when it suits its purposes to do otherwise, a natural consequence in a system of self-regulation.

379. *Op. cit.* ref. 309, testimony of Glen E. Keller, Jr.

380. Press release, Colo. Dept. of Public Health, Oct. 29, 1971.

381. "Infants and Radioactive Sands: Small-Town Doctor Wins Fight," by Anthony Ripley, *New York Times,* Oct. 3, 1971.

382. *Op. cit.* ref. 309, testimony of Dr. C. Henry Kempe and Dr. Robert Ross.

383. See "Dear Sir: Your House Is Built on Radioactive Uranium Waste," by H. Peter Metzger, *New York Times Magazine,* Oct. 31, 1971.

384. "Warnings on Tailings Peril Set," by James Crawford, *Rocky Mountain News,* Nov. 18, 1971, p. 5.

385. "Rocky Flats Dow Head to Retire," Denver *Post,* Nov. 25, 1971.

386. *Op. cit.* ref. 74, pp. 110-11, 152.

387. *Annual Report to Congress of the AEC for 1964,* USAEC, January 1965.

388. *Annual Report to Congress of the AEC for 1961,* USAEC, January 1962.

389. *Op. cit.* ref. 34, p. 62.

390. *Ibid.*, p. 68.

391. All of these methods were failures. The "indirect cycle" which isolated the nuclear reactor from the airstream by using a heat exchanger turned out to be too heavy and produced still more unsolvable technical difficulties. "Shadow shielding," another failure, works only in outer space, where an air-breathing engine cannot.

392. York, *op. cit.* ref. 34, p. 63.

393. *Ibid.*, pp. 64-66.

394. *Aviation Week,* Dec. 1, 1958.

395. York, *op. cit.* ref. 34, pp. 72-73.

396. Authorizing legislation hearings, JCAE, April–June 1957.

397. Authorizing legislation hearings, JCAE, May–June 1958.

398. "Aircraft Propulsion Conversion System Analysis," XRFP (513/255-3937), Directorate of R & D Procurement, Wright Patterson Air Force Base, Ohio 45433.

399. *Atomic Energy Clearing House Reports,* Jan. 25, 1971, p. 1.

400. "Air Force Grounds C5s After Engine Falls Off One," AP dispatch in the Denver *Post,* Oct. 8, 1971.

401. "Entire C-5A Fleet Grounded by U. S.," by Richard Witkin, *New York Times,* Oct. 13, 1971.

402. "Lockheed Accused of Waste and Deceit on C-5A," *ibid.,* Sept. 30, 1971.

403. "Advent of Nuclear Aircraft Predicted," dateline Burbank, Calif., *Rocky Mountain News,* Jan. 31, 1971.

404. *Nuclear Rocket Engine Development Program,* joint hearing before the Senate Committee on Aeronautical and Space Sciences and the JCAE, Feb. 23 and 24, 1971. See testimony of Rep. Robert L. Leg-gett, 4th Cong. Dist., Calif. (pp. 15-19). Also see testimony of the following: *from Pennsylvania* (testifying for Westinghouse), Sen. Hugh Scott (pp. 130-31), Rep. Thomas E. Morgan (p. 133), Rep. James G. Fulton (p. 52) and A. P. Zechella, mgr., Astronuclear Laboratory, Westinghouse Electric Corp., Large, Pa.; *from California* (testifying for Aerojet), Sen. Alan Cranston (p. 134), Rep. John E. Moss (p. 132) and Alvin L. Friedman, pres., Aerojet Nuclear Systems Co., Sacramento; *from Nevada* (testifying for the Nuclear Rocket Development Station), Sen. Howard Cannon (p. 9), Sen. Alan Bible (p. 13) and Rep. Walter S. Baring (p. 129); *from New Mexico* (testifying for Los Alamos Scientific Labs), Sen. Joseph M. Montoya (p. 130), Sen. (Chairman) Clinton P. Anderson (p. 1) and Dr. Harold Agnew, dir., Los Alamos Scientific Laboratory (p. 74).

405. *Op. cit.* ref. 6, p. 284.

406. *Op. cit.* ref. 404, pp. 62-63.

407. *Ibid.*, p. 99.

408. Some military missile systems which have been developed, deployed and since abandoned: Hermes, Dart, Loki, Terrier, Mobile Minuteman, Sparrow, Regulus, Talos, GAM-63 Rascal, GAM-87 Skybolt, Mauler, SM-72 Goose, MMRBM, BOMARC A, Mace A, Thor, Pluto, Q4 Drone, GAM-67 Crossbow, Petrel, Nike-Ajax, Eagle, Lacrosse, Dove, Polaris A1, Houndog A, Snark, Corvus, Redstone, Rigel, Jupiter, Oriole, Navaho, Titan 1, Entact, Meteor, Corporal, Triton, Typhon, Atlas D, E, F.

409. *Op. cit.* ref. 404, p. 71: testimony of Milton Klein, mgr., Space Nuclear Systems Office.

410. *Ibid.*, p. 103: testimony of Alvin L. Friedman, pres., Aerojet Nuclear Systems Co.

411. *Ibid.*, pp. 29-31: testimony of USAEC Commissioner James T. Ramey.

412. *Ibid.*, p. 57: testimony of Dr. Glenn T. Seaborg.

413. The efficiency of any rocket engine is inherently limited not only by the energy contained within, but also by a theoretical maximum which, among other things, is determined by the molecular weight of the propellant. Specifically, its highest exhaust velocity is proportional to the square root of the reciprocal of the molecular weight. Accordingly, propellants of low molecular weight can achieve substantially higher exhaust velocities than propellants of higher molecular weight such as hot air (as with Pluto and the ANP) or chemical combustion products (as with conventional rockets). Air-breathing nuclear jet engines and chemical rockets can't "choose" their propellants, but a nuclear rocket can; and so NERVA uses hydrogen, the lowest-molecular-weight substance available. In this way, at least theoretically, NERVA can generate twice the power efficiency (or "specific impulse") of conventional rockets.

414. "Summary of Hypothetical Whole-Body Gamma Exposures and Infant Thyroid Doses Resulting Off-Site From Project Rover Nuclear Reactor/Engine Tests at the Nuclear Rocket Development Station," by R. F. Grossman, Southwestern Radiological Health Lab., USDHEW, PHS, Las Vegas, Nev., August 1970.

415. "Final Report of Environmental Surveillance for Phoebus 2A Reactor Test Series, May–July 1968," Southwestern Radiological Health Labs, October 1970.

416. "Particulate Effluent Study: Phoebus 1B, EP-IV," Southwestern Radiological Health Labs, April 1970.

417. "Particulate Effluent Study, Phoebus 2A-EP-IV and EP-V," Southwestern Radiological Health Labs, June 1969.

418. "Final Report of Off-Site Surveillance for the KIWI B4D Experiment," Southwestern Radiological Health Labs, July 23, 1964.

419. "Draft Environmental Statement for Reactor Test during FY 1971 at the Nuclear Rocket Development Station, Nevada," USAEC-NASA, January 1971, p. 18.

420. *Op. cit.* ref. 404, p. 21: testimony of George M. Low, admin., NASA.

421. *Ibid.*, p. 92: testimony of Dr. Wernher Von Braun.

422. *Ibid.*, p. 92: testimony of Milton Klein, mgr., Space Nuclear Systems Office.

423. *Ibid.*, p. 27: testimony of Dr. Glenn T. Seaborg.

424. *Ibid.*, p. 10.

425. *Ibid.*, p. 53.

426. Letter from Ralph Decker, asst. mgr. for nuclear propulsion safety and reliability, Space Nuclear Systems Office, USAEC, to H. Peter Metzger, Dec. 13, 1970.

427. Public law 91-190, S.1075, 91st Congress, Jan. 1, 1970.

428. Metzger v. Klein, [SNSO], Seaborg [AEC] and Low [NASA], Civil Action C-2787, U.S. Dist. Court, Denver, Colo., Jan. 28, 1971.

429. "Brief in Support of Motion for Summary Judgment," by James L. Treece, U.S. attorney.

430. *102 Monitor,* Environmental Impact Statements from the President's Council on Environmental Quality, February 1971.

431. *Ibid.*, March 1971.

432. *Ibid.,* April 1971, p. 7; June 1971, p. 11.

433. *Op. cit.* ref. 404, p. 82.

434. *Atomic Energy Clearing House Reports,* May 31, 1971, p. 60.

Also Senator Symington press release dated May 22, 1971.

435. *Op. cit.* ref. 430, August 1971.

436. "Costs of Operating the NS Savannah," Review B-136209, General Accounting Office, June 28, 1970.

437. House floor debate on the Maritime Admin. Authorization Bill for FY 1971, week of Feb. 27, 1970.

438. *Atomic Energy Clearing House Reports,* July 6, 1970, p. 1.

439. See remarks by Dr. Glenn T. Seaborg, chairman, USAEC, at the George Washington Univ. Medical Alumni Banquet, Washington, D.C., June 5, 1964 (AEC Press Release S-12-64). Also remarks by Dr. Charles L. Dunham, dir., Div. of Biology and Medicine, USAEC, at the Frueauff Foundation Radiation Center, Danville, Pa., Sept. 26, 1964 (AEC Press Release S-21-64).

440. For example, the nonspecific destruction of brain tissue, using atomic radiation, to treat depression and anxiety. See *Spectrum,* No. 51 (1958); abstract in *The Sciences,* Vol. 9, No. 2 (February 1969).

441. "National Mandate for Atomic Energy: A Twenty-five-Year Review," speech on the 25th anniversary of the signing of the Atomic Energy Act, Dept. of State, Washington, D.C., Aug. 1, 1971 (USAEC Press Release S-16-71).

442. "Harold Agnew New Boss of Los Alamos," *Empire Magazine,* Denver *Post,* Aug. 2, 1970.

443. General review articles on the cardiac pacemaker: "Artificial Cardiac Pacemakers" by B. Lown and B. D. Kosoweky, *New Eng. Jour. Medicine, 283,* 907, 971, 1023 (1970); "A Decade of Permanent Pacing of the Heart," by Victor Parsonnet, M.D., in *Cardiovascular Clinics,* Albert N. Brest, M.D., ed. in chief (F. A. Davis Co., Philadel-

phia, 1970); "The Failure of Triggered Pacemakers," by Furman and Escher, *American Heart Jour., 82,* 28 (1971).

444. *Annual Report to Congress of the AEC for 1966,* USAEC, January 1967.

445. "First Implantation of a Nuclear Cardiac Stimulator Ever to Be Implanted in a Human" (in French), *Newsletter* (information bulletin on isotopic generators and batteries), European Nuclear Energy Agency, Paris, June 1, 1970.

446. "Development Abroad on Radioisotope-Powered Cardiac Pacemaker," *Isotopes and Radiation Technology, 8,* 360 (1970).

447. *Major Activities in the Atomic Energy Programs, January–December 1969,* USAEC, January 1970.

448. *Nucleonics Week,* Dec. 25, 1969.

449. *Annual Report to Congress of the AEC for 1970,* USAEC, January 1971, p. 194.

450. "The French Nuclear-Powered Pacemaker Program," by M. Alais *et al., Nuclear News,* December 1970, p. 42.

451. *Nucleonics Week,* July 9, 1970.

452. *Science News,* June 27, 1970.

453. "Implantable Nuclear-Powered Cardiac Pacemaker," by J. C. Norman, G. W. Sandberg, and F. N. Hoffman, *New Eng. Jour. Medicine, 283,* 1203 (1970).

454. Written guarantee for Cardiac Pacemaker Model 5862, Medtronic, Inc., 3055 Old Highway Eight, Minneapolis, Minn. 55418.

455. "Elective Replacement Policy for Implantable Pulse Generator," Medtronic, Inc., July 26, 1971, p. 4.

456. Panel Discussion, *Annals of N.Y. Acad. of Science,* Oct. 30, 1969, p. 676.

457. *New York Times,* Dec. 1, 1970.

458. *Op. cit.* ref. 456, p. 674.

459. *Isotopes and Radiation Technology, 7,* 192 (1970).

460. "Nuclear Materials and Equipment Corp. Radioisotope-Powered Pacemaker," USAEC Report NUMEC-3731-3, April 19, 1968.

461. The maximum permissible lung burden is 16×10^{-9}g for each worker; see *op. cit.* ref. 228.

462. *The Director,* (National Fueral Directors Assn., 135 West Wells St., Milwaukee, Wisc. 53203), April 1971, p. 7.

463. "High Cost of Dying Spurs an Increase in Cremation and Burial at Sea among Southern Californians," by Everell R. Holles, *New York Times,* Nov. 14, 1971.

464. *Nucleonics Week,* Dec. 25, 1969.

465. FRC Report No. 1, approved by the President May 30, 1960.

466. See Denver *Post,* July 5, 1970. Also *op. cit.* ref. 456, p. 678; "Principles and Techniques of Cardiac Pacing," by Furman and Escher (Harper and Row, New York, 1970), p. 46; "Biologically Energized Cardiac Pacemaker: *In vivo* Experience with Dogs," by Enger and Simeone, *Nature, 218,* 180 (1968); and "Cardiac Pacemakers," by Howard J. Sanders, *Chemistry, 44,* 14 (1971), p. 16.

467. *Atomic Energy Clearing House Reports,* July 26, 1971, p. 58.

468. *Ibid., 17,* No. 32.

469. *Ibid., 17,* No. 34, Aug. 23, 1971, p. 1.

470. Private companies in the nuclear-pacemaker business: Nuclear Materials and Equipment Corp., Donald W. Douglas Labs., Medtronic, Inc.

471. Joseph L. Angello, U.S. Army Electronics Command, at the Power Sources Symposium, Atlantic City, N.J., 1970.

472. "Science and You," by Dr. Leonard Reiffel, syndicated in many newspapers by World Book Science Service, 1970.

473. *Atomic Energy Clearing House Reports,* Sept. 29, 1969, p. 22.

474. "AEC's Radioisotope-Powered Heater for Diving Suits to Get U.S. Navy Test" AEC Press Release K-234, Oct. 6, 1967.

475. *The Sciences* (publication of the N.Y. Acad. of Science), *9,* 35 (1969).

476. *Fed. Register,* April 24, 1969.

477. *Atomic Energy Clearing House Reports,* July 20, 1970, p. 28.

478. *Ibid.,* Aug. 18, 1969, p. 1.

479. Testimony of E. E. Fowler, dir., Div. of Isotope Development, USAEC, at FY 1971 authorizing hearings before the JCAE, Feb. 18, 1970.

480. AEC Press Release PR-K-214, Aug. 31, 1967.

481. "Status of the Food Irradiation Program," Joint Committee on Atomic Energy, July 18, 20, 1968, foreword.

482. *Ibid.,* p. 59.

483. *Atomic Energy Clearing House Reports,* Dec. 9, 1968, p. 1.

484. *Annual Report to Congress, 1968,* USAEC.

485. *Atomic Energy Clearing House Reports,* Feb. 17, 1969, p. 16.

486. *Ibid.,* Feb. 16, 1970, p. 1.

487. *Ibid.,* Feb. 23, 1970, p. 23.

488. *Ibid.,* May 11, 1970, p. 1.

489. "Plowshare Chronology through July 31, 1971," issued August 1971, available from DPNE, USAEC, Washington, D.C. 20545.

490. *The Constructive Uses of Nuclear Explosives,* by Teller, Talley, Higgins and Johnson (McGraw, Hill, New York, 1968), pp. 212-15.

491. *Ibid.* See also "Miniata Observer Program" brochure, July

1971, available from USAEC, NVOO, Las Vegas, Nev. 89114; also Press Release NV-71-44, July 2, 1971. Also see "Hopes for Faster Development of Gas Stimulation Explosives," *Nuclear Industry,* July 1971. For news coverage, see "New Atomic Device Fired in U. S. Project to Tap Gas," by Anthony Ripley, *New York Times,* July 9, 1971.

492. *Op. cit.,* ref. 490, p. 216.

493. See "Project Chariot," *Nuclear Information,* June 1961, an entire issue devoted to the "probable gains and risks of the AEC's Plowshare [harbor] project in Alaska." Also "Nuclear Digging," by Michael Friedlander, *Scientist and Citizen,* November 1964, and "Plowing a Nuclear Furrow," by E. A. Martell, *Environment,* April 1969, p. 2.

494. *AEC Authorizing Legislation, Fiscal Year 1972,"* JCAE hearings, Part IV, March and May 1971, p. 2345. Also "Status of the Interoceanic Canal Study," by Brig. Gen. R. H. Groves, USA, Jan. 14, 1970, available from DPNE, USAEC, Washington, D.C. 20545.

495. Interview with Hal H. Aronson, v.p., CER Geonuclear Corp., Las Vegas, Nev., July 28, 1971, in Grand Junction, Colo.

496. Interview with Glenn C. Werth at Los Alamos, N.M., Nov. 12, 1971.

497. See "Project Gasbuggy and Catch-85," by H. Peter Metzger, *New York Times Magazine,* Feb. 22, 1970.

498. Most of this work has been done at Oak Ridge National Laboratory, Oak Ridge, Tenn., and is available there, using their code numbers:

"First Quarterly Progress Report on the Theoretical Safety Evaluation of Consumer Products from Project Gasbuggy," ORNL-TM-2427, Feb. 19, 1969.

"Second . . . [idem]," ORNL-TM-2513, March 1969.

"Third . . .," ORNL-TM-2657, July 1969.

"Fourth . . .," ORNL-TM-2721, October 1969.

"Fifth . . .," ORNL-TM-2862, February 1970.

"Quarterly Progress Report on Radiological Safety of Peaceful Uses of Nuclear Explosives: Consumer Products from Nuclearly Stimulated Gas Wells," ORNL-TM-3123, September 1970.

"Radiological Consideration in the Use of Natural Gas from Nuclearly Stimulated Wells," ORNL-TM-3216, November 1970.

See also *Proceedings, Symposium on Engineering with Nuclear Explosives, Jan. 14-16, 1970, Las Vegas, Nev.,* available from the American Nuclear Society and DPNE, USAEC; and *Proceedings, Symposium on Public Health Aspects of Peaceful Uses of Nuclear Exposives, Las Vegas, Nev., April 1969,* available through USAEC, Washington, D.C. 20545.

499. Gasbuggy: "Summary of Results of Underground Engineering Experience," by Fred Holzer, UCRL-71489, March 18, 1969; "Project Gasbuggy Operational Experience," by Kase *et al.,* UCRL-71356, Jan. 10, 1969; "Gasbuggy Experiment," by Fred Holzer, UCRL-71624, March 10, 1969; "Studies of Chemical and Radiological Composition of Natural Gas from the Cavity Produced by the Project Gasbuggy Nuclear Shot," by Smith and Momyer, *Radiological Health Data and Reports,* July 1969, p. 281.

Rulison: Three preliminary reports have been prepared on Project Rulison and are available from the Office of Peaceful Nuclear Explosives, NVOO, USAEC, Las Vegas,

Nev. 89114. NVOO is preparing a final report containing all pertinent information already released. See also "The Rulison Project in Retrospect," by Paul Haas, *Nuclear News,* May 1971.

500. There have been several reports on the economics of nuclear gas-well stimulation. CER Geonuclear Corp., Las Vegas, can supply "Economics of Nuclear Stimulation" and "Economics of Nuclear Gas Stimulation" (1970). The Atomic Industrial Forum, 475 Park Ave. South, New York, N.Y. 10016, has "Economics of Stimulating Natural Gas Reservoirs with Nuclear Explosives" (1970), available for $6. Lawrence Radiation Laboratory has produced several reports, the best of which is "An Analysis of Nuclear-Explosive Gas Stimulation and the Program Required for Its Development," by Werth *et al.,* available as UCRL-50966 (April 20, 1971). Resources for the Future, Inc., has published *Peaceful Use of Nuclear Explosives: Some Economic Aspects,* by Brooks and Krutilla, available from the Johns Hopkins Press, Baltimore, Md. 21218. And the DPNE of the USAEC has commissioned several detailed economic studies by Mathematica, 1 Palmer Sq., Princeton, N.J.; see "General Report on the Economics of the Peaceful Uses of Underground Nuclear Explosions" (PNE-3005), "The Economic Potentials of Natural Gas Production Stimulation by Nuclear Explosion" (PNE-3007) and "A Cost-Benefit Model for Nuclear Explosive Stimulation of Natural Gas Reservoirs" (PNE-3013).

501. *Naval Nuclear Propulsion Program, 1969,* JCAE hearings, April 23, 1969, p. 110.

502. "The Causes of Pollution," by B. Commoner, M. Corr and P. J. Stamler, *Environment, 13,* 2 (April 1971). Also *The Closing Circle,* by Barry Commoner (Knopf, New York, 1971).

503. "Thoughts on Nuclear Plumbing," by Ralph E. Lapp, *New York Times,* Dec. 12, 1971.

504. "Safety Gear Untried at A-Power Plants," by Anthony Ripley, *ibid.,* Dec. 11, 1971, p. 1.

505. "Con Ed Assesses Indian Point Fire," *New York Times,* Dec. 12, 1971.

506. "A Critique of the New AEC Design Criteria for Reactor Safety Systems," by D. F. Ford, H. W. Kendall and J. J. MacKenzie, (Oct. 1971), available for $1 from Union of Concerned Scientists, P. O. Box 289, MIT Branch Station, Cambridge, Mass. 02139.

507. "Nuclear Reactor Safety: An Evaluation of New Evidence," by I. A. Forbes, D. F. Ford, H. W. Kendall and J. J. MacKenzie (July 1971), see above.

508. "Developments in Nuclear Power Economics, January 1968–December 1969," a report prepared for the JCAE by Philip Sporn, in *Prelicensing Antitrust Review of Nuclear Power Plants,* Part I, Nov. 18, 19 and 20, 1969, pp. 300-1.

509. Estimates submitted by Alvin M. Weinberg, Oak Ridge National Laboratory, to *Bulletin of the Atomic Scientists,* June 1971, p. 3.

510. For an opposing view on the insurance question, see "Price Anderson and Nuclear Insurance," a lecture by Burrell C. Lawton, secretary of the Hartford Insurance Group, at the Topical Conference on Nuclear Public Information, Bal Harbour, Fla., March 21-24, 1971, reprinted as "Background Info" by the Public Affairs and Information Program of the Atomic Industrial Forum, Inc., 475 Park Ave. South, New York, N.Y. 10016.

511. *New York Times,* June 3, 1971, p. 1.

512. *Op. cit.* ref. 508, *Prelicensing Antitrust Review,* Part II, p. 462.

513. *Ibid.,* p. 554.

514. *Ibid.,* p. 351.

515. *Atomic Energy for Military Purposes,* by Henry D. Smyth (Princeton Univ. Press, 1945).

516. *Op. cit., Environmental Effects of Producing Electric Power,* Part II, Vol. I, p. 1140.

517. "The Risk/Benefit Calculus in Nuclear Power Licensing," an address by Harold P. Green, Symposium on Nuclear Power and the Public, Univ. of Minnesota, Oct. 10 and 11, 1969.

518. *Long Island Press,* New York, March 20, 1971.

519. *Nucleonics Week,* May 13, 1971, p. 4.

520. "Plutonium Revisited," speech by Dr. Seaborg at the Univ. of Utah, Oct. 8, 1970 (AEC Press Release S-34-70).

521. Claude E. Barfield, "Science Report: Nuclear Establishment Wins Commitment to Speed Development of Breeder Reactor, *National Journal, 3,* 1494 (July 17, 1971), and "Science Report: Breeder Reactor Program Likely to Make It Despite Industry's Default, Environmental Fears," *ibid.,* 1602 (July 31, 1971).

522. *Ibid.,* p. 1496.

523. "Use of a Deep Nuclear Chimney for the *in-situ* Incorporation of Nuclear Fuel-Reprocessing Waste in Molten Silicate Rock," by J. J. Cohen, A. E. Lewis and R. L. Braun, Lawrence Radiation Laboratory, Livermore, Calif. (UCRL-51044), May 4, 1971.

524. "Comments on Plowshare Waste Disposal Report," UCRL-51044 (3 pages), dated July 26, 1971.

525. Letter to Dr. Kenneth S. Pitzer, pres., Stanford Univ., from Francesco Costagliola, commissioner, USAEC, May 7, 1969.

526. Letter to Dr. Howard W. Johnson, pres., MIT, from Francesco Costagliola, May 7, 1969.

527. *Nucleonics Week,* June 5, 1969, p. 2.

528. Letter to Dr. James A. Perkins, pres., Cornell Univ., June 9, 1969.

529. Letter to Dr. Lincoln Gordon, pres., Johns Hopkins Univ., June 9, 1969.

530. Letter to Dr. Malcolm C. Moos, pres., Univ. of Minnesota, June 9, 1969.

531. "Warned on Defense Jobs," Providence *Evening Bulletin,* May 21, 1969.

532. *Op. cit.* ref. 493, p. 15.

533. "The Mess in Montana," by Leverne Hamilton, *Frontier* (1434 Wilshire Blvd., Los Angeles, Calif.), September 1963, pp. 13-14.

534. Minutes of the Zoology Staff Meeting, May 15, 1963, Univ. of Montana, Missoula, Mont. 59801.

535. Letter to H. Peter Metzger from Prof. E. W. Pfieffer, April 19, 1971.

536. "Colorado Environmentalists: Scientists Battle AEC and Army," by Bryce Nelson, *Science, 168,* 1324 (1970). Also "Taking on a Nuclear Giant," by Tom Wicker, *New York Times,* March 1, 1970.

537. "Plutonium Contamination in the Denver Area," press release by the Colo. Committee for Environmental Information, Boulder, Colo. See "Colorado Atom Plant Is Called Radiation Hazard," by Anthony Ripley, *New York Times,* Feb. 11, 1970, p. 1.

538. Letter to Dr. Glenn T. Seaborg, chairman, USAEC, from Dion W. J. Shea, Ph.D., and Robert H. Williams, Ph.D., Colo. Committee for Environmental Information, 2595 Stanford Ave., Boulder, Colo., Feb. 18, 1970.

539. Letter to Dr. Seaborg, from E. A. Martell, Ph.D., D. W. Shea,

Ph.D., P. D. Goldan, Ph.D., R. H. Williams, Ph.D., and H. P. Metzger, Ph.D., Colo. Committee for Environmental Information, Feb. 18, 1970.

540. Letter from Dr. Seaborg to Dr. H. P. Metzger, pres., Colo. Committee for Environmental Information, March 2, 1970.

541. *Op. cit.* ref. 7, p. 143.

542. *Memoranda for the President of the United States: Establishment of a Department of Natural Resources,* submitted by the President's Advisory Council on Executive Organization (U.S. Govt. Printing Office, 1971) (O-420-791).

543. For the President's message to Congress, March 25, 1971, see *Papers Relating to the President's Departmental Reorganization Program —A Reference Compilation* (U.S. Govt. Printing Office, 1970) (O-416-631), p. 3.

544. S. 1431, Department of Natural Resources Act, 92nd Cong., April 1, 1971.

545. Price, *op. cit.* ref. 541, p. 11.

546. *Executive Reorganization Proposals,* hearings before the Senate Committee on Government Operations, first session on S. 1430-1433, Part I, May, June 1971, pp. 29-30.

547. "Reorganization of Atomic Energy Operating Functions," AEC Announcement No. 216 to all AEC employees, Dec. 7, 1971.

548. "AEC Reorganized in Move Stressing Civilian Programs," by Richard Lyons, *New York Times,* Dec. 8, 1971.

549. "Is the AEC Obsolete?" by John W. Finney, *The Reporter,* Nov. 19, 1964, p. 44.

550. *Nuclear Explosion Services for Industrial Applications,* JCAE hearings, May and July 1969, testimony of Hollis M. Dole, asst. secretary of the Interior, pp. 99-118. Also see Asst. Secretary Dole's testimony before the Senate Interior and Insular Affairs Committee (on Oil Shale Development), Nov. 15, 1971.

551. "Proposed Chairman of the AEC," by Robert H. Phelps, *New York Times,* July 22, 1971.

552. "New AEC Chairman Tells Power Officials Agency Won't Promote Private Industry," *Wall Street Journal,* Oct. 21, 1971. Also "AEC Shifts Role to Protect Public," by Richard D. Lyons, *New York Times,* Oct. 21, 1971.

553. "Expectations and Responsibilities of the Nuclear Industry," speech at the American Nuclear Society annual meeting, Bal Harbour, Fla., Oct. 20, 1971 (AEC Press Release S-21-71).

554. Statement made in Denver, Colo., Dec. 2, 1971, as reported by Howard Pankratz, reporter, appearing in the Jan. 2, 1971 edition of the Kansas City *Star,* 1729 Grand Ave., Kansas City, Mo. 64108.

555. U.S. Dist. Court, Minnesota, vs. Northern State Power Co., Dec. 22, 1970.

556. U.S. Dist. Court, Washington, D.C., May 25, 1971.

557. U.S. Court of Appeals, Dist. of Columbia Circuit, July 23, 1971 (No. 24839 and No. 24871); the complete opinion can be found in *Atomic Energy Clearing House Reports* for July 26, 1971, and *102 Monitor* (from the President's Council on Environmental Quality), September 1971.

558. U.S. Dist. Court, Washington, D.C.

559. *Op. cit.* ref. 187, p. 45.

560. *Atomic Energy Clearing House Reports,* Aug. 9, 1971, p. 3.

561. "AEC Plans No Appeal of Court Decision" AEC Press Release 0-147, 8-26-71.

562. "Anti-AEC" citizen activist groups are both local and national, both rustic and urbane. Local opposition to Colorado's Project Rulison was organized by "only a common

workingman on a small farm" (Citizens Concerned About Radiation, Box 34, Rural Route 1, Cedaredge, Colo. 81413); New York City has its Independent Phi Beta Kappa Environmental Study Group (115 Central Park West, New York, N.Y. 10023). The largest "anti-AEC" citizens group publishes a regular newsletter, *Watch on the AEC*. That is the National Committee to Stop Environmental Pollution (113 2nd Street N.E., Washington, D.C. 20002).

563. *New York Times,* March 17, 1972, p. 22.

INDEX